PRIVACY AND THE NEWS MEDIA

Critically examining current journalistic practices using both theoretical and applied approaches, this book addresses the interplay between the right to free expression (and what that means to a free press) and the right to privacy.

Privacy, and the criticism that journalists unreasonably and regularly invade it in order to get a "good story", is the most significant ethical dilemma for journalists, alongside accurately reporting the truth. Where is the line between fair exposure in the public interest and interesting the public? This book explains what privacy is, why we need it and why we go to some lengths to protect it. The law, the regulators, the key court cases and regulator complaints are covered, as well as issues raised by new technological developments. The book also briefly examines regulators in Ireland as well as privacy and free expression elsewhere in Europe and in North America, considering the contrary cultures of the two continents.

This insightful exploration of privacy and journalism combines theory and practice to provide a valuable resource for both Media and Journalism students and working journalists.

Chris Frost is emeritus professor of Journalism at Liverpool John Moores University, formerly working as a journalist and editor. He was Chair of the Association for Journalism Education, President of the National Union of Journalists, NEC member and Chair of its Ethics Council. He has written extensively about journalism.

PRIVACY AND THE NEWS MEDIA

Chris Frost

Routledge
Taylor & Francis Group

LONDON AND NEW YORK

First published 2020
by Routledge
2 Park Square, Milton Park, Abingdon, Oxon OX14 4RN

and by Routledge
52 Vanderbilt Avenue, New York, NY 10017

Routledge is an imprint of the Taylor & Francis Group, an informa business

British Library Cataloguing-in-Publication Data
A catalogue record for this book is available from the British Library

Library of Congress Cataloging-in-Publication Data
Names: Frost, Chris, 1950– author.
Title: Privacy and the news media / Chris Frost.
Description: London ; New York : Routledge, 2020. | Includes
bibliographical references and index.
Identifiers: LCCN 2019027629 (print) |LCCN 2019027630 (ebook) |
ISBN 9780367140212 (hardback) |ISBN 9780367140236 (paperback) |
ISBN 9780429029813 (ebook)
Subjects: LCSH: Journalism–Social aspects. | Privacy, Right of. |
Freedom of expression. | Press law. | Mass media–Law and legislation.
Classification: LCC PN4749 .F76 2020 (print) | LCC PN4749 (ebook) |
DDC 302.23–dc23
LC record available at https://lccn.loc.gov/2019027629
LC ebook record available at https://lccn.loc.gov/2019027630

ISBN: 978-0-367-14021-2 (hbk)
ISBN: 978-0-367-14023-6 (pbk)
ISBN: 978-0-429-02981-3 (ebk)

Typeset in Bembo
by Swales & Willis, Exeter, Devon, UK

Dedicated to the memory of my wife Vanessa and to the many wonderful women in my life: daughters Emma, Julia, Alice, Liz and granddaughters Madeleine and Margot. Also to grandson Freddie.

Also Sue: thanks for the hard work and support in helping me to finish.

CONTENTS

List of figures   *ix*

1 Introduction   1

2 Human rights and journalism ethics   4

3 What is privacy?   20

4 Privacy development   31

5 Gossip and celebrity   48

6 Issues in privacy   58

7 Public interest   74

8 Personal reputation   86

9 Law of privacy   92

10 Data protection   104

11 New technology and privacy   111

12 Media regulators   126

13 Privacy case studies   153

14 Privacy in Europe   177

15 Privacy in North America   182

Appendices   188
Bibliography   202
Index   205

FIGURES

2.1	Flow chart of ethical decision making	18
5.1	Falling newspaper circulations since 1999	54
5.2	Gossip plotted against circulation 2004	55
9.1	Privacy injunctions and undertakings in the UK courts	94
12.1	Number of complaints made to IPSO by year	130
12.2	Fate of complaints made to IPSO that are investigated	131
12.3	Fate of adjudicated complaints to IPSO	132
12.4	Number of programmes complained about to Ofcom	150
12.5	Ofcom standards adjudications	150
12.6	Ofcom privacy and fairness adjudications	151
12.7	Ofcom sanctions applied	151

1

INTRODUCTION

Are you a private person? Do you like to keep details of your life hidden away and do you shy from the internet and social media for fear of the data that will be stolen from you or are you what American privacy expert Alan Westin describes as a privacy pragmatist? Someone willing to take a risk in order to enjoy the pleasures of social media, online shopping or more.

Now more than ever in the history of humanity privacy is a critical issue in our lives. Our financial security depends on protecting our data, and our family and home life is something most of us prefer to keep to ourselves.

When it comes to journalism though, and the national press in particular, privacy is more complex. The national press likes to expose the privacy of celebrities and even the ordinary public at times in pursuit of a good story. But why do editors think that salacious intrusion into people's privacy is a good idea? The general view of editors, publishers, academics and journalists seems to be that such stories drive circulation and increase readership, offering a wider audience to advertisers and therefore an opportunity to charge higher rates for the same advertising space. Circulation also increases income from cover sales. So is it all about sales? Well not according to Colin Myler, the then editor of the *News of the World* when it ran the Max Mosley sadomasochistic orgy story. So why did he run it? "It was a very good story", he told the parliamentary select committee on Culture, Media and Sport, justifying it by telling the MPs that: "you only have to look at the manner in which it was followed up." So was he aiming for a specific audience? No again, he told the committee. He disagreed with fellow editors Paul Dacre and Peter Hill who had told the committee they would not have run it in their "family papers" (*Daily Mail* and *Daily Express*) as he considered the *News of the World* was also a family newspaper: "Yes, I do. I don't agree that it was an unsuitable story for a family newspaper, no, I don't", he told the committee. Nor was it used to boost circulation, he told the committee, dismissing the idea that the story was used for commercial gain: "rarely in these situations is there any commercial advantage, despite what many people think". The last reply is almost certainly true – a look at the plummeting circulation figures of national newspapers over the last 50 years makes it clear that boosting circulation is not the prime reason. However, that doesn't mean editors don't think that intrusive stories are the best way to keep their head above water; that invading someone's privacy will draw enough readers to at least slow circulation falls when competing against social media, the internet and TV. That said, the circulation figures of national newspapers over the last ten years shows a fairly straight, downward line and extrapolating those lines terminates at zero in about 2026 for the redtops, 2031 for the midmarket press and 2034 for the so-called quality press. Of course none will go that far. Newspapers are usually axed or go online when their circulations fall too low. The closure of national papers in the 1960s happened when circulation hit around the 1.3m mark (*News Chronicle* and the *Daily Herald*), papers died in the 1990s when circulations fell to around 200,000 (*Today* and the *Sport*). The *Independent* went online at 55,000 in 2016, despite attracting quality advertising and it is doubtful if the redtops and the mid-market papers could survive at that level of circulation. With the *Daily Express* and the *Daily Star* presently on just over 300,000 circulation, their days are probably numbered.

What about readers – do they want intrusive stories? Well, they say they don't and research supports this but can we believe what we are told? Again, there is no supportive evidence that intrusive stories boost circulation, but no evidence that they damage it either and there is certainly little doubt that most people enjoy a little gossip and magazines and newspapers that are full of celebrity tittle tattle still sell. It's also true that occasionally a privacy intrusion is required to expose the wrongdoings of some important or influential person.

I return to the editors for advice on this. Does privacy and the newspapers' intrusion into it have an important part to play in the commercial life of the press? Yes, said Paul Dacre, then editor of the *Daily Mail* talking to the Society of Editors about what he sees as the dangers of privacy laws:

> Concentrate instead on how inexorably, and insidiously, the British Press is having a privacy law imposed on it, which – apart from allowing the corrupt and the crooked to sleep easily in their beds – is, I would argue, undermining the ability of mass-circulation newspapers to sell newspapers in an ever more difficult market.
>
> *(www.pressgazette.co.uk/society-of-editors-paul-dacres-speech-in-full*
> *accessed Sept. 2019)*

It would appear that Dacre's main concern about privacy laws is not the occasional need to intrude on privacy to expose wrongdoing in the public interest, but that they may undermine the ability of newspapers to sell in an "ever more difficult" market. So the evidence from editors, the people who decide what goes in our papers, is that privacy invasions can be justified to publish "good stories" that "sell newspapers". Interesting definitions since one is unqualifiable (who says they're good and on what criteria?) and the other is unquantifiable (circulations are still falling). It's a debate from which I will stay aloof, having no evidence to prove either that intrusions help circulations or hinder. However, I have laid out in this book research and guidance on the approach to privacy that journalists who are proud of their craft might consider.

The book starts with a look at the ethics of human rights, since the law in the UK and Europe is strongly tied to the Human Rights Act and the European Convention on Human Rights. Chapter 2 shows that understanding the ethical positioning of human rights can help both with performing ethically and with better reporting. From there it moves to looking at privacy itself, in Chapter 3, what is privacy, why do we think it important and in Chapter 4 how privacy has developed in the UK over the past 150 years. From Chapter 5 the book starts to examine the privacy issues that affect journalists, starting in Chapter 5 with gossip and celebrities before moving on in Chapter 6 to look at the range of issues that need to be considered ethically when potentially intruding on personal privacy. Chapter 7 introduces the concept of public interest and its interaction with privacy and this is followed by Chapter 8 dealing with reputation and then Chapter 9 looking at the law surrounding personal data in the UK. Chapter 10 examines the complex area of data protection and its many issues for journalists. New technological developments raise significant issues in the area of journalists, news gathering and privacy that are dealt with in Chapter 11 while Chapter 12 introduces the concept of regulation and the various regulators in the UK and the Republic of Ireland. Much of the ethical area of privacy is dealt with by common law, that is, court rulings based on statute or previous court decisions. These play a major role in how the media handle privacy and so there are detailed descriptions in Chapter 13 of the key court cases dealing with privacy. Chapters 14 and 15 take a look outside the UK to give an idea of how privacy is dealt with in Europe and the US and investigate the difference a constitution makes and then examine the contrary cultures of the two continents. The appendices give access to the various codes for easy reference.

I hope you find the book useful both as a student and as a working journalist.

2

HUMAN RIGHTS AND JOURNALISM ETHICS

Human rights are a system of ethics, of moral thinking, that allows those who use it to determine what is fair and reasonable treatment for each individual on an equal and unprejudicial basis. Human rights are closely linked to but distinct from civil rights.

It is one of several systems of ethics that are widely used throughout the world but has gradually become popular over the past couple of centuries as religion has slowly been usurped, in the West at least, as the sole arbiter of morality. As much of humanity has slowly moved from religions, whose sacred texts are all too often used to treat others badly, forms of human rights have slowly been taken up either piecemeal or as a convention fully formed. Human rights are often converted to civil rights by governments or constitutions. The basic form remains the same but civil rights bring with them government protection. One has human rights wherever one lives, whether upheld by government or not, but civil rights are only available in a country that offers constitutional or statutory protection.

There are other systems of ethics that will be considered later in this chapter, but it is worth understanding that for the notion of privacy as an ethical issue, human rights is the system that best deals with both the importance and contradictions of privacy.

Morality and ethics

Morality is about having a set of standards by which one lives one's life. They determine such matters as how one treats other people, honesty, fair dealing and applying a set of understood standards to one's professional life. Ethics is about how one thinks about those moral standards – the philosophy that underpins the professional standards that you use.

Some of journalism's standards are fairly obvious. If I were writing fiction, it would be understood that what I wrote was invented; that while places and events might be based in reality, the characters I wrote about, their escapades and interactions were not. By writing non-fiction or journalism the intention should be to provide accurate, truthful information about people, places and events that would assist people to model their world and understand the pressures that mould it so that they work out the best way of living to suit them.

Fiction allows for fantastical adventures, strange places and fanciful events all developed from the mind of the author (unless it is plagiarised from another writer, in which case this is also unethical and possibly unlawful). Journalism might also present similarly fanciful events but this time the expectation is that they are truthful. If they are not, then they are not journalism and if they are represented to be journalism, the publisher or broadcaster has broken trust with its customers. Whilst entertaining readers or viewers is always something a journalist needs to consider as a tool to attract an audience, the reason people read journalism is to get a truthful, if abbreviated report of what is going on in the world and their small portion of it. They have a right to be informed, and this applies a duty to journalists to do that and do it truthfully.

Journalism is not a style of writing (although much journalism is identifiably stylistic, some of it even worth reading in its own right as literature). Journalism can use comedy, poetry, prose, it can tell stories of love, war and death, just like fiction, but it must be true and tell its story accurately.

But journalistic standards are not just about accuracy and truth, even if that is the most important aspect. There are several other ethical issues where taking the moral high road is not always easy or not even easily apparent when seeking the best interests of the public. This is where ethics comes in: a way of thinking about the moral standards we apply to our work to ensure that our journalism lives up to the trust our readers and viewers must place in journalists for their journalism to be useful. Broadcasting should educate, inform and entertain according to Lord Reith, the founder of the BBC, and it is a good description of excellent journalism. Journalism should entertain its readers and viewers. Few people want to read or see a dull report, no matter how important. So as well as informing people and educating them with accurate information, journalists need to make their stories entertaining, whether that is through choice of story such as gossip or stranger than truth tales, or by good writing, design and image. If the government issues an important report, for instance, few people will take the trouble to access it and read it, no matter how important, even though the internet has made this easier than ever before. We prefer to read a well-written synopsis that picks out the main points for us.

Human rights

Human rights developed from European political thinking in the 18th century and the early 19th century. They coincided with the move away from absolute rule, favoured by such thinkers as Thomas Hobbes (1588–1670), who, whilst postulating the idea of rights and a social compact, believed that the only way to ensure firm control and peace with people adhering to the rule of law was to have an absolute ruler. Living in admittedly difficult times, Hobbes believed that life "in the state of nature is solitary, poore, nasty, brutish and short" (Hobbes, 1968: 186). Society – an agreement to stick to the rules or social compact – was the only way around this but, according to Hobbes, required an absolute power to ensure the "terror of some punishment" for infringing the rules. Having a single ruler – preferably a king whose interests would be tied directly to the land of his kingdom – meant that there could be no debate, so no internal conflicts, no changing of mind and no compromising of secrecy.

Of course this would mean there would be no democracy and no need of a western-style news-based media. Challenging government and trying to hold the leadership to account is pointless if you believe in a single ruler, right or wrong – a danger many Trump supporters face. Exposing what is wrong with that world only leads to unhappiness and potential conflict, the very thing those supporting this system were trying to avoid. This is not to suggest that tyrants are only muzzling the media and free speech out of the kindness of their heart or a belief in a benevolent system. A look at any dictator around the world or those supposedly democratic leaders who find challenge inconvenient makes it clear that they find a Hobbesian system very useful. Any democratic leader who starts to talk about firm rule, praises patriotism and the "special nature" of the people he or she leads, or calls on the people to work together on a common project should be eyed with deep suspicion because, whilst they may pay lip service to democracy, they would probably prefer a more Hobbesian system.

Hobbes was a thinker of his time, as are we all, and that time was slowly changing. Abolishing slavery was a passionate campaign with its legal roots in a 1772 judgment in the British courts that ruled that slavery was not supported by the law in England. Abolitionists such as William Wilberforce (1759–1833) and Henry Brougham (1778–1868) brought about the Slave Trade Act 1807, outlawing global trading in slaves, followed in 1833 by the Slavery Abolition Act which ended slavery throughout the British empire. Other countries followed suit over the next few years. Slavery is now outlawed in the UK under the Human Rights Act, although it would be foolish to consider this means there are no slaves.

The anti-slavery movement coincided broadly with several thinkers and campaigners developing the ideas of human rights. John Locke (1632–1704) was one of the earliest to suggest that human equality meant that slavery was wrong. Locke saw slavery as simply a continuation of a state of war between lawful conqueror and a captive, a condition that would be ended by agreement:

> ... for if once compact enter between them, and make agreement for limited power on the one side and obedience on the other, the state of war and slavery ceases as long as the compact endures; for, as has been

said, no man can by agreement pass over to another that which he hath
not in himself – a power over his own life.

(Locke, 1947: 86)

Locke was an early essayist to consider the ideas of limited liberal government
and human rights. For Locke, the state of nature is one in which a man who is
wronged by another has the right to punish him, but Locke accepted there are
several reasons why this may not work because of power, strength, position, age
and so on. To get around this, Locke believed people should come together and
give up their right to escape punishment by authorising society to punish them
and therefore gain the right to have those who transgress against them, punished.
For this to work, there had to be law above all, and, unlike Hobbes, he believed
that tyranny or absolute power must be wrong as law by caprice of a monarch
or dictator would lead to chaos and fear rather than stable government.

> For he that thinks absolute power purifies men's blood, and corrects the
> baseness of human nature, need read but the history of this, or any other
> age, to be convinced to the contrary. He that would have been insolent
> and injurious in the woods of America would not probably be much
> better on a throne, where perhaps learning and religion shall be found out
> to justify all that he shall do to his subjects, and the sword presently silence
> all those that dare question it.

(Ibid.: 120–1)

Therefore, people must come together in a commonwealth and give up their
right to escape punishment to people they appoint to make the laws and punish
transgressors.

> Every man, by consenting with others to make one body politic under one
> government, puts himself under an obligation to everyone of that society to
> submit to the determination of the majority, and to be concluded by it; or
> else this original compact, whereby he with others incorporates into one
> society, would signify nothing, and be no compact if he be left free and
> under no other ties than he was in before in the state of nature.

(Ibid.: 124)

The legislature and magistrates so appointed would then be able to treat all
equally and there would be a right of appeal should they not. To ensure these
appointees carry out their duties fairly, those appointees would be responsible to
those who appoint them. This would mean people have rights; rights that are
not granted by society so society cannot remove them.

Thomas Paine (1737–1809) was another Englishman, described by
Saul K. Padover as "a corsetmaker by trade, a journalist by profession, and
a propagandist by inclination". He certainly delighted in being controversial,

spending time in jail in France for his beliefs and being found guilty in absentia for seditious libel in the UK. He was involved in two revolutions – the American and the French – because of his loathing of the monarchy and his belief in government by the people of the people.

Paine was instrumental in sparking the American civil war, producing his pamphlet *Common Sense* which inspired Ben Franklin and Thomas Jefferson and was proportionately the all-time best-selling American title. This was very widely read and helped inspire those involved in the revolution, with many believing the revolution would not have succeeded without it. Much of the subsequent US constitution was written from his beliefs by Thomas Jefferson.

Paine moved to France to live in the 1790s and wrote *Rights of Man*. This opposes the idea that hereditary dictatorial government is *necessary* because of Man's corrupt, bestial nature and insists that the people have the right to hold the government to account. This was duly attacked in England and a writ for his arrest was issued. He was later found guilty of seditious libel in his absence.

One of key points in this important essay was that human rights originate in nature, and so cannot be *granted* because that would imply privilege not rights. Privilege would be legally revocable, but rights are not. Paine saw government's prime purpose as being to safeguard the individual and protect their rights. This is the change between natural rights, human rights and civil rights. Paine believed that when we enter society, we surrender some rights which "though perfect in the individual, the power to execute them is defective" (Paine, 1993: 90) in exchange for a protection of our civil rights by the law and government. Paine explained:

> He deposits this right in the common stock of society, and takes the arm of society, of which he is part, in preference and in addition to his own … Society grants him nothing. Every man is a proprietor in society and draws on the capital as a matter of right.
>
> *(Ibid.)*

A vital element of human rights is equality. Locke, Paine and many others explain that, although there may be differences in physical or mental ability between persons, these are not so marked as to set us apart. We are all born equal; all born into humanity with the same natural rights and so these cannot be removed and so we are equal in terms of our rights and our opportunities. Because of this we can all have the same expectation of government that it should protect our civil rights because that is government's role and because we all have, or should have, equal access to that protection as we have deposited our rights in the common stock of society. We live by society's laws, give up our ability to escape punishment for our crimes and participate in society's democracy. That is why slavery must be wrong and why people should be treated without prejudice no matter what their colour, ethnicity, gender or age. Those accused of a crime should get a fair trial and should be presumed innocent until found guilty by a properly convened court of law. Equality does not mean we are all the same or can only have the same things; it means equality of treatment under the law and equality of opportunities. If you like listening to music and I don't then you should be able to listen to it when you want provided you are not obliging me to listen to it when I don't want. The same applies to the whole of life. We should have the same opportunities even if we make different choices of the opportunities granted us.

Another important idea underpinning human rights that needs to be understood is that of the inalienable nature of rights both natural and civil. Inalienability means that your rights cannot be removed. You are born with them and they remain with you. No government or individual can remove your rights. However, it would be foolish and would ignore evidence to the contrary that some states do not uphold people's civil rights and do ignore their human rights despite their loud claims to the contrary. Whilst those with sufficient wealth, power and influence may be able to uphold their human rights without government assistance, that is not the case for most of the population. Governments in democracies are obliged to uphold civil rights for all to ensure the law applies to all.

Inalienability means that people's natural rights cannot be bought, sold or given away. They cannot be disposed of by the person whose rights they are or by someone else on their behalf. They are not a privilege granted by government or some leader. Locke's and Paine's description of the inalienability of human rights has permeated much of western radical political thinking of the past three hundred years and is an important component of democracy and universal suffrage. John Stuart Mill (1806–73) supports Paine's and Locke's view on government, saying there is no difficulty showing that the best form of government is one that is:

> vested in the entire aggregate of the community; every citizen having not just a voice ... but being called upon to take an actual part in the government, by the personal discharge of some public function local or general.
>
> *(Mill, 2008: 244)*

This is often called the social compact or social contract from the French: *Du contrat social ou Principes du droit politique,* a 1762 book by Jean-Jacques Rousseau (1712–78) that discusses similar ideas to Hobbes and Locke. As citizens, we give up the right to escape punishment under the law and in exchange we gain the power to elect a government of and for the people with the right to hold it to account and to dismiss it. The compact guarantees us protection of our civil rights and it also guarantees us equality.

Paine wrote (quoting Dr Price, a radical cleric in London) that the people of England had three fundamental rights:

- To choose their own governors;
- To cashier them for misconduct;
- To frame a government for themselves.

(Paine, 1993: 64)

> Civil power ... is made up of the aggregate of that class of the natural rights of man, which becomes defective in the individual in point of power ... But when collected to a focus becomes competent to the purpose of everyone.
>
> The power produced from the aggregate of natural rights ... Cannot be applied to invade the natural rights ... In which the power to execute is as perfect as the right itself.
>
> *(Paine, 1993: 90)*

Although the basic idea of human rights is now widespread, the principles are often applied in different ways around the world and this has a significant effect on journalism. Some rights are individual and some are collective. Mature western democracies tend to emphasise individual rights whilst some developing cultures might concentrate more on collective rights: rights for children, groups of workers or slum dwellers might be seen as more significant than some individual rights.

Thinkers in the European Continental tradition such as Jean-Jacques Rousseau tend to emphasise positive rights such as the right to education, employment and health care. The British and American tradition concentrates more on what are often called negative rights, protecting the individual from the state with the right to a fair trial and the right to free speech. The UK has a Human Rights Act that mirrors the European Convention of Human Rights. The Act and the Convention lay down rights available to citizens in the UK and the rest of Western Europe. These include the right to:

- Life;
- Own property;
- Freedom of speech;
- Freedom of worship;
- Be free from torture;
- Be free from slavery and forced labour;
- Liberty and security;
- A fair trial;
- No punishment without law;
- Respect for private and family life;
- Freedom of thought, conscience and religion;
- Freedom of expression;
- Freedom of assembly and association;
- Marry and found a family;
- Prohibition of discrimination;
- Protection of property;
- Education;
- Free elections;
- Abolition of the death penalty.

It is government's job to protect those rights on our behalf. There needs to be a balance throughout, though. An overzealous attempt to protect our property, liberty, security and ultimately our lives, for instance could lead to restricting our rights to privacy, fair trial, presumption of innocence, right to association and free speech.

Virtue

Although human rights have become increasingly more important as arbiters of behaviour in a society that has become increasingly more individualistic since the Second World War, there are still other moral systems that have their uses when making professional journalism decisions.

The ancient Greeks developed some of the earliest non-religious moral systems that concentrated on the concept of virtue. Philosophers such as Socrates (470–399 BC), Plato (428/427–348/347 BC), Aristotle (384–322 BC) developed ethics (or ways of thinking about morality) around goodness, or virtue. Socrates left nothing for future generations in terms of his writing, but his work was developed by Plato and used in his own writings. Plato founded his Academy, the forerunner of modern universities, in the 380s. Aristotle later became a member of the Academy.

Plato believed that the world contained moral entities in the same way it contained physical entities and that goodness was absolute and could be identified by a person. Aristotle often contrasted his views with those of his teacher, Plato, so whilst we are able to see Plato's views, we also learn where Aristotle's diverge. For Plato, ethics was about goodness itself but for Aristotle it was about the good for human beings. Aristotle felt we could learn goodness. He said we should pursue happiness (or in Greek *eudaimonia,* often translated as flourishing) or "virtuous activity of the soul". He believed that happiness could not be achieved without training: "none of the moral virtues arise in us by nature; for nothing that exists in nature can form a habit that is contrary to its nature" (Aristotle, 1980: 28). Aristotle thought that virtuous acts brought a good man pleasure and so that a man who was good would find happiness (*eudaimonia*) in doing good acts. "Anyone who does not delight in fine actions is not even a good man; for nobody would say that a man is just unless he enjoys acting justly" (Aristotle, 1976: 79). However, critics accuse Aristotle and Plato of *ethical egoism*. H. A. Prichard argues that "if justice is advocated on the grounds that it is advantageous to the just person, it is thereby reduced to a form of self-interest." (Cited in Norman, 1983).

Aristotle described the "Doctrine of the mean" where men had to balance their lives between extremes: "it is in the nature of moral qualities that they are destroyed by deficiency and excess" (Aristotle, 1976: 94).

He believed that this is why it is important to train from "infancy to feel joy and grief at the right things" (i.: 95). The doctrine of the mean can be very useful in everyday living but does not work so well in journalism. Virtue ethics cannot always help us decide what to do in each moral dilemma. For instance, there is no path of moderation between telling the truth and telling lies.

Deontology

One of the main school of ethics believes that decision making should be done on the basis of duty and obligation. Immanuel Kant (1724–1804) and his followers believe that only an action done through duty – where the motive for the action is the only determiner of whether a decision is moral – can be considered a moral action. In other words, only if your motive for your decision is virtuous can an action flowing from it be called moral. The consequences of your action, good or bad, have no part to play in whether your action is moral.

Those who use motive as their only test of right and wrong are called motivists. Kant believed that man's will should be paramount and that whilst:

> intelligence, wit, judgment and other talents of the mind … or courage, resoluteness, and perseverance as qualities of temperament, are in many respects good and desirable, they can become extremely bad and harmful if the will, which is to make use of the gifts … is not good.
>
> *(Kant, 1990: 9)*

Kant believed that a good will was important not because of what it achieved, but because it had been willed: "The good will is not good because of what it effects or accomplishes … ; it is good only because of its willing" (ibid.: 10).

Kant explains this by pointing out that, if we accept that "no organ will be found for any purpose which is not the fittest and best adapted for that purpose", then nature would have hit on a very poor way of doing things if the creature's happiness were determined by its will and reason. Kant says that nature would have used instinct rather than reason, if happiness had been the only aim. Since we have been given reason, he argues, it must be so that we can use it to guide our will for good, and not necessarily for happiness. Kant tells us: "An action done from duty does not have its moral worth in the *purpose* which is to be achieved through it but in the *maxim* whereby it is determined" (Kant, 1990: 16).

Kant identifies three *imperatives* – objective principles we *ought* to do or refrain from doing:

- *Technical imperatives:* These are actions of technical skill. To be a good teacher, doctor or journalist means being skilled in those tasks, not that one is necessarily morally good, after all both physicians and poisoners have skill with poisons.

- *Hypothetical imperatives:* These are described as pragmatic actions carried out for reasons of prudence not at the direct command of our reason. We may carry them out because some authority (God, our parents, our boss) tells us to or because they are in our best interests, such as moving out of the way of fast-moving traffic. We don't do them because they are a good thing to do, but because they are a sensible thing to do.
- *Categorical imperatives:* These are actions done objectively for no other reason than the rightness of the action. These command conduct without any reference to the purpose to be reached by it. It can be determined by reason and carried out on the basis of good will. "I will not steal" would be a categorical imperative if you thought it was objectively the right thing to do and you therefore refrain from stealing without thought to the consequences for or against. Kant believed we should only act in such a way that we could also will that our maxim should be a universal law.

People who use duty as a guiding force are called deontologists because they believe in doing what is their duty. Deontologists believe that one should carry out a moral act simply because that is the kind of act it is, not because of the motive or the consequences. Kant said it is right to keep one's promises because that is the universal maxim; because it is your duty. One cannot fail to keep promises just because it might be in one's interests so to do. Duty ethics are supported by philosophers such as William David Ross (1877–1971) and Harold Arthur Prichard (1871–1947). They stress the importance of duty and obligation. One should do something because it is right to do it.

W. D. Ross believed we had a number of duties:

- Of fidelity (keeping promises);
- Reparation (compensation for harm done);
- Gratitude (repaying a kindness);
- Justice;
- Beneficence (improving the condition of others);
- Self-improvement; and
- Non-maleficence (not injuring others).

These duties are forms of categorical imperatives that one should do, not because it is in your interests, but in the interests of others. Kant tells us that rational beings are ends, not means. He warns that man "is not a thing, and thus not something to be used merely as a means; he must always be regarded in all his actions as an end in himself". We should be careful not to use others in a way we would oppose for ourselves.

Universal laws and codes of practice

Universal laws, when applied in professional practice, can be described as codes of practice or, in the NUJ's case, a code of conduct. These are rules (universal laws), drawn up by the profession they apply to, that should be adhered to by all in that profession. Journalists have several codes of practice including those of the National Union of Journalists, Independent Press Standards Organisation, Impress, BBC and Ofcom. Codes of practice can be identified with deontology as a series of universal maxims that journalists can apply in all circumstances. These maxims make it easier to behave ethically, and easier to police conduct. They are like laws we either uphold or ignore at our peril. Deciding a code of conduct based on objective principles can be easier than working everything out from basics.

If, for instance, you have decided that stealing is wrong you would be able to justify that from first principles but, having decided that, a code saves you from constant major decision making.

Deontological moral decision making

Without a rule saying that stealing is wrong and something you should not do you would have to decide what you intended to do every time you saw something. You would need to go through a series of questions as shown in Table 2.1.

I'm not suggesting one should behave morally simply because to do otherwise is complicated, but it is certainly true that no one wants to go through all those questions every time they see something. Presumably, if you do not have a moral code, then tough, you must; even if your technical knowledge speeds up the answering of at least some of those questions. For those with a code, it's simple. Is it wrong to steal? Yes. Therefore the rest of the list is redundant.

TABLE 2.1

Action	Imperative
Is it wrong to steal?	Categorical
Will someone be harmed by my stealing it?	Categorical
Does someone need it?	Technical
Is that worth stealing?	Technical
Can I steal it; weight, tools needed?	Technical
Will I get away with it?	Hypothetical
Will anyone see me and call the police?	Hypothetical
Am I fast enough to run or drive away?	Technical
Could I sell it?	Technical and hypothetical
Could I sell parts of it?	Technical
Is the price worth the risk?	Hypothetical

Utilitarianism

Whilst deontologists use motive and duty to determine their moral decisions, believing that only a decision made to moral rules can be a moral decision, there are others who say that this is not a good method of deciding morality as choices made for good moral reasons can often have bad consequences. One paper criticising Kant's views by a French philosopher, Benjamin Constant, in 1797, concerned an example of a murderer who comes to your house determined to kill your friend who is inside. The paper argues that you would be right to lie about your friend's whereabouts. Kant responded in a famous paper "On a Supposed Right to Lie from Altruistic Motives" (www.unc.edu/courses/2009spring/plcy/240/001/Kant.pdf accessed 2/8/18) explaining that, even if several of the perfectly good responses to this inquiry that did not involve lying could not be used for various reasons, it would still be wrong to lie. This is not the place to go into the detailed arguments of Kant and the scores of philosophers who have pawed over his reasoning since, but it does bring into stark relief the difference between those who believe that duty and right should underpin moral decision making and those who believe that the consequences that flow from your decisions should be the arbiter.

Utilitarians are those who seek the greatest utility or general happiness by determining the consequences of their actions rather than motive. This is sometimes called teleology, in that it examines the purpose to which the decision leads rather than its cause. Those things that have a good consequence are seen as desirable. Those that do not as undesirable.

However, this involves deciding what is a good consequence or a bad consequence.

Consequentialists

Jeremy Bentham (1748–1832) and John Stuart Mill (1806–73) were the two most famous utilitarians. They argued that an action is right in so far as it tends to produce the greatest happiness for the greatest number. J. S. Mill called this the Greatest Happiness Principle: actions are right in proportion as they tend to promote happiness, wrong as they tend to produce the reverse of happiness such as pain and the privation of pleasure. In his defence of utilitarianism, Mill rejected the idea that actions are right because God says so or because they have any inherent moral properties of their own.

These ideas were controversial at the time they were first described, although they seem uncontroversial to us now, and were condemned as outrageous and "worthy of swine". Many of these critics were devout and believed in the morality laid down in the Bible and driven by God. We are much more likely to consider consequences today as a way of making moral decisions.

Utilitarianism is a useful tool for moral decision making in a number of circumstances because it can allow you to focus on what you want to achieve, and it can allow you to measure an increase in the balance of happiness. There can be a clear and direct consequence to your moral actions in a way that is not always clear with duty.

However, there are a number of difficulties with it as a moral process. Are all pleasures/pain identical and therefore measurable? Could an immediate pleasure have longer term consequences that might make it less desirable and how do we measure those and still ensure the greater happiness? Are all people equal and is their happiness or pain equal? Is something that is desirable for one less desirable or even anathema to another? Can we balance the increase in happiness in one or more people and balance it with the potential pain and harm to others? Utilitarianism can also ignore individuals in an attempt to identify the greater good for all. Would it be right to increase someone's happiness enormously at the cost of a small amount of pain for many?

Riotous living might seem the ultimate pleasure, but it is unlikely that continuous pleasure of this sort would bring happiness over an extended period. Are there different types of pleasure? Can the transient pleasure of scratching an itch match the pleasure of producing a major work of art?

Pleasure must vary by type and quantity and so we must take these into consideration. If you were offered a choice of the life of Paul McCartney or an oyster (even if it went on for millions of years) which would you choose?

Can we give more emphasis to higher pleasures than lower pleasures? Should I prefer to watch opera rather than the *Simpsons* or are both of equal quantities of pleasure? The questions just go on and on as we try to work out the balances of consequences, and these are just the foreseeable consequences. Many a comedy takes as its basic principle the action done in the belief of good consequences but which is followed by appalling consequence piling on top of bad consequence. There are also other problems that arise if one is simply looking for the greatest good.

Whilst it might be morally good to sacrifice yourself to save the many (again a central plot line of many books and movies) it's not the same if the decision is made for you. If we were to agree to kill a homeless person who had no family or job in order to harvest their organs to save the lives of seven or eight people bringing happiness to them and their families, improving the lives of 50 to 100 people, that might increase the general sum of happiness but I doubt that anyone would see that as morally acceptable.

Critics of utilitarianism do not believe that we are all equal in consequence. If I saw two people drowning in a river and had a lifebelt to hand, would I throw it first to my mother or to the stranger floundering nearby? Friedrich Nietzsche (1844–1900) was a fierce critic of utilitarians as he did not accept that what was right for one person was right for another. He felt that one could not compare one man with another: "there exists an order of rank between man and man, consequently also between morality and morality". Whilst this flies in the face of the equality that underpins human rights, it's certainly the case that we are more likely to value those close to us rather than strangers or a hardworking doctor or nurse than the town drunk.

A further complication of utilitarianism concerns acts of omission. If we do not do something that leads to harm are we as culpable as if we did do something that led to good? If we were to drive past a road accident without stopping to see if we could help, we could hardly claim to be as morally responsible as if we had not seen the accident unless there were already emergency services or other assistance already there.

Utilitarianism also seems to reduce individual human rights, subsuming them by collective rights. If the majority is happy, then the pain of a few may not be important. This is widely accepted in democracies. A few suffer so that the majority can be safe. However, with the move away from collectivism towards individualism over the past half century this seems less acceptable in many western countries.

Mill argued that justice and individual rights are something society should defend – a form of trump card that demanded a higher level of proof than ordinary pleasure or pain.

> To have a right, then, is, I conceive, to have something which society ought to defend me in the possession of. If the objector goes on to ask, why it ought? I can give him no other reason than general utility.
>
> *(Mill, 2008: 189)*

General utility in this context would mean that a person's individual utility may well be tied to the general utility, that is the utility of all, and vice versa. General utility may be damaged if a person's utility is damaged. There are differing forms of utility either relating to a specific act or to the applying general rule, a sort of hybrid deontological utilitarianism (see works in the References by Frost, Warburton, Norman for more detailed discussion). However, when it comes to journalism this may be something that we need to consider. Duty, through the code of practice, allows us to discuss what is right and how journalists should behave.

Codes of conduct and their interplay with ethics systems

Human rights have played an increasingly important role in journalistic ethics over the past 20 years, encouraged by the Human Rights Act which was implemented from the early part of this century.

The legal pressure for human rights and therefore the government's duty to uphold them has led to more concern about issues such as reputation, fair trial and privacy. Whilst the law in the UK already upheld reputation and fair trial and had some things to say about privacy, or at least its practical application, the Human Rights Act emphasised the ethical importance of these rights and ensured that none took precedence over another, including the right to free speech. Although this means that journalists need to think carefully about the justification for exercising their right to free speech and whether it traduces

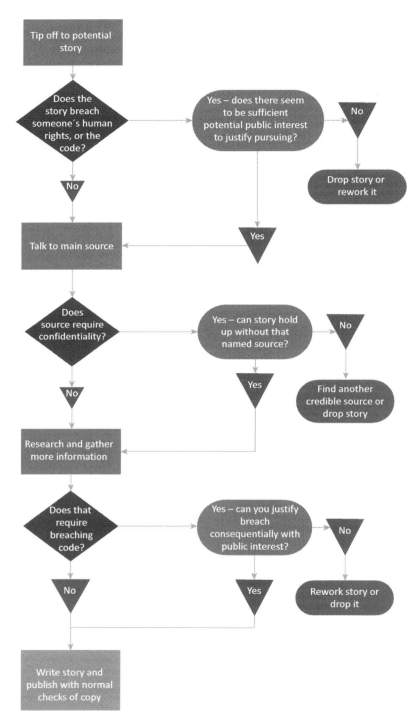

FIGURE 2.1 Flow chart of ethical decision making

someone's other rights, it has left the basic ethical concepts of truth and doing no harm untouched and so ethical codes still have an important part to play. In discussing professional ethical conundrums, the journalist may start with human rights, but will quickly move to deontology and the need to consider a code of practice.

A strict code, whilst saving the journalist from having to ponder every professional decision against the usual tight deadlines to which journalists must adhere, cannot cover all cases. It is also often set against the public interest or the rights of individuals. Are we right to deceive if that is the only way in which we can get a story? Are there other things we might do that breach the code we are working to but are needed to produce a story? The journalist can set out a basic principle but, on seeing that the story is likely to be of major public interest (see Chapter 7 for a fuller discussion of public interest), he or she can then move on from the deontological limitations of codes and universal maxims to utilitarianism. This will allow the journalist to examine the consequences of publishing the story, gauging the level of harm caused to the subject or subjects of the story in terms of their reputation or privacy as measured against the general increase in human happiness that might be brought about through people's right to be informed about criminal or anti-social activity. We need to consider the harm caused as well as the significance of the story as it is probably impossible to consider all the likely consequences that may flow from publishing.

This means we can set up a taxonomy of decision-making to lead us through a difficult ethical dilemma. We can start looking at the various rights involved. There is a right to free expression that allows journalists to write what they want and a commercial right for broadcasters and publishers to publish that writing provided it breaches none of the several laws that protect individual rights.

Next we need to consider if there is an individual right that might prevent us from publishing, such as invading someone's privacy or removing their right to a fair trial. If there is not, then we go on to consider the code. If there is no prohibition there, then the article can be published. If there is a prohibition or a breach of an individual right, then we move on to utilitarianism and try to work out what the possible consequences may be and whether the public interest in the story is significant enough to raise the general level of human happiness higher than any pain we may cause an individual. Whilst this sounds complex, it is in fact a lot easier than deciding every question from scratch alongside the difficulties of researching, gathering information and presenting it. Figure 2.1 helps describe the process.

Flow chart of ethical decision making

This flow chart describes general journalistic ethical decision making that can be applied to any ethical dilemma. However, future chapters will deal solely with privacy and its linked dilemmas such as harassment, intrusion or confidence. For more general ethical issues, please see Frost, 2016.

3
WHAT IS PRIVACY?

Privacy is a basic human right protected under the UK Human Rights Act, the European Convention on Human Rights and the UN Declaration of Human Rights that allows people the right to respect for their private and family life, home and correspondence. This means that no one should interfere with or intrude on another's privacy without good reason. This applies to government, government authorities and others, including the media, although I will generally be talking about privacy in terms of its relationship with the media in this chapter.

However, we cannot ignore governments and government agencies entirely even when considering privacy only in connection with the media. Journalists have a right to privacy as well as a duty to protect the privacy of their sources, so they need to be aware of the pressures governments can apply and the tools they can use in the UK and other developed countries so as to resist such intrusions from the authorities and protect their sources.

Privacy is a complex matter, made more complex by modern technology and the ability to collect and store huge quantities of personal data, requiring us to consider privacy both in terms of protecting a personal right to privacy and a right to protect the personal data that is part of that privacy. Generally speaking, the right to privacy is recognised around the world. Article 12 of the UN Declaration of Human Rights says:

> No one shall be subjected to arbitrary interference with his privacy, family, home or correspondence, nor to attacks upon his honour and reputation. Everyone has the right to the protection of the law against such interference or attacks.
>
> *(www.un.org/en/universal-declaration-human-rights/*
> *accessed January 2019)*

This is a broad definition and includes protection of honour, something covered by laws of defamation in the UK and many others. The European Convention on Human Rights (ECHR) has a similar clause, Clause 8, echoed in the UK Human Rights Act:

> 1. Everyone has the right to respect for his private and family life, his home and his correspondence. 2. There shall be no interference by a public authority with the exercise of this right except such as is in accordance with the law and is necessary in a democratic society in the interests of national security, public safety or the economic well-being of the country, for the prevention of disorder or crime, for the protection of health or morals, or for the protection of the rights and freedoms of others.
>
> *(www.echr.coe.int/Documents/Convention_ENG.pdf*
> *accessed January 2019)*

Clause 1 is very similar to the UN declaration. The key elements to remember are that privacy is protected if it concerns someone's family life, their home or their correspondence. In this context correspondence has generally been taken to mean personal correspondence between two people. It's worth remembering that these declarations were drawn up shortly after the Second World War, well before computers and the huge advances in communication they would bring. Correspondence meant sitting down and writing a letter to a specific person. In order to contact more than one person, copies needed to be made either by using carbon paper to copy the handwritten or typewritten letter, or by making a mimeograph – typing or drawing onto a stencil that could then be used on a duplicator to produce up to a couple of hundred copies. Whilst slightly cumbersome, such technology was cheap and widely used in offices and schools for circulars and bulletins, but would not normally be considered as correspondence in the sense of it needing privacy. The introduction of computers, the internet and social media has changed all that and correspondence includes emails and social media messages that are being capable of posting to thousands of people. This ability to post to large numbers probably removes any attempt to identify social media postings as private. However, it also increases the risk of them being defamatory.

Whilst there is no tort of intrusion on privacy in the UK, despite a number of attempts to introduce one, there are laws of trespass, harassment, breach of confidence and data protection all of which flow the basic human right outlined above. The law in the UK and many other countries requires the police and other authorities to seek a warrant from a magistrate or judge showing reasonable grounds for believing that a search will produce evidence pertinent to the crime the officers are investigating. These various laws give considerable protection of our privacy from those in authority.

Breach of confidence, however, is the one that has been most widely used in order to protect the privacy of those in public positions. Many people, over the years, have offered to sell to the newspapers their stories about life with celebrities or important people. With the public's seemingly inexhaustible interest in celebrity most newspapers see these as certain circulation boosters, improving sales and justifying higher advertising rates. However, a number of celebrities have prevented publication by gaining an injunction from the courts. Cherie Blair, the wife of UK prime minister Tony Blair gained an injunction to prevent her children's former nanny Ros Mark publishing in the *Mail on Sunday* part of a book she had written about her experiences. Whilst some early editions contained the story, the injunction prevented further publication and the book Ms Marks was writing was never published. Ms Mark had a duty of confidence to her employer, just as the Blairs had a duty of confidence to her as an employee.

Singer and musician Loreena McKennitt similarly prevented publication of a book written by her former friend as it contained details of Ms McKennitt's private life and was deemed by the courts to breach the confidence expected of a friend. The McKennitt case is highly significant in UK law as it introduces a number of points of law at the Appeals Court and will be examined in detail in a later chapter. Breach of confidence means, according to Lord Denning, a former Master of the Rolls, that one "should not take advantage of information disclosed in confidence". Of course the information concerned is rarely disclosed to the journalist and never in confidence – the whole point is to publish; but the courts will prevent publication if they believe it has flowed from a source that did receive the information in confidence.

Why is privacy important?

Why is privacy important to people? We regularly mix with people and tell them about ourselves; many of us go on social media to tell others of our day's adventures.

First it is important to understand there are different forms of privacy.

The individual

We all need somewhere to retreat in order to manage our identity and to rest and relax. This is why home is such an important part of our privacy. Whether it is a mansion or a simple one-room apartment, we would not welcome people wandering through uninvited. We may not be doing anything more exciting than sitting in an armchair enjoying a cup of tea or lying in bed trying to get to sleep but having strangers wandering in and out uninvited would be considered intolerable. Everyone from the most widely known celebrity down to the humblest citizen shares the same desire and right to expect privacy in their home. Even the homeless or those in multiple occupancy do what they can with cardboard boxes or blankets hung on ropes to give some semblance of privacy. This is the basic expectation that we all have to control at least some aspects of our lives, keeping us apart from others. We can control what we do in our own home, with whom we like. One of the many definitions of privacy is "Time to our self, the right to be let alone." But privacy is not the only state we need to consider. *Intimacy* is a form of privacy that has to be shared with another. This can be a friend or lover, life partner or spouse but the key to intimacy is the exchange of private information with someone special that is controlled by us but exhibits a level of trust in the other person that identifies them as someone special. Because of this, the unauthorised revelation of that information to others is a breach of that trust. This has ramifications for the relationship; it would be seen as a betrayal if the other person were a friend or lover and a breach of confidence if the other person was involved in some contractual arrangement that could be actionable at law. Privacy and intimacy are not the same as *secrecy*. Secrecy involves keeping information private that, were it to be revealed, would damage the person whose secrets they are, either financially or emotionally. We all have some secrets: passwords to bank accounts, pin numbers to use credit cards, which could damage us financially if they were to be revealed: some of us have secrets that could embarrass us or worse if they were revealed, but we have a perfect right to keep secrets. Matters of confidence arise from these intimacies and secrets. They are matters of privacy that are known to someone who has a right to know them, but a duty to keep them confidential. The courts are clear that spouses cannot kiss and tell even during a bitter divorce and a nursery nurse cannot reveal family information to outsiders any more than she can safely reveal the pin number to the family credit card or the password to the family home.

Where is privacy?

As we have already seen, there are different levels of privacy. Equally there are different ways and times at which privacy can be invaded. A privacy invasion can come from the state, a corporate body or the media and none is more welcome than another if the contact is seen as an invasion of privacy. It should be remembered that privacy is a complex matter of personal control and so the levels vary from person to person. Some like to boast about their earnings or how much money they have; others prefer to keep such matters private. There may be a variety of reasons for these differences: one may think displaying wealth is vulgar, another may need to show off their financial success, a third may wish to minimise their lack of financial success, a fourth may think it more likely to attract a mate, whilst another might think a display of wealth would harm their left-wing credentials. There are probably scores of other reasons. My point is that the person has the right to control how their wealth (or lack of it) is displayed in order to control how they are perceived and therefore how they control their persona. A lot of work was done by Prof. Alan Westin (1929–2013) in the US in the 1960s and 1970s looking at privacy and he wrote one of the first, ground-breaking books on the subject. His later work in the 1990s through a non-profit think tank, *Privacy and American Business*, was significant as computers became all powerful and his research was crucial in determining data protection laws and raising awareness of the importance of privacy in a computer age. Westin identified two main types of people with regard to privacy: privacy fundamentalists and privacy pragmatists. Privacy fundamentalists are very concerned with their privacy and careful not to let people have any information. Privacy fundamentalists are unlikely to do much online in terms of social media, shopping or any other access that requires them giving data over the internet, including credit card details and any personal details. Privacy pragmatists on the other hand are aware of their privacy and its importance but don't see some details as crucial and are willing to exchange that data in return for the convenience of online shopping, social media, messaging and other advantages of computer life. Since Westin, a number of researchers have followed up on his work and expanded the range of types to add intermediate types: fundamentalist, intense pragmatist, relaxed pragmatist, marginally concerned and cynical expert (Elueze and Quan-Haase, 2018). The research was carried out with older subjects (65+). Only 13% of their study group were fundamentalists. Some were cynical experts, believing privacy breaches online are inevitable, but who take maximum precautions and are willing to take the risk for the gains. The others were varying levels of pragmatist, identifiable by the type of online use they were prepared to risk.

The UN Special Rapporteur on Privacy, Prof. Joe Cannataci, appointed in 2015, has set out to gain a better understanding of privacy in a world where surveillance and collection of big data is easier than ever before. His mission is to analyse privacy as "an over-arching fundamental right to the free, unhindered development of one's personality" (www.ohchr.org/documents/issues/privacy/a-72-43103_en.docx accessed January 2019).

His report specifically concentrates on the use of computers to surveil people's internet activity and the gathering of big data as this is the latest threat to personal privacy The basic principle remains the same, however. People have a right to control information about themselves to decide how they present to the world, how they develop their personality and their dealings with others.

Privacy covers:

- **Physical** – whether we are happy to expose more or less of our bodies and bodily functions. We like to keep control of how much we expose because of our culture, embarrassment, religion, pride or social expectation (swimwear that might be totally acceptable on the beach, would not normally be acceptable at a formal ceremony). It is our decision how much we reveal. Consider how much of your home is designed simply to protect you from public view to a greater or lesser extent: fences, hedges, doors, curtains. Locks might provide security but are mainly there to protect your privacy.
- **Emotional** – this is affected by similar concepts. Our cultural, social or religious background might well condition how we are prepared to portray our emotions and in what circumstances. Many at a funeral, for instance,

would wish to keep their emotions to themselves, whilst others from different cultures prefer to show their feelings to memorialise their loss.

- **Intellectual** – this is more subtle. It is not a matter of simply deciding whether to show how bright (or dim) we are or how much we do or do not know about a topic. It will be about controlling our perceived intellect to suit our purpose.
- **Information** – this spans a wide range of information from data that we require to keep secret for our own safety from data that might be embarrassing were it to be revealed, to data that we wish to control simply because it is about us. I have no real problem revealing to the world that I have recently refurbished my kitchen, buying a range of new appliances. However, that does not mean that I am happy for data collection tools to gather that information through my online investigations and purchases in order to present a detailed picture of my spending habits to potential advertisers or others with even more sinister motives.

I will discuss in detail later on the difference between private people and public people but, as far as privacy goes, we are talking about potentially invading the privacy of people who are of interest to the public. Interesting the public through gossip, "would you believe it" type of stories and yes, pictures of cats, has long been a way of drawing reader and viewer interest raising circulation or views. I will talk about this in depth in a later chapter.

Health, home and personal correspondence

Health, home and personal correspondence are central elements to the right of privacy. Leveson identified these as the keys to the personal autonomy that makes sense of the need for privacy. It is a reasonable working definition of the significant elements of privacy and one that journalists should bear in mind. Any story about someone's health, or their family and home life, would need a public interest defence in order both to research it and to publish or broadcast it. Personal correspondence (in its broadest sense, including social media, phone calls, voice messages, personal notes, cards and emails) is also protected in the same way. People have a right to assume that their correspondence, especially if tidied out of sight in a drawer or cabinet, should be considered private, but even if left openly on a desk or table, common decency would normally prevent the reading of such correspondence and professional ethics should prevent reading it unless there is a strong reason to believe it is pertinent and that there will therefore be a public interest defence. It may be for instance that the subject will make it clear that they can't show you the letter or report, but that if you should happen to see it and read it on the desk while they are out of the room then well, that's not their fault, is it? Also if circumstances make it clear that a letter or email on the screen is an important part of the current investigation then it may well be that public interest would trump the subject's right to privacy. However, it must be clear that looking without either a heavy hint, or what the law calls "probable cause", would be an invasion of privacy, even if there was no subsequent publication. It always needs to be remembered that intrusion starts with the investigation.

Defining privacy

The UN rapporteur is not the first person to attempt to define privacy and present a reasoned case for why we consider it important. I've concentrated on looking at those who have tended to define it in light of intrusions from the press. Much of what has been written about privacy in recent years has been biased heavily in favour of looking at our privacy in cyberspace and how our data can be accessed legally or illegally by criminals, commercial enterprises or governments. The work of Westin was crucial in this area. Whilst much of the Leveson inquiry examined the intrusion of privacy by the media through phone hacking and personal contact, surprisingly little was made of the evidence provided by the Information Commissioner's Office in its reports to parliament *What Price Privacy* and *What Price Privacy Now*, both published in 2006. The reports revealed that 305 journalists working for 31 UK publications has been identified as driving the illegal trade in confidential information. It is clear that the media are as likely as anyone else to invade privacy using any methods available. Most of the key definitions of the importance of privacy concentrate on the element of being in control of our personas and information that concerns our personal integrity and home life. There is a clear and important distinction between our private and our public lives. How we are known professionally or in our workplace may not be the same as how we view ourselves or how those close to us see us. Many, if not all, people present a mask in their professional life that is a filtered presentation of their persona. This is something they are entitled to do, provided the presentation is merely filtered, not inaccurate, and it provides a basic protection in everyday life. Some "Billy Liars" may invent elements of a fantasy personality in order to impress but this rarely fools people for long and the person themselves can become lost between fantasy and reality and suffer some mental health problems. More usually, people are honest in their exchanges of information but carefully filter what they tell others to modify perceptions.

One of the earliest definitions of privacy appeared in a law paper written by Samuel D. Warren and Louis Brandeis in 1890 for the *Harvard Law Review*. In it they quote Judge Cooley who said that there was a right "To be let alone". This was seen as an extension of the rights of property and life and the right to enjoy life that were current at the time. This new right was still struggling through the courts in the 1800s. Prince Albert won a significant victory, still a key case today, when in the 1849 *Prince Albert v Strange*, the Court of Chancery granted him an injunction preventing Strange from publishing a catalogue of etchings by the prince and Queen Victoria. The royal couple both enjoyed sketching and often gave these to friends. Strange exhibited a number of the pictures and then attempted to publish a catalogue of the collection. On this basis he was breaking no law of property as he was not publishing the etchings but merely a catalogue. Nor was that catalogue defamatory in any way: there was no criticism contained within. At the then present state of the law in both the UK and America the idea that such work should be injuncted simply because it contained information whose circulation the prince would prefer to control was not often supported by the courts. Several cases appeared in both jurisdictions where private letters were published but the courts refused redress simply because the letters had no literary merit – surely a double insult to the poor plaintiff.

Warren and Brandeis went on to identify several reasons for a right of privacy. They saw the development of common law as able to adapt to the requirements of developing society, economy and technology. They identified that this right was founded upon broader rights to enjoy life and to be let alone, both leading to support for a right to control privacy. They identified and discussed that privacy is essential to the individual and his/her need for retreat from the world. Even as early as 1890, they saw the increasing importance of protecting privacy as developing technology made it easier and easier for privacy to be invaded and more difficult for the individual to achieve the level of solitude they required. They were also concerned to protect against the "evils of gossip", an issue I will discuss in more depth in a later chapter.

More recent writers have picked up the same themes. David Archard (1998) talks of keeping personal information non-public or undisclosed whilst Wendy Parent (1992) defines it as the condition of not having undocumented personal knowledge about one possessed by others. Raymond Wacks, who has written extensively about privacy, talks about intrusion being the use or abuse of personal facts, communications or opinions which that individual might regard as intimate or sensitive. (Wacks, 1995: 23). Sissella Bok, in her excellent book on secrets, follows a similar theme:

> Being protected from unwanted access by others ... Claims to privacy are claims to control access to what one takes – however grandiosely – to be one's personal domain.
>
> *(Bok, 1984: 11)*

Judith Innes is one of the more interesting investigators on privacy and its link to intimacy which is what makes privacy both so special and so difficult to identify. She claims (1992: 90) that privacy protects a realm of intimacy:

> intimate matters draw their intimacy from their motivation dependency. An examination of a range of paradigmatic examples of intimate matters produced an account of intimate acts and activities: to claim that an act or activity is intimate is to claim that it draws its meaning and value from the agent's love, liking, or care. Intimate decisions concern such matters. Hence they involve a choice on the agent's part about how to (or not to) embody her love, liking, or care.

This is an incredibly interesting observation, hinted at by the previous writers but not fully examined. Privacy clearly spans a range of matters of health, home, family life and correspondence, some of which we would share with others from necessity but not love or caring. I will tell my bank manager about my financial affairs and discuss my health with my doctor, but whilst these are discussions of private matters, my discussions are not intimate and I rely on their professional discretion and ethics to keep those matters private. I share through necessity for my overall well-being. But I don't tell my bank manager about my health (unless I am putting my affairs in order pending my imminent death) nor does my doctor need to know about my wealth or lack of it in a country that has a national health service. But with intimacy, I tell those I love or care about what I want them to know and what I feel they need to know in order to become closer and develop a stronger relationship. Privacy allows us levels of intimacy that could not exist without that privacy. What is important is not that this thing or that is private (although there is a large level of cultural agreement about what should or could be private if only to make these exchanges of intimacy easier) but that we have private things and that we can choose whom we share them with. We can build up levels of trust and intimacy over a period that will vary depending on the levels of intimacy *we believe* is required to suit that relationship. Acquaintances would get to know basic information; things that are barely private at all. Are we married, do we have children, where are we going on holiday and so on? This level of exchange might suit chats with neighbours, local shop-keepers, work colleagues or people we meet regularly but incidentally in the workplace, pubs or clubs. With people we count as friends, the level of intimacy will be much deeper, with things we would prefer to keep from most people being the confidentialities exchanged. Family, life partners and possibly best friends would be people with whom we would share our deepest privacies. These would be things that require a high level of trust before we would expose our potential vulnerability; things that would dent the public image we are trying to project, that might be embarrassing or even shaming should they be revealed by another. They might or might not include secrets. A person might share a pin code for a credit card or ATM to life partner or family member, or they might prefer to keep it a secret; they might even have things they specifically want to keep secret from someone with whom they otherwise share a strong bond of intimacy, whether that is as innocent as the choice of their Christmas present or the more reprehensible affair they are having with a colleague.

Innes cites Charles Fried and his theories about the commodification of intimacy:

> close relationships involve the voluntary and spontaneous relinquishment of something between friend and friend, lover and lover. The title to information about oneself conferred by privacy provides the necessary something ...
>
> *(Ibid.: 81)*

Intimacy requires these exchanges of private information, partly to show compatibility of personality and to gain a better understanding of a potential friend or lover and partly simply as tokens of that trust and intimacy that must be built up in order to develop a firmer bond. In the sense of true intimacy, it is not just the items exchanged that is important but the motivation behind them and their selection.

The principle of exchange, however, is widely used by much of the media to encourage viewers or readers by pretending intimacy with celebrities. Publishing items of seemingly private information for fans to share gives a false sense of intimacy with celebrities and influencers that can be used to help drive the marketing of goods and lifestyles either directly or through supporting advertising. Much of the supposed private information is of course carefully calculated to construct an image that will be desirable to those who follow the celebrity. This desire can sometimes build to infatuation and even lead to the stalking of the celebrity. The false image of the celebrity is in reality a manufactured avatar that may be very different from the reality. Marketeers and the media use social media, celebrities and performers in reality shows or other public figures as avatars for gain. A celebrity is often just a character that we are encouraged to get to know who is as fictional as the part they might being playing in a TV soap or the face they present to the public. That fictional character often has a minimal connection to their real persona. These avatars are built up over a period by sharing tokens of intimacy carefully manufactured for their public consumption.

If articles or pictures expose a side of their life that does not fit the carefully cultivated persona, they will often attempt to prevent publication and invoke claims of privacy invasion, "invasions" they were happy to accept when it supported the manufactured persona.

Levels of privacy: public v private

Whilst the definition of privacy covering home and family life and correspondence is relatively clear, the water generally becomes muddied by these elements of public and private personas. If a celebrity (or indeed anyone) is presenting a false picture of themselves in public then there is always a risk that the media will attempt to expose this falsehood.

There are many examples of celebrities or politicians who have tried to present a particular lifestyle only to be caught out and have the reality exposed. A number of football stars, amongst others, who have attempted to present themselves as loving family men whilst having affairs on the side have seen their true story published in the newspapers.

This brings me on to the difference between public and private. There are choices to be made by the individual about what they consider private in terms of using the information as tokens of intimacy. This can cover anything from such inconsequentials as favourite colour, food or music. Practically any dating site will see those seeking partners explaining their choices in hobbies or music but as they get to know a new date, they will exchange more and more personal information. When it comes to publishing or broadcasting information about people it is important to understand that there are differences between those who seek normal levels of privacy, even if they release some information on social media of various kinds, and those whose lives are more public.

People who seek a more public life, where they hold positions of authority or influence that give them social respectability, must inevitably expect more risk of privacy invasions. For instance, a GP who has sexual relations with patients must expect more scrutiny than a tennis coach who does the same thing with his clients.

Privacy of the dead

Whilst the general view is that the dead have no privacy, and they certainly cannot sue for defamation, their memory does need to be handled with care and respect for the protection of the private memories of those who loved and cared for them. Of course, it may well be in the public interest to tear down a false image or expose previously hidden private information. Jimmy Savile, for instance, became widely reviled after exposure of his considerable sexual abuses during his life. His fame and personality had protected him until his death, but this opened the way for people to challenge that memory. It is appropriate to remember that the dead cannot protect themselves and present contrary evidence to support their actions and so decent standards of evidence will be required before attacking, in print or online, someone whose record is otherwise good.

4

PRIVACY DEVELOPMENT

Identifying what privacy is and its importance to people is difficult enough, coming down, as it does, to the importance of the individual's feeling of a need for separation from the mass. This can be a chance to feel individualistic and have opportunities to commune with one's soul or one's maker, to involve ourselves in personal activity that can be grandly identified as spirituality. Of course we also enjoy private time for more practical or baser activities.

Privacy law development in the UK and US

There is plenty of evidence that a concern for privacy goes back as far as there have been opportunities or circumstances that can lead to intrusions. David Vincent gives examples taken from the London Assize of Nuisance back in 1341 of Isabel, the relict of John Luter, complaining that a neighbour and his servants could see into her garden (Vincent, 2016: 1). Whilst this is unlikely to have been the first ever official complaint, it does emphasise that concerns about privacy go back a long way. As Diana Webb had it:

> there was surely never a time when individuals, families or groups did not sometimes claim the right to withdraw from public scrutiny into a space of their own.
>
> *(Webb cited in Vincent, 2016: 1)*

Vincent goes on to identify three reasons for this:

1. The nurturing of intimate relations whose conduct required a realm of protected discourse.

2. The search for an inner sanctum where individuals could manage their mental archive and conduct their bodily functions.
3. The defence of thought and behaviour from invasion by external structures of authority.

The law in the UK grudgingly accepted that privacy needed protection and developed alongside a society that provided both more opportunities for privacy but also more requirements for it. Larger houses had more private rooms. The growth in literacy brought with it a need for privacy and secrecy in correspondence. A postal service allowed correspondence between distant friends and relatives but bringing with it the fear of intrusion into that very correspondence that was proving so popular. The development of the telegraph and then the motor car, film, television, cameras and the whole paraphernalia of modern life all added their burden and requirement of privacy. Privacy of the post was brought into legislation in 1710 as an early part of privacy protection in the UK.

At the start of the 20th century, privacy was already seen as an important right by many. The etchings of Queen Victoria and Prince Albert had been protected by the courts and other cases had protected privacy in private homes.

The growth of the media brought further risks to privacy. Various periodicals soon saw the financial benefits of publishing gossip:

> If the journalistic flag-bearers of the public sphere were claiming the right to hold governments to account, their counterparts in the lower reaches of the press were courting prosecution with every issue. A succession of entrepreneurs with close connections to the burgeoning market for pornography were discovering how to monetize privacy.
>
> *(Ibid.: 70)*

Very soon some editors realised there might be even more money to be made by taking payment not to publish a juicy nugget of gossip and neighbours would take money not to pass on the gossip to the paper in the first place. This blackmail led to some journalists facing court proceedings and the law was changed. Section 3 of the Libel Act 1843 (later repealed by the Larceny Act 1916) made it an offence punishable by up to three years prison with hard labour to publish or threaten to publish a libel or to propose abstaining from publish anything with intent to extort money. (www.legislation.gov.uk/ukpga/Vict/6-7/96/section/III/enacted accessed February 2019)

The 1857 Matrimonial Causes Act brought fresh story matter to newspapers and their growing readership. There was domestic scandal aplenty as the courts heard scandalous details of marriages gone wrong, with more marriages dissolved in the next two years than in all the preceding century.

Gradually the newspapers moved on to covering the sexual misconduct of the rich and famous. This expanded into concerns about behaviour behind closed doors and potential mistreatment of more vulnerable members of a household.

Tabloid newspapers encouraged readers to send in their stories, offering, in the case of the Daily Mirror, a "pledge of secrecy" in return for anonymized accounts of private suffering and discontent. Beginning with Leonora Eyles in Woman's Own in 1932, the agony aunt dispensed advice that was now less easily available from a nearby neighbour or relative. Eyles, "the woman who understands", was particularly concerned with communication itself, who should share what confidences with whom within the family circle.

(Ibid.: 96)

The public's appetite for gossip and scandal proved to be almost limitless whether as news or agony aunt advice. In 1936 the National Union of Journalists agreed a code of conduct that instructed its members:

In obtaining news and pictures, reporters and Press photographers should do nothing that will cause pain or humiliation to innocent, bereaved, or otherwise distressed persons. News, pictures, and documents should be acquired by honest methods only.

(Frost, 2016: 265)

The following year proprietors' and journalists' organisations came together to condemn methods of news gathering which caused distress to private persons.

The Second World War limited the press's more serious outrages as newspapers, hit by paper rationing, concentrated on war reporting. The requirement for news at a time of national peril drove the popularity of radio and, whilst newspaper circulations were at their record levels after the war, there were concerns about competing with radio and then TV.

Parliament agreed to examine the press in a royal commission chaired by Sir William David Ross the philosopher; it started work in 1947, submitting its report in 1949. It did not consider privacy as its main focus but it did inevitably have some thoughts about it. The report outlines its concerns about intrusion into the privacy of the bereaved, particularly in cases that attracted the attention of the national press and the risks of a press pack. The report goes further though:

The pain given to individuals is, however, only part of the evil of this practice. The greater evil lies in the degradation of public taste which results from the gratification of morbid curiosity, and in the debasement of the professional standards of the journalists who, whether willingly or otherwise, minister to it.

(Ross, 1949: 132)

Despite these concerns the Commission decided against recommending a law of privacy:

> We have given considerable thought to this suggestion, but it would in
> our view be extremely difficult to devise legislation which would deal
> with the mischief effectively and be capable of enforcement.
>
> *(Ibid.: 170)*

The Commission felt it best to allow the proprietors and unions to make good
on their resolutions about distress to private persons and suggested that the proposed General Council of the Press could enunciate those principles afresh.
A General Council was one of the key recommendations of the Commission.
The Commission was surprised there was not already one single organisation
that represented the press "to maintain either the freedom of the press or the
integrity on which its reputation depends" (ibid.: 165). They proposed a council
representing the entire industry, to regulate such matters as professional standards, recruitment and training. The chair of the council would be independent,
as would 20% of the members, with none having a link to the industry or government. The rest of the committee, 25 in all, would be proprietors, editors and
journalists. In fact the General Council did not get going until 1953, following
significant pressure in parliament.

Privacy continued to be an issue. Lord Mancroft introduced a Bill to parliament
in 1961. This would give a person a right of action against anyone who published
without consent details of his personal affairs or conduct calculated to cause distress or embarrassment. There were defences provided for public interest and privilege. The Bill gained some support but was later withdrawn.

The press was coming under increasing scrutiny during the 1960s. The Royal
Commission on the Press 1961–1962 was chaired by Baron Shawcross. Set up
largely to look at economic and financial factors affecting the press, it did take the
time to express its regret that the General Council of the Press had not taken on
board all of the Ross Commission's recommendations, in particular that it did not
have any lay members sitting on the council. Following these criticisms, the council changed its name to the Press Council and included lay members on its board.

Pressure on the press over privacy continued and a joint working party of
JUSTICE (the British section of the International Commission of Jurists) and
the British Committee of the International Press Institute was set up under the
chairmanship of Lord Shawcross and their report was published in 1965 (Vincent, 2016: 153). Part of this growth in concern about privacy was not so much
worries about the press but about the storing and usage of personal information
on computers. Whilst still limited to large mainframe computers, owned solely
by government departments or large corporations, it was clear that the use of
computers would expand and that private data needed protection. The JUST-
ICE committee's work was significant and the pressure continued in parliament
with Alexander Lyon MP introducing another Private Member's Bill, this time
to the Commons in 1967, and Peter Bessell MP introducing a Bill to prevent
unauthorised phone tapping. Neither Bill made it to second reading but they
did identify public concerns.

Brian Walden MP introduced yet another Bill in late 1969. Both the JUST-ICE Committee and the National Council for Civil Liberties circulated potential draft Bills and Walden finally accepted the JUSTICE committee Bill as the basis for his Bill. However, this Bill also fell.

Kenneth Younger was appointed to chair a Committee on Privacy in 1972. The committee looked extensively at the question of privacy, but concluded "that we should not attempt a single and comprehensive definition of 'privacy'". Finding by a majority that:

> Privacy is ill-suited to be the subject of a long process of definition through the building up of precedents over the years, since the judgements of the past would be an unreliable guide to any current evaluation of privacy. If, on the other hand, no body of judge-made precedent were built up, the law would have to remain, as it would certainly have to begin, highly uncertain and subject to the unguided judgments of juries from time to time.
>
> *(Younger, 1972: 206)*

- A further Bill from Tom Litterick MP in 1977 on Freedom of Information and Privacy followed but was again unsuccessful. A new royal commission had been announced in 1974 and this reported in 1977. It was chaired by Professor Oliver McGregor. Whilst it made a number of recommendations, few of them were acted on by the Press Council at which they were aimed and none specifically concerned privacy.
- More Bills, this time from William Cash MP in 1988 and in 1989 from John Browne MP continued to pursue a right of privacy but both fell. By this stage the Press Council was seen as a failing organisation. The NUJ had quit in disgust and Louis Blom-Cooper QC was brought in as chair in a last-ditch bid for reform.

Finally in 1989 the Calcutt Committee on Privacy and Related Matters was commissioned by the government to examine the issue of privacy with particular reference to the media. As it took up its task, *'Allo, 'Allo* actor Gorden Kaye was seriously injured during a major storm when a piece of advertising hoarding smashed through his windscreen piercing his forehead. Whilst he was in hospital and still severely ill, a *Sunday Sport* reporter and photographer entered his room, interviewing and photographing him. He later sued for invasion of privacy, but the Court of Appeal said there was no remedy in English law for such an invasion of privacy. The Press Complaints Commission later included privacy in a hospital in its code of practice.

The Committee on Privacy and Related Matters under the chairmanship of David Calcutt QC reported in June 1990. The committee came up with a definition of privacy, but decided against legislation to support it:

> An individual's personal life includes matters of health, home, personal
> relationships, correspondence and documents but does not include his
> trade or business.
>
> *(Calcutt, 1990)*

It took the view that the case for a tort of privacy had not been made out, it
rejected the introduction of a statutory right of reply and felt that in general
freedom of expression should take precedence over privacy of the individual.

The committee's report recommended three changes in the law with the
introduction of new criminal offences: of trespass on private property to obtain
personal information for publication; of planting a surveillance device on private
property to secure information for publication; and of taking a photograph, or
recording the identifiable voice, of someone on private property for publication.
All three offences would allow a defence of public right to know, for example,
when done to expose crime or other wrongdoing. The then Home Office minister, David Waddington, told the House that the government were initially
attracted by these proposals as a possible remedy against the worst excesses of
the press and accepted them in principle and he promised to report to the
House later in the year. The committee also recommended extending anonymity to victims of sexual offences as well as rape.

The Committee reported that it felt that reforms of the Press Council had not
gone far enough and that a new Press Complaints Commission, modelled on
the existing Broadcasting Complaints Commission, should be set up in its place
specifically to adjudicate on complaints. The Commission would be non-
statutory, composed of 23 independently selected members. Should the Commission's rulings be flouted by an individual publication or should the industry
fail to set up a commission or not enforce its decisions, the committee recommended that a publicly funded statutory tribunal with more far-reaching powers
should be set up in its place.

Mr Waddington told the House that:

> "The Government recognise that the industry has made some attempt
> in the past year to respond to the public concern about press abuses...
> In the view of the Calcutt committee, however, the reforms have not
> gone far enough, the two distinct functions of defending the freedom
> of the press and adjudicating on complaints of press malpractice sit
> uneasily together, and only an independent body can effectively carry
> out that second task.
>
> This is positively the last chance for the industry to establish an effective
> non-statutory system of regulation, and I strongly hope that it will seize the
> opportunity that the committee has given it. If a non-statutory commission
> is established, the Government will review its performance after 18 months
> of operation to determine whether a statutory underpinning is required. If
> no steps are taken to set up such a commission, the Government, albeit with

some regret, will proceed to establish a statutory framework, taking account of the committee's recommendations."

(https://api.parliament.uk/historic-hansard/commons/1990/
jun/21/calcutt-report accessed April 2019)

The Press Complaints Commission was launched in 1991, taking over the staff of the former Press Council, and was chaired by Professor Oliver McGregor who had chaired the 1974–9 Royal Commission on the Press.

The PCC failed to impress many people as being a either a good press regulator or a decent complaints handler. David Calcutt, by now Sir David, was asked to look at the PCC's performance and he reported in 1993. He said he had considered three matters:

- Regulation of the press. Has non-statutory self-regulation since the establishment of the PCC been effective?
- Better protection against physical intrusion.
- The possible introduction of a new statutory tort of infringement of privacy.

Sir David was blunt:

> The Press Complaints Commission is not, in my view, an effective regulator of the press. It has not been set up in a way, and is not operating a code of practice, which enables it to command not only press but also public confidence. It does not, in my view, hold the balance fairly between the press and the individual. It is not the truly independent body which it should be. As constituted, it is, in essence, a body set up by the industry, financed by the industry, dominated by the industry, and operating a code of practice devised by the industry and which is over-favourable to the industry.

(https://assets.publishing.service.gov.uk/government/uploads/system/
uploads/attachment_data/file/271963/2135.pdf
accessed April 2019)

Sir David went on to say that in his view the press would not be willing to make the changes needed and that therefore the government should introduce a statutory regime to:

- draw up a code of practice;
- restrain publication of material in breach of the code;
- receive complaints;
- initiate its own investigations;
- rule on alleged breaches;
- enforce publication of its adjudications;
- impose fines;
- award costs and compensation.

Calcutt also recommended that there should be a criminal offence in England and Wales of:

1. entering or remaining on private property, without the consent of the lawful occupant, with intent to obtain personal information with a view to its publication; or placing a surveillance device on private property without the consent of the lawful occupant with intent to obtain personal information with a view to its publication; or
2. using a surveillance device (whether on private property or elsewhere) in relation to an individual who is on private property, without the consent of the individual to such use with intent to obtain personal information about that individual with a view to its publication; or
3. taking a photograph, or recording the voice, of an individual who is on private property, without his consent to the taking or recording, with a view to its publication and with intent that the individual shall be identifiable.

Calcutt did suggest a public interest defence:

1. for the purpose of preventing, detecting or exposing the commission of a crime or other seriously anti-social conduct; or
2. for the purpose of preventing the public from being misled by some public statement or action of the individual concerned; or
3. for the purpose of informing the public about matters directly affecting the discharge of any public function of the individual concerned; or
4. for the protection of public health or safety; or
5. under any lawful authority.

He also recommended that the government gave serious thought to the introduction of a new tort of infringement of privacy.

The government of the time was led by John Major with a very slim majority and decided that the introduction of a tort of privacy was not appropriate despite the Select Committee on National Heritage (the forerunner of the Select Committee on Digital, Culture, Media and Sport) recommending the introduction of a Privacy Bill. It rejected all the National Heritage Committee's proposals.

John Major's government lost the 1997 general election and the Labour party introduced the Human Rights Act in 1998, bringing the European Convention on Human Rights directly into UK law. This included a right of privacy although S12 of the Act makes it clear that this should always be balanced against the right to free expression.

Despite a period of relative calm during the 1990s concerns about privacy became an issue again in the new century. This was partly triggered by the furore that surrounded the death of Princess Diana in 1997, who, it was claimed, was pursued by paparazzi through the streets of Paris at high speed, leading her car to crash, killing her, Dodi Fayed and her driver Henri Paul. The suggestion that pictures had been taken of the princess, badly injured in the car, brought fierce criticism. This emphasised the double nature of privacy invasion. First the intrusion or harassment at the point of gathering the story and then the invasion of privacy through publication or broadcast. No one denied the public interest in the story and therefore its newsworthiness, but pictures of the wrecked car and the bodies inside were generally considered a serious and unnecessary intrusion and no British newspaper had the nerve to use them.

The Human Rights Act, which had been enacted around the same time but did not come into force until 2000, encouraged a number of court cases around privacy, both publication and intrusion that provided precedents whilst parliament investigated the operations of the press with regard to privacy through the Culture, Media and Sport Select Committee in 2003, 2007 and 2010.

The 2003 committee met at a time of some uncertainty. The introduction of digital mobile phones at the end of the 1990s led to increasing claims of voice mail tapping and computer hacking. Journalists and the private investigators they often employed were finding rich territory for stories about the rich and famous by tapping into their voice mail. New laws in 1998 on Data Protection and Human Rights were still bedding down and their impact was still to be determined. Broadcasting had only recently been reformed with the introduction of the Office of Communication (Ofcom) and the Communications Act, neither of which had had a chance to show how they would work. The committee made 34 recommendations, most of them concerning the PCC that were largely ignored. It particularly recommended that:

> Ofcom and all the broadcasters should engage with the PCC and the press industry to develop ways of tackling the media scrums that still seem to gather at the scent of a story. Described by Lord Wakeham as "a form of collective harassment" this is a matter that must be capable of being sorted out – especially when it is the victims of violent events, or their families, that are involved.
>
> *(Culture, Media and Sport Committee, 2003: 4*
> *accessed February 2019)*

The committee went on to recommend that the PCC should set up a pre-publication team to handle issues related to media harassment, including liaison with the broadcasters and the transmission of "desist messages" from those who do not want to talk to the media. The committee said the first job for the pre-publication team should be the collaborative work with Ofcom on "media scrums".

The committee also called on the government to reconsider its position on privacy legislation and:

> bring forward legislative proposals to clarify the protection that individuals can expect from unwarranted intrusion by anyone – not the press alone –

into their private lives. This is necessary fully to satisfy the obligations upon the UK under the European Convention of Human Rights. There should be full and wide consultation but in the end Parliament should be allowed to undertake its proper legislative role.

(Culture, Media and Sport Committee, 2003: 7
accessed February 2019)

Once again the government ignored this recommendation preferring not to upset a press that was at that time generally supportive of the Blair government.

The CMS select committee took up its cudgels again in 2007, looking at the self-regulation of the press. This arose because of current events including the conviction of Clive Goodman, the royal editor of the *News of the World*, for phone hacking and the hounding of Kate Middleton, the then girlfriend of Prince William. The Committee criticised the PCC for failing to question *News of the World* Editor Andy Coulson over the matter. The committee said in its report:

We are, however, concerned at the complacency of the industry's reaction to evidence presented by the Information Commissioner showing that large numbers of journalists had had dealings with a private investigator known to have obtained personal data by illegal means. Although no malpractice by journalists has been proved, that does not mean that no malpractice occurred, and we are severely critical of the journalists' employers for making little or no real effort to investigate the detail of their employees' transactions. If the industry is not prepared to act unless a breach of the law is already shown to have occurred, then the whole justification for self-regulation is seriously undermined.

(Culture, Media and Sport Committee, 2007: 3
accessed February 2019)

The committee went on to say that it thought a privacy law to be almost impossible and in any case they were not persuaded there was significant public support for such a law.

The year 2007 was a significant one for privacy and the media. First Clive Goodman pleaded guilty to illegally intercepting phone messages from the royal household and was jailed for four months along with co-conspirator Glen Mulcaire, a private investigator who was jailed for six months. Goodman was later awarded a £240,000 settlement for unfair dismissal. This was the tip of the phone hacking scandal iceberg. The Information Commissioners Office had published two reports in 2006 starting with *What Price Privacy* and following that six months later with a report on progress: *What Price Privacy Now?* These were reports on halting the unlawful trade in confidential personal information. The ICO noted the police had revealed in its Operation Motorman a "widespread and organised" undercover market in personal information.

Among the ultimate "buyers" are many journalists looking for a story. In one major case investigated by the ICO, the evidence included records of information supplied to 305 named journalists working for a range of newspapers. Other cases have involved finance companies and local authorities wishing to trace debtors; estranged couples with one party seeking details of their partner's whereabouts or finances; and criminals intent on fraud or witness or juror intimidation.

(ICO, 2006a: 5)

The Select Committee said it did not consider "the Information Commissioner should feel debarred from releasing to their own employers the names of individual journalists identified in invoices obtained under Operation Motorman".

The second privacy report had gone further and named the newspapers concerned (see Table 4.1), but not the journalists. The press was somewhat shy about reporting these two important reports and, although editors claimed to the PCC and the Select Committee that they agreed strongly with the recommendations and were carrying out additional training, in fact little changed.

The CMS Select Committee held special sessions again leading into 2010, this time to look at press standards, privacy and libel. Their report was published in February 2010 only months before the lid blew off the phone-hacking scandal. Their inquiry was prompted by the persistent libelling of the McCann family after their young daughter Madeleine went missing on holiday in Portugal. They also examined privacy cases including the Max Mosley case and the Bridgend suicides. They also returned to phone hacking, considering the allegations contained in the *Guardian* in July 2009 that the *News of the World*'s parent company had paid more than £1m in damages and costs to settle three civil actions relating to phone hacking. The committee said they took these claims very seriously as "they cast doubt on assurances we had been given during our 2007 inquiry Privacy and media intrusion that the phone-hacking at News of the World had been limited to one 'rogue reporter', Clive Goodman" (Culture, Media and Sport Committee, 2010: 6 accessed February 2019).

The Committee was scathing in its criticism:

We find that it is likely that the number of victims of illegal phone-hacking will never be known, not least because of the silence of Clive Goodman and Glenn Mulcaire, their confidentiality settlements with the News of the World and the "collective amnesia" at the newspaper group which we encountered during our inquiry. It is certainly more than the "handful", however, cited by both the newspaper and the police ... We find, however, that the newspaper group did not carry out a full and rigorous inquiry, as it assured us and the Press Complaints Commission it had ... The readiness of all concerned – News International, the police and the PCC – to leave Mr Goodman as the sole scapegoat without carrying out full investigations is striking. The verdict

TABLE 4.1 Publications involved in illegal trade in confidential information

Publication	Number of transactions positively identified	Number of journalists/clients identified using services
Daily Mail	952	58
Sunday People	802	50
Daily Mirror	681	45
Mail on Sunday	266	33
News of the World	182	19
Sunday Mirror	143	25
Best Magazine	134	20
Evening Standard	130	1
The Observer	103	4
Daily Sport	62	4
Sunday Times	52	7
The People	37	19
Daily Express	36	7
Weekend Magazine (Daily Mail)	30	4
Sunday Express	29	8
The Sun	24	4
Closer Magazine	22	5
Sunday Sport	15	1
Night and Day (Mail on Sunday)	9	2
Sunday Business News	8	1
Daily Record	7	2
Saturday (Express)	7	1
Sunday Mirror Magazine	6	1
Real Magazine	4	1
Woman's Own	4	2
Daily Mirror Magazine	3	2
Mail in Ireland	3	1
Daily Star	2	4
Marie Claire	2	1
Personal Magazine	1	1
Sunday World	1	1

Source: ICO, 2006b: 9.

of the PCC's latest inquiry, announced last November, we consider to be simplistic, surprising and a further failure of self-regulation. In seeking to discover precisely who knew what among the staff of the News of the World we have questioned a number of present and former executives of News International. Throughout we have repeatedly encountered an unwillingness to provide the detailed information that we sought, claims of ignorance or lack of recall, and deliberate obfuscation. We strongly condemn this behaviour which reinforces the widely held impression that the press generally regard themselves as unaccountable and that News International in particular has sought to conceal the truth about what really occurred.

(Culture, Media and Sport Committee, 2010: 7 accessed February)

The committee made a number of recommendations, including that it was still too early following the introduction of the Human Rights Act to consider legislation for privacy. However, in the months that followed the *Guardian* and other media continued to provide stories on phone hacking, including the revelation that murdered teenager, Milly Dowler, had had her phone hacked, leading the detectives and her family to believe she was still alive. This sparked such public outrage that finally, in July 2011, Prime Minister David Cameron announced an inquiry into phone hacking and the ethics and practices of the press to be led by Lord Justice Leveson.

Leveson inquiry

The Leveson Inquiry took evidence for around a year before spending four months writing the almost 2,000 page inquiry report to published in November 2012.

Although publishers and editors had claimed over the previous 20 years that the PCC was improving standards, those claims became unsustainable after the evidence heard at the Leveson Inquiry when even its former director Tim Toulmin told the inquiry: "It thinks it's a complaints body. I've always preferred to think of it as an ombudsman. I don't think it is a regulator." The Prime Minister, David Cameron, told the inquiry that the PCC was: "ineffective and lacking in rigour" whilst the leader of the opposition, Ed Miliband, called it a "toothless poodle" (Leveson, 2012: 12). Both demanded the PCC be closed and a new body set up. Lord Hunt, the last PCC Chairman, and the PCC itself unanimously decided before the Leveson Inquiry ended, to close. Lord Hunt said: "I decided early on that the problem really was that the PCC was being criticised for not exercising powers it never had in the first place, so I recommended we start again with a new body with a Press regulator with teeth." (www.independent.co.uk/news/media/press/lord-hunt-defends-decision-to-scrap-pcc-7546356.html accessed March 2019). The PCC continued to take complaints pending the setting up of the IPSO.

Lord Leveson also identified in his report the failings of the PCC and supported the views of many witnesses. His report said:

In practice, the PCC has proved itself to be aligned with the interests of the press, effectively championing its interests on issues such as S12 Human Rights Act 1998 and the penalty for breach of S55 Data Protection Act 1998. When it did investigate major issues it sought to head off or minimise criticism of the press. It did little in response to

Operation Motorman; its attempts to investigate phone hacking allegations, which provided support for the News of the World, lacked any
credibility: save for inviting answers to questions, no serious investigation was undertaken at all. It may be that no serious investigation could
be undertaken: if that was right, it was of critical importance that the
PCC said so.

The PCC has not monitored press compliance with the Code and the
statistics which it has published lack transparency. Even what the organisation undoubtedly was able to do well, namely complaints handling and anti-
harassment work, was restricted by a lack of profile and a reluctance to deal
with matters that were the subject of civil litigation. That latterly high profile complainants almost invariably turned to the courts instead of using the
PCC speaks volumes.

(2012: 12)

He went on to recommend in his report that he felt a genuinely independent
but effective system of regulation was required. However, he did not feel that
the two proposals from the industry – one from Lord Hunt and one from Lord
Black of Brentwood, as Chair of the Press Standards Board of Finance (Press-
BoF) – met his earlier criteria and failed to be sufficiently independent of the
press. He wrote:

An independent self regulatory body should be governed by an independent Board. In order to ensure the independence of the body, the Chair
and members of the Board must be appointed in a genuinely open, trans-
parent and independent way, without any influence from industry or
Government.

(Ibid.: 32)

He made a number of other recommendations but crucially called for wider
powers for such a body, including the power to fine newspapers up to £1m.
The body should take and consider complaints from individuals and groups of
people where there was no identifiable complainant. There should be an arbitration service to limit the need to go to law on matters such as libel and privacy
and that membership should be open to all publishers and could include different types of membership.

The PCC had already accepted that it was doomed and had agreed it would
remain solely as a transitional body until the Leveson recommendations could be
considered. Leveson's recommendations for a new regulator called for it to be
governed by a board independent of the industry and government. He identified
how this might be done and made further recommendations designed to
strengthen self-regulation. He recommended little about privacy except to
toughen up the Data Protection Act requiring journalists processing data were
doing so for publication not simply with a view to publication.

He also recommended there be an immediate review of damages available for breach of data protection and privacy.

There were a number of other recommendations but Leveson had not examined the corporate basis for phone hacking – because of a number of outstanding court cases, it was decided to leave this second part of the inquiry until later. Leveson 2, as it was known, was due to examine the extent of unlawful or improper conduct within News International and other newspaper organisations and investigate the way the police investigated allegations of unlawful conduct by persons connected with News International. It was also to examine the extent of corporate governance and management failures at News International and other newspaper organisations.

In the event, Leveson 2 was cancelled in March 2018 by the government with the minister for Digital Culture, Media and Sport saying that most of the key issues had been dealt with.

The publication of the Leveson Report was followed by lengthy negotiations between government and publishers. In March 2013 the government was forced to accept a plan to set up a Press Recognition Panel with a list of criteria for an acceptable regulator in March 2013, after the Lords bombarded the Commons with amendment after amendment of every Bill they were sent, none of which the government dared to put to the Commons because they would be agreed against the government's wishes. The government agreed to a royal charter and some supporting legislation to provide incentives for the press to join a recognised regulator in the Crime and Courts Act 2013. Newspaper employers opposed the royal charter and submitted one of their own, but eventually parliament's charter was signed by the queen.

The royal charter set up an independent appointments committee to a recognition panel and a Press Recognition Panel (PRP) to validate self-regulators and ensure they meet the basic criteria.

The PCC handed over the baton of self-regulation to the Independent Press Standards Organisation on 8 September 2014. The new regulator took on the old code which remained unchanged from the code that had failed to deal with the phone hacking, although they later made some changes. Meanwhile a group of concerned citizens set up Impress in 2015 and sought recognition from the PRP. This was granted and an increasing number of small publishers joined up.

Broadcast media and privacy

Leveson and most of the criticism of the media in parliament and elsewhere focused largely on the press, leaving broadcasters to watch on smugly. This was mainly because of the historic development of broadcasting. Coming much later than newspapers as an entirely new technology it was handled very differently. For the first time, the media could grab their audience directly in their living rooms and it's no surprise that broadcasting was treated with caution, with licences limited to the BBC with its royal charter limiting what it could do.

Privacy was an issue even in the early days of the BBC but the limits on news in early years meant it was not a big worry.

Through the early development of TV the BBC had its own standards set by its royal charter, to which broadcasters adhered firmly. When it was joined by commercial broadcasting in 1954, the Television Act 1954 that set up the regulator was more concerned with the technicalities of an additional broadcaster and the dangers and difficulties of commercials being broadcast for the first time than they were about the risk of broadcasters invading people's privacy. Professor Dennis Lloyd of the University of London wrote a critical commentary on the Television Authority and particularly the Act that created it. He said, after expressing his concerns at flaws he saw in the Act:

> Not surprisingly, no criterion is afforded as to how such quality is to be assessed or by whom, and this provision, like many others in the Act, may be regarded as a pious hope or as brutum fulmen, according to whether one adopts the viewpoint of the legislator himself or of the aggrieved viewer desirous of securing the implementation of this particular statutory duty. As the enforceability of this duty gives rise to questions similar to those evoked by other provisions of the Act, it is proposed to postpone any general comment on this matter until some of the other detailed provisions of the Act have been referred to.
>
> *(https://scholarship.law.duke.edu/cgi/viewcontent.cgi?referer=&httpsre dir=1&article=2745&context=lcp accessed Sept. 2019)*

Prof. Lloyd died in 1992 – it would have been interesting to hear his views on modern regulatory legislation. The Television Act gave the Television Authority the duty to ensure programmes broadcast:

- did not offend against good taste or decency, encourage crime or disorder, offend public feelings or refer offensively to any living person;
- maintained a proper balance as to subject matter and a high general standard of quality;
- presented any news with "due" accuracy and impartiality.

Since the ITA had the power of prior restraint, programmes that might have breached these rules were usually referred to the ITA and any programme that seriously breached the privacy of a person would almost certainly be censored.

In 1972, the Sound Broadcasting Act that introduced commercial local radio to the UK replaced the ITA with the Independent Broadcasting Authority that took a more robust approach to regulation but otherwise made little change to editorial regulation. The Broadcasting Act 1996 transformed the broadcasting scene by introducing the concept of digital broadcasting and various other structures of the modern broadcasting framework. It also added the Broadcasting Standards Commission to the Broadcasting Complaints Commission as regulation mechanisms. The BSC was responsible for standards and fairness, including privacy and concern over bereavement. It gained some notoriety as a body introduced to regulate sex and violence on TV during a period when this was perceived to be on the increase. It was replaced by Ofcom in 2003.

The BBC had its royal charter renewed in 2017 but paid the price of series of historic errors including the revelations about Jimmy Savile and other sex abusers and alleged sex abusers. The BBC Trust, set up in 2006 to protect viewers, was seen as a failure and scrapped and Ofcom was ordered to take over the role of editorial regulator.

5

GOSSIP AND CELEBRITY

Interesting the public is an important aspect of journalism. Whilst journalists have a responsibility to inform the public about what is happening in their world, they also need to do it in a way that attracts an audience. Writing dry, highly detailed geopolitical analyses is important for a small intellectual elite, but most people would not be prepared to invest their time and effort in such a piece of reporting. A major part of a journalist's work is to educate and inform their audience about issues in an entertaining way. More serious reporting can also be supported by stories that are more heavily entertainment-led. These types of stories are about the lives of ordinary people or, more often, about the lives and loves of celebrities. To investigate important political stories as well as the lives of celebrities often involves breaching a person's privacy. Revealing evidence of a corrupt politician or the adulterous doings of a famous film star means invading elements of their lives, something that they may not be happy about. Around 58 privacy suits were heard in the High Court in the UK in 2014/15 (www.telegraph.co.uk/news/2016/06/12/celebrity-injunction-and-privacy-cases-double-in-five-years/ accessed February 2019), although only 11 of these were celebrities or politicians.

So why are we interested in celebrities and their lives? The general view seems to be that, while it is often seen as reprehensible, such gossip is covered because it is of interest to readers and so helps increase sales and circulation. However, there is much evidence in the literature that gossip is more than merely entertainment and that it plays an important part in setting the structure and moral tone of society. As broadcasting has taken over the alerting role of newspapers, so newspapers, particularly the tabloids, seem to have come to rely more and more on the importance of gossip to their readers in order to hold, or at least slow the fall of, circulation and therefore profits.

As Paul Dacre, then Editor-in-Chief of the Daily Mail group, said:

> if mass-circulation newspapers, which also devote considerable space to reporting and analysis of public affairs, don't have the freedom to write about scandal, I doubt whether they will retain their mass circulations, with the obvious worrying implications for the democratic process.
>
> *(www.pressgazette.co.uk/society-of-editors-paul-dacres-speech-in-full/*
> *accessed June 2019)*

This is an argument used by many, that newspapers need to intrude on the privacy of others in order to attract the readers required to make it worth providing news in the public interest. The risk, of course, is that in a commercially difficult market, newspapers will concentrate solely on the gossip and scandal that people want to read rather than ensuring that the stories they perhaps ought to read are presented in a sufficiently attractive way and written entertainingly enough to keep them buying the newspaper.

There is, though, a difficult link between gossip, scandal and how newspapers handle them. As Dacre has said elsewhere, the nature of celebrity and its connection to our desire to read about celebrities is not always as it seems:

> Many of the people who are covered in our papers – film stars like Hugh Grant, celebrity chefs and singers – are famous because they choose to be. Their publicity experts arrange interviews and photo-shoots.
>
> Their agents ring when they are going to be in a certain place for a "candid shot". We review their films and give a huge amount for space to their TV appearances ...
>
> The publicity tap is not something you can turn on and off. Stories emerge that do not flatter these stars. To ignore the truth behind the carefully manipulated images would provide only a partial picture. To do that would be to betray the readers.
>
> *(www.pressgazette.co.uk/why-a-free-press-cant-be-dismantled-to-accommo*
> *date-the-foibles-of-the-rich-and-famous-51320/ accessed June 2019)*

It is this public interest in knowing the truth about celebrities, rather than fiction often presented by their various agents and advisers, that is important and can be a justification for intrusion. Carrying reports about a celebrity that have been provided by a publicity agent is to play along with the image presented for the enrichment of the celebrity and the newspaper. Getting behind the mask is to play to the public interest.

Dacre is right to point out that gossip is enjoyed by many at work or with friends but that it is simultaneously condemned as being at best trivial and at worst destructive. It is often described as a malicious force that should be halted. Despite this, many anthropologists and psychologists say that gossip is important to a society and that its role is often underplayed. Gossip in news-papers is also widely condemned either as intrusive or as evidence of "dumbing down".

Talking about one's friends, neighbours and relations is probably as old as language, but Tebbutt (1995) and Rosnow and Fine (1976) identify the term gossip as being derived from the old English term *godsibb* meaning god-parent (Rosnow and Fine, 1976: 86), (Tebbutt, 1995: 19). This term became extended to mean female friends of the mother who would gather at the birth and chattered idly amongst themselves about their neighbours and their lives. Joke Hermes (1995) states that gossip has gathered a bad reputation over the years, to the point where most people consider it either trivial or malicious:

> It is considered a typical women's pastime and is often taken to be highly malicious talk about persons who are not present. Academic sources underline that gossip creates in-groups and out-groups and that it is a social menace ...
>
> *(Hermes, 1995: 119)*

Hermes believes there are three varieties of gossip published in magazines: mali-cious gossip and scandal, friendly stories about celebrities and friendly stories about royalty (1995: 118). Much of the gossip in newspapers follows a similar pattern.

Rosnow and Fine (1976) offer several definitions for the meaning of gossip:

> The unabridged Random House dictionary gives rumor as a synonym for gossip, which it defines as "idle talk". Niehoff, however, has suggested drawing a distinction between "positive gossip" and "negative gossip," and preserving rumor as a synonym for the latter expression [180]. Cooley writes that rumor deals with events and gossip deals with people [49], but Thomas and Znaniecki have qualified this distinction slightly in arguing that rumor deals only with important events and gossip deals with trivial personal occurrences [249].
>
> *(Rosnow and Fine, 1976: 83)*

There seem to be two main themes to gossip. First that it can be positive or negative and, second, that it is almost always trivial and without consequence, unless it is malicious. Rosnow and Fine certainly identify positive and negative gossip but emphasise that this is not really essential to its definition (1976: 87). They define gossip as:

> news about the affairs of another, to one's own memoirs or confessions, or to any hearsay of a personal nature, be it positive or negative, spoken

or in print. In that shadowy area between gossip and rumor, where the significance of the message is unclear or debatable, either term will suffice. The question now posed is how something characterized as trivial can be of value as a social resource.

(Ibid.: 87)

There are two further elements to gossip identified by Spacks (1986). One is the character of the exchange of information; Spacks believes that no more than two or three can "engage in what I call a serious gossip" (1986: 4) and she believes that the level of gossip deteriorates as the group expands. It is certainly axiomatic that only a limited number of people can gossip, and close observation of groups in social settings such as pubs will show that a group of six or more friends will usually split into sub-groups of three or four in order to talk, although these sub-groups may change membership regularly over a period.

The second element is that the gossip always "involves talk about one or more absent figures" (ibid.). One might question a friend or exchange confidences, but discussion about an absent subject is gossip.

Why do we gossip?

Hermes identifies gossip, certainly when it comes to reading gossip magazines, as a pleasurable pursuit:

Some of the women's magazine readers … do occasionally read gossip magazines … and enjoy their unpretentious, undemanding stories. Others are fascinated, but express puzzlement at their fascination or defend their taste for this low-level genre by making it clear they are aware of this low status and that they are not taken in by the magazines and what they write.

(Ibid.: 122)

Rosnow and Fine also point out that gossip is not always seen as being entirely bad. They give an example from Lumley in which in 1888 "The girls of North Hall, Newnham, debated the question whether life without gossip would be worth living". They came to the conclusion it would not and the principal defended this decision (1976: 86).

Many anthropologists now see gossip as playing an important part in a number of social and community roles. Dunbar believes that primates use their social intelligence to form complex alliances with each other. He has found considerable evidence to suggest that the normal size for a human social grouping is between 100 and 200, with a natural grouping being in the 120 to 150 range (1992: 30). He believes that a group that size could only be maintained if humans had moved away from more typical primate group activities such as grooming which limits interaction to two, to language in which a 1:2.7 ratio could be achieved. One talker and 2.7 listeners – well within Meyer's "good gossip" limits, suggesting as it does an average group of between three and four. Dunbar takes this a stage further and suggests that the way men and women use gossip could suggest that:

> language evolved in the context of social bonding between females ... The suggestion that female-female bonding, based on knowledge of the relationships of other individuals, was more important fits much better with views about the structure of nonhuman primate societies where relationships between females are all important. That conversations allow us to exchange information about people who are not present is vitally important. It allows us to teach others how to relate to individuals they have never seen before. Combined with the fact that language also makes it easy to categorise people into types, we can learn how to relate to classes of individuals rather than being restricted to single individuals as primates are in grooming.
>
> *(Ibid.: 31)*

So gossip can help us to place people into types and groups making it easier to understand them and to deal with them on a day to day basis. Gossip can help prevent us making damaging mistakes and speeds up the development of relationships.

Gluckman (1963: 312) supports this with a case study that shows how insiders use gossip to ensure their position within the community by using the lack of knowledge of outsiders against them. Tebbutt also explains how women's gossip was used to hold together communities at the turn of the 19th century (1995).

Gossip – dividing the sexes?

Tebbut, Hermes and Rosnow and Fine identify gossiping as being something that is often seen as a women's pastime. Where men are involved in gossip (and Rosnow and Fine point out that "one need not search very far to find gossipy men" (1976: 83)) the description is different. Men are usually described as being involved in "shop talk" or "shooting the breeze" (Rosnow and Fine, 1976: 82), the implication of this is that men's gossip is of more worth than that of women. Tebbut also identifies this trend and points out that women tend to be patronised, where their voices are documented at all, as "a second class version of 'real' language" (1995: 1). She agrees that where men's talk "performs the same function as women's gossip it is simply called something else" (ibid.). It's possible that with a western view of developing equality this is becoming a less obvious distinction.

The aspirational nature of gossip

Several authors identify (if only in passing) the aspirational nature of gossip. The ability of gossip to define clear groups of people: insiders and outsiders – what Paine calls "we groups" (1967: 278) – has been identified by several writers (Tebbutt, Rosnow and Fine, Gluckman, etc). Gluckman expands on this theme by pointing out that the more exclusive the group, the greater the amount of gossip (1963: 309). He gives as an example groups whose social status becomes so exclusive that they tend to become hereditary and then it also becomes necessary to gossip not only about present members of the group but also the dead members. These high social groups, whether hereditary or professional, are adept at excluding parvenus by using gossip.

> ... old practitioners of a subject can so easily put a comparative new-comer into his place, can make him feel a neophyte. They have only to hint in a technical argument at some personal fact about the person who advanced the theory discussed, to make the eager young student feel how callow he is.
>
> *(Ibid.)*

This ability to retain exclusivity amongst a high status group by using gossip to exclude is often reversed by gossip magazines and newspapers so that they could be seen as providing this exclusive gossip to low status "wannabes" who would then feel they were "in the know" and could take their "rightful" place as part of the high status group.

If gossip is as important to readers as any other form of factually based, time-dependent information, then it is likely that newspapers, even those that are aiming for an audience not normally associated with gossip or the cult of celebrity, will use significant amounts of gossip amidst their news output.

A survey of national newspapers carried out by the author in 2004 showed the extent of gossip in UK national newspapers. Although the survey was limited to one day, it threw up some interesting statistics. It is certainly a survey worth repeating.

It supports the hypothesis that the amount of gossip in the red tops at least, far outweighs the amount of news. The surprise was the middle market papers and particularly the *Daily Telegraph*. The *Daily Telegraph*'s circulation approached that of the *Express* and was easily ahead of its other broadsheet rivals, but it did this with a much higher gossip quotient than the other broadsheets. Indeed, its gossip quotient was very close to that of the *Daily Express*, whose circulation it lagged by only 61,000. The biggest surprise was that, with the exception of the *Daily Star* (whose circulation was about a third to a quarter of what would be expected for its content) and *The Times*, charting gossip against circulation showed a surprisingly straight line. This suggests that the amount of gossip has a direct effect on the sales of the newspapers. If an average is taken of the four main groups as outlined in the data analysis (excluding the *Daily Star*) and the circulation figures are charted against gossip, the result is as identified in Figure 5.2.

If the literature is right, this should not be surprising. One of the reasons for language is as a social–control mechanism and so it can hardly be surprising that this should also be an important role in the newspapers.

It seems possible that some newspapers are intending to use this effect in a bid to increase circulation. Using Figure 5.2, the amount of gossip contained in *The Times*, should give it a circulation at just over 1.1 million instead of 725,000 (circulation in 2019 is only 417,298 according to the Audit Bureau of Circulation). If the chart is reliable, then this either means *The Times* had too much gossip or, it was offering readers more gossip in a bid to increase its circulation towards 1.1m. Although the circulation has fallen dramatically since 2004, this is true of all national papers with all now on circulations that are at best half what they were in 2004 (see Figure 5.1).

Similarly, the *Daily Express* (with the same gossip quotient as the *Daily Telegraph*) was also underperforming marginally according to the chart. If the graph is redrawn, this time averaging the figures for the four main groups of newspapers, there seems to be a direct relation between gossip and circulation.

Of course gossip is almost certainly not the only criterion affecting circulation. *The Sun* picks up many readers with its sports coverage, while the *Daily Mail*

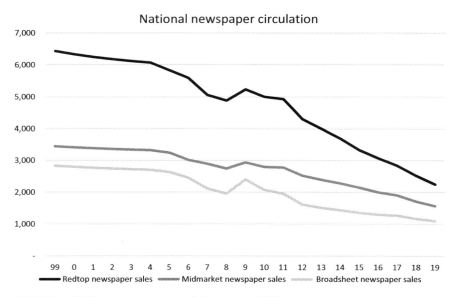

FIGURE 5.1 Falling newspaper circulations since 1999

Gossip v circulation

Calculated by averaging the circulation and gossip quotient for each of the four groups.

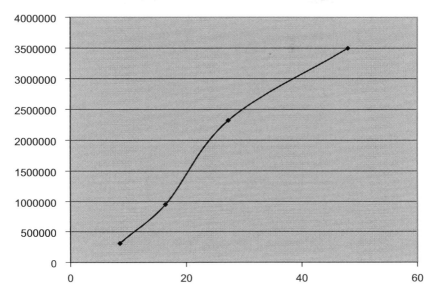

FIGURE 5.2 Gossip plotted against circulation 2004

targets a female audience with great success. Design, presentation, marketing, news choices and writing styles must all play a part in the approach and of course newspapers now face fierce competition from social media, Google, Amazon and others. However, the measure of gossip against circulation is stark enough to explain why editors like Dacre are so keen to fill their papers with gossip.

What is a celebrity?

Although we still gossip about our friends, work colleagues and family, we also gossip, or enjoy reading gossip, about people outside our personal circle. The modern mass media and social media allows us to engage with a large number of people famous for their abilities, talents, positions, wealth or simply for being famous. We can follow our favourite music, film or sport stars on Facebook or twitter. This allows us to feel that we know these people and that we are actually involved in some kind of relationship with them, even if they normally have no knowledge of our existence. Big stars have long had fan clubs where fans could get special messages, Christmas cards and early access to tickets and other "brand" benefits in order to make them feel part of the in group and to keep them loyal.

Public and private images

Social media and its ability to draw readers into the loop has not gone unnoticed by celebrities and their various business managers. Many celebrities, especially those who are not particularly tied to one specific industry such as acting, music, politics, or sport but have, perhaps, gained their popularity through reality shows or some other method of being in the public eye, have found it useful to publicise their public persona – a sort of avatar that presents a picture to the world of their life that may be far from their true personality. I discussed this method of using intimacy to draw fans into the inner circle in Chapter 3. It is done to keep them loyal to the brand and requires this one-way exchange of intimate revelations to make them feel special. This can be (and often is) done through the mass media or social media putting out information that may be built up or even fabricated. Posed pictures, designed to look like secretly snatched shots of two celebrities meeting secretly for a romantic rendezvous; interviews that reveal "personal" details that follow a carefully cultivated fictional characterisation; acts of generosity at a charity event – all may be designed simply to keep the celebrity in the public eye and to present a particular characterisation. Some celebrities keep their status simply by putting their lives on view. Social media is great for this and many celebrities have hundreds of thousands even millions of followers picking up their beloved's every tweet and message, often not realising that a busy celebrity is almost certainly paying a press agent to do the tweeting for them, putting out semi-fictional messages to support their public image. Many reality TV programmes are simply "real life" soaps – semi-scripted interactions between people whose programmes differ from the likes of *Eastenders* and *Coronation Street* simply by being allegedly real rather than fictional. This has not stopped many of the favourite characters from these shows becoming celebrities appearing regularly on "celebrity" versions of TV game shows and elsewhere.

Of course this level of characterisation can be a double-edged sword. Whilst a newspaper or magazine may be happy to go along with these stories if circulation is helped, they may decide at any time that if the characterisation drifts too far from the truth that there is more benefit to circulation in exposing the failings and hypocrisy of the celebrity. There is certainly an argument for saying that those who have relied on publicity to gain their position and status lose some right to privacy over their lives. It's a view that is certainly supported by the IPSO which says in its code:

> In considering an individual's reasonable expectation of privacy, account will be taken of the complainant's own public disclosures of information and the extent to which the material complained about is already in the public domain or will become so.
>
> *(www.ipso.co.uk/editors-code-of-practice/#Privacy*
> *accessed February 2019)*

So, if a celebrity has, for instance, built up a characterisation of someone devoted to their spouse and family, then exposure of adultery and the necessary intrusion this would require, may be justified in order to expose their hypocrisy. Such a fate befell footballer Rio Ferdinand. He sought damages against the *Sunday Mirror* over its 2010 kiss-and-tell story of Carly Storey who talked of her alleged relationship in return for £16,000. Ferdinand sued for a "gross invasion of his privacy", saying he had not seen Ms Storey for six years. He claimed to be a reformed and responsible character. This was important, as the *Mirror*'s lawyer, Gavin Millar QC, told the court, as Ferdinand had just been appointed England captain replacing John Terry after allegations that Terry had had an affair. Millar argued that the case was not about Ferdinand's privacy but about the public pretence that he was a reformed character.

The judge, Mr Justice Nicol, said:

> Overall, in my judgement, the balancing exercise favours the defendant's right of freedom of expression over the claimant's right of privacy.
>
> At one level it was a "kiss and tell" story. Even less attractively, it was a "kiss and paid for telling" story, but stories may be in the public interest even if the reasons behind the informant providing the information are less than noble.
>
> *(www.bbc.co.uk/news/uk-15114365 accessed Sept. 2019)*

Turning to the issue of the England captaincy, the judge said:

> It was a job that carried with it an expectation of high standards. In the views of many the captain was expected to maintain those standards off, as well as on, the pitch.

The judge refused Ferdinand permission to appeal, and the footballer faced a costs bill of about £500,000, with £100,000 to be paid to MGN within 14 days on account of its £161,000 costs. Of course had Ferdinand been a celebrity with a well-known hedonistic lifestyle for which they were celebrated then such coverage would simply be expected.

Intruding into the privacy of lives of celebrities should be measured in much the same way as those of ordinary people. The only difference is measuring what is already in the public domain and how much that is increased by further revelations.

As is explained in Chapter 7, it may be entirely appropriate to intrude into a person's public life in order to:

- Hold those in authority to account;
- Expose undeserved reputations;
- Expose political hypocrisy;
- Expose incompetence or corruption in public life.

Celebrities only differ in that we may find that their public life already intrudes heavily into their private life by their own hand.

6

ISSUES IN PRIVACY

This chapter examines a range of issues concerning privacy and their ethical dilemmas for journalists. It needs to be fully understood that privacy becomes an issue at each point during the story production process: gathering information, researching and data storage, writing and publishing a story. Accuracy and an attempt to tell the truth should always come first when producing a story for publication or broadcast so gathering accurate information is vital, but gathering information about a person will mean collecting data that is identified by the Data Protection Act 2018 as personal data, that is data that can lead to the identification of an individual, and may also be special category personal data (see Chapter 10 for full details). Personal data processing involves collecting and recording data, using and disclosing it to others, tasks a journalist should only be doing if they intend to use the data for the publication of a story, otherwise they may not have a legitimate reason to either collect or store the data. The data collected should be accurate and journalists should do their best to ensure this is the case to prevent the risk of the Information Commissioner's Office becoming involved. So right from the start of researching any story, a journalist needs to consider privacy. What information is needed for the story, how will it be stored and how will it be protected? As a staff journalist, security is the responsibility of the employer, although the journalist does need to know and apply the employer's regulations. Contact books and research data for stories need to be stored in a secure place and, if carried about, then they should be kept on an encrypted memory stick, laptop or mobile device. Freelance journalists (including photographers, researchers and videographers) are responsible for securing and managing their own data collection and processing. This means they should apply to the Information Commissioner's Office to become recognised as a data collector (see Chapter 10). Having collected some basic research information it's likely that the journalist will want to visit the subject and talk to them and also visit other witnesses or contacts (all of whom will have had some level of personal data stored). Journalists need to inform people from whom they collect data that they are collecting data and how it will be used. This is normally done as part of the introductions: "Hi, I'm Fred Bloggs from the Daily Examiner, I want to speak to you about the road accident, I believe you were a witness?" So long as it's clear that the data collected will be stored and might be used in a story that will be published or broadcast, so the person has the information to make an informed decision about whether they would like their data published, that's fine. Of course some people may refuse either because the want to preserve their privacy or because revealing personal data such as a name or address could endanger them or their family — if, for instance they were trying to avoid a violent partner or had some baser motive. Since no one is obliged to talk to journalists and give information if they don't want to, all the journalist can do is to try to persuade them; it depends how important their statement will be to the story. If it is critical to giving the story credibility then compromises should be sought. Can one use a pseudonym? Can one collect the data but promise source confidentiality? However, if that person's evidence is no more crucial than a dozen or so other witnesses then a polite thank you before moving to the next witness is all that's required.

That approach also includes photographs, which the ICO considers a type of personal data, although no cases of illegal collection of data in the form of photographs have yet been through the courts. To use data about a peripheral witness or onlooker without their permission is to risk breaching the law and potentially putting them at risk. If the person is important to the story either as a subject or as a witness a refusal may be more complicated to deal with. That doesn't apply to large group shots or scene shots though. A crowd watching a big fire or gathering at a road accident or a sporting event in public, for instance, can all be photographed without worrying about informing every person there. However, taking pictures of patrons in a pub or restaurant or similar private place, even one where you might not expect total privacy, would require at least alerting patrons who might appear in the picture, and gaining permission from the restaurant owner. The Press Complaints Commission found against papers that published pictures of diners in a restaurant.

Journalists do get some protection under the Data Protection Act 2018 with regard to collecting and storing personal data as journalism is considered a special purpose (see Chapter 10) and collecting data for the purposes of journalism does allow more leeway in terms of the Act but we are still not in a position to force people to tell us who they are.

There are potentially three key elements of privacy invasion and intrusion:

1. The actual publication or broadcast of private details;
2. The potential invasion into a person's privacy at the point of researching the story;
3. The potential invasion of privacy in collecting data and storing it in pursuit of a story.

Breach of privacy through publication

Invasion of privacy at the point of publication, whether this is in print, online or broadcast, is a matter of concern to many people who see journalists as being needlessly intrusive and concerned only with selling newspapers or raising viewing figures by publishing the private affairs of others unnecessarily. Publishing stories that can be invasive of someone's privacy can be justified as being in the public interest provided there is always a public benefit, such as exposing criminal activity or corruption, that makes it clear that the person concerned is undeserving of privacy in that particular area of their life. However, a number of commercial media outlets have noticed that people are inordinately interested in the private lives of other people, whether those people are their friends, family, neighbours or celebrities. I discussed the enthusiasm for stories about celebrities and the reasons for this in the previous chapter and I hope that helped explain why we want to read about celebrities, although of course we should remember that celebrities seem to live more interesting, glamorous lives than we do and this alone attracts attention. They are better-looking, better dressed and seem to float through life unencumbered by the everyday grind of meal preparation, the daily commute, home cleaning, child rearing and the other seemingly endless domestic chores. Of course we forget that we only see the highlights of their lives, just as we only talk to friends and family about the more exciting elements of our own lives – one of the big problems with social media is that people only publish edited highlights in order to make their lives seem more exciting. Our chores are only mentioned if there is a disaster or funny story connected to them – the road accident on the way to work, the exploding vacuum cleaner whilst cleaning the home or the strange things that young children do – but all of this does explain why we like to see glamorous celebrities in their scruffs, with no makeup.

Not all stories invade privacy, but many do. In the examples I mentioned above, imagine the road accident happens in a public place and involves a work colleague who you know. Speaking to that person to get a witness report is fine as it is their story to tell. Speaking to other bystanders is also fine, telling their story is not invasion of privacy. The journalist can report on the accident, as that happened in public and was a public event that might lead to arrests, or changes in road signalling or layout or other public factors. However, someone else in the accident may well have been badly hurt. This affects their health and so is a matter of privacy. We need to check whether they are happy for that private information to be published. This can be difficult if they are in a hospital ward, which are not public areas, as IPSO says journalists should seek permission before entering – permission that is unlikely to be granted unless the patient agrees. Whilst a celebrity may realise that this might be a useful sympathy boost, a chance to get some silver lining from a horrible situation ("*Voice* winner's agony after car crash", or "*Eastenders* star may lose leg"), for most people the privacy required by health concerns means journalists might find it difficult to get information about injuries.

Intrusion at point of researching a story

Invasion of privacy at the point of investigation, whether this is early research or attempts to contact the subject for comment, can also be an intrusion.

When invading someone's privacy it is best to seek them out for comment about the story. However, editors or journalists are often nervous that doing so would warn the subject and allow them to seek an injunction (see Chapter 9) so they wait until publication of the story and then seek comment for a follow-up story. This prevents the risk of an injunction and guarantees a story for the next publication but it also fails to give the subject a right to respond until after publication.

Public figure v private figure

People who choose to move into public life whether as a politician, a performer or simply someone who has a responsible role in society can expect to have reduced privacy in certain areas of their lives. There are some people who make a conscious decision not to live their lives in public and they will deliberately avoid any kind of activity that will bring them into the public eye, but unless one chooses to be a hermit, most people will have some exposure to public life and will therefore have some potential to be accountable to the public for their actions. Only in our thought and dreams can we guarantee absolute privacy.

The level of privacy will vary throughout one's life. Children and young people should be able to guarantee considerable privacy. The law even protects children and young people charged and found guilty of criminal offences. There are only very rare exceptions to this. Thompson and Venables, the killers of Jamie Bulger in the 1990s in Liverpool, for instance, were named but only in order to protect other Liverpool families who were being falsely accused during the trial. Once they were released from prison, there were given new names and injunctions were granted preventing their identity being revealed for life. The 16-year-old killer of 6-year-old Alesha MacPhail in Bute in 2018 was eventually named after the media launched a bid to have the injunction overturned but only after he was found guilty. Will Cornick, then 15, who was found guilty of murdering 61-year-old teacher Audrey Maguire in Leeds. *The Sun* named him after the killing but before his arrest, but his name could not be used during the trial.

Nor should children suffer invasions of their privacy simply because they are the children of famous people. Ofcom, Impress and IPSO are all clear that children of the famous should not lose their right to privacy simply because of who their parents are.

As people become adults they move into public life and are more likely to have their privacy invaded. Sometimes this is chosen, sometimes it is something that has to be accepted and sometimes privacy is sought, but undeserved.

Those who choose to give up much of their privacy are usually those who aspire to be celebrities or performers of all kinds who know they have to sacrifice some privacy in order to entertain and advance their career.

For most people, their lives will evolve around a workplace and they will be obliged to give up some element of privacy in order to be accountable for the position they hold. This can vary from the clerk, who would be responsible for ensuring things are done according to company rules, through administrators and managers whose interaction with staff, the public and others is open to scrutiny, potentially invading their privacy, to professionals with serious responsibilities to the public. These would include health professionals, teachers, social workers, businessmen, senior civil servants and others whose interactions with people, children and public money should make them accountable. Then there are those whose very business requires them to be open – politicians and the like. Finally there are those who become accountable to the public either because they have become involved against their will in some major event or because they have been involved in criminality. When investigating a story a journalist needs to be constantly remined of why this person's privacy is being invaded. If a headteacher is misusing public funds or abusing children, then these are areas for which he or she is responsible to the public and they sacrifice their privacy in that area in order to gain the benefits of being a respected member of society. However, if they belong to a local wife-swapping club or go out night-clubbing every weekend, then that is not directly connected to their responsibilities to parents, children or the school governors and is a private area the courts are likely to uphold.

Someone who does not seek such recognition in society could certainly not expect to have their privacy invaded in that area of their life. A ditch digger, for instance, who has minimal dealings with the public should be able to expect their lives to be private unless they commit a crime or become involved in a major event against their will such as a terrorist outrage but even then the intrusion should only be about the outrage and their limited connection to it and nothing else.

Private places

There is a distinction to be made between public places and private places. This is particularly important for photographers and videographers. Whilst, as a general rule, journalists, including photographers, can operate confidently from a public place such as the street, taking pictures and interviewing people, that is not so in a private place. Permission needs to be obtained from whoever is responsible for the place. Whilst this is obvious in someone's home it may not be so obvious elsewhere. Shopping malls and even some streets are often private property and if you are asked to move on it would be aggravated trespass to refuse. There is also a difference between journalists writing about something and taking pictures. It might be acceptable to say that someone famous was spotted dining out but it would probably be unacceptable to take pictures of them in the restaurant without their permission and the permission of the restaurant owner. It might also be an unacceptable intrusion to name any dining partners unless there was a particular public interest. Out on the streets though things are different. It is legitimate to picture celebrities out and about but even here there may be limitations. Children for instance have a higher right to privacy than their parents and filming or picturing them out on the streets merely because they were with their famous parents would not be acceptable. In 2014, three children of singer Paul Weller were awarded £10,000 damages in the UK High Court after the *Mail Online* ran pictures of them out on a shopping trip with their father in Santa Monica, California (see Chapter 13).

Regulators, the PCC and now IPSO, have occasionally identified other areas that are open to the public but which they identify as having a reasonable expectation of privacy and therefore requiring a strong public interest defence. Hospitals have their own clause and it would be inappropriate and unethical to picture someone in hospital. However, if a famous politician, for instance, was spotted in a hospital A and E gushing blood or clutching a broken arm, then clearly there is the potential for a story, even if it would be potentially be unethical, as an invasion of privacy, to take a picture. However, it is difficult to imagine any journalist worthy of the name not ensuring that a picture was taken of the person as they left the hospital heavily bandaged. The point of the picture is not to show us what the politician looks like in bandages – an artist's impression can do that – but to provide evidence to back up the story.

Similarly restaurants, public houses and public areas of hotels have been identified as areas where people can have a reasonable expectation of privacy in respect of photographs, but again a married politician would be wise not to rely on the privacy of a restaurant to meet someone with whom they were having an affair. A decent public interest defence can trump privacy protection in such places.

Death and private grief

Private grief following a death requires care as does dealing with suicide both at the time and at the later coroner's inquest. Death should always be considered as a time when the potential for intrusion into privacy and an invasion of someone's dignity is high. People grieving the death of someone close are in a highly sensitive emotional state, easily upset and working hard to keep themselves together. It may not take much irritation for them to lose control. For some of the worst of the paparazzi this is their aim, but this is not ethical and is not good journalism. Deliberately provoking someone in order to record the outcome is both appallingly insensitive and a type of fishing expedition. The reporter or photographer is not recording opinion or action but anger and reaction. We have all experienced times of high emotion when we have reacted in a way we later regret. Invading someone's privacy, especially at a time of heightened vulnerability, to provoke such an untypical reaction is unethical and should be resisted.

Suicide in the news

Suicide is a particular kind of death that requires consideration when reporting it. Suicide, as with many deaths, makes for a good story. Death is an important part of our lives that affects everybody and suicide is one side of that.

Suicide has two faces for the journalist:

- It can be a dramatic story of human tragedy that makes good reading;
- It is an ethical dilemma of complex decisions and choices made under intense time pressure.

To make a suicide story newsworthy, the journalist needs to present it in a form that will help the reader understand both the nature of the death and some of the underlying issues that led to the death. This is extremely problematic as those who take their own life have obviously been going through a very troubled period, but it is often tempting as a journalist to try to present the death as an unambiguous and familiar event triggered by a single cause such as a split from a girlfriend/boyfriend, failed exams or the loss of a parent. But often the supposed cause is just in fact another paving slab on the long walk from good mental health to depression and suicide and it would be wrong to present the one single event as the cause. A journalist always needs to bear in mind that incidents are always part of a wider story.

The NUJ guidelines on mental health and suicide say:

> The chances are that at some time in your career you will have to report on a death by suicide. Sadly, the chances in your lifetime of someone you know dying by suicide – or trying to – are frighteningly high. Reporting suicide requires sensitivity and compassion. It is therefore important you are aware that how you report suicide can have a direct effect on vulnerable people. Irresponsible reporting can potentially cause copycat suicides: the words used can be damaging; referring to the method and location is dangerous; providing excessive detail of the method used goes against media guidelines; and romanticising the story or ill-thought out use of pictures can also cause huge problems.
>
> Reports about suicide can be in the public interest, for example they can provide vital information that can help educate the public, so they should be based on the most reliable information. Gathering the views of health experts, researchers into suicide and self-harm and relevant community leaders can assist with this.
>
> *(www.nuj.org.uk/news/mental-health-and-suicide-reporting-guidelines/*
> *accessed May 2019)*

The guide has some very useful advice on the coverage of suicide including:

- Care over language and terminology to be used in the story;
- Avoid using the term suicide in other contexts, such as "political suicide";
- Avoid sensationalist headlines that might glamorise suicide.

Of more significance to a consideration of privacy around a suicide, journalists should take care about location and method of suicide. Pictures of the place of death should be avoided as they often contain unwitting information about the suicide mission – a tall building perhaps or a bridge – that might make them attractive to those seeking a way out. Unusual methods of suicide should also not be spelt out as research shows that people are more likely to take on a method that has been successful for others and whilst it would be wrong to assume that an unsuccessful suicide attempt is simply a cry for help, there are certainly plenty of people who have later been grateful that their method of choice did not work. Research led by Professor Keith Hawton in Oxford showed a 17% increase in the number of people attempting overdoses of a well-known, over the counter drug after the TV show *Casualty* featured a similar suicide bid in 1999. The researchers did not identify an impact on deaths, but this was mainly because mortality from an overdose of the drug is "relatively low".

The IPSO upheld a complaint against the *Northampton Chronicle and Echo* for carrying a story that gave considerable detail of an unusual method of suicide. The report of their findings said:

> The article had provided extensive details regarding the method of suicide the woman had used. The Committee was concerned that this level of detail had been included, and the details included were sufficient to support an individual, in a number of ways, in engaging in a simulative act. This was concerning when the article related to a relatively unusual method of suicide, as there was a risk of increasing the awareness of this method among the population. The level of detail included in the article was excessive in a number of respects, and this represented a breach of Clause 5 (Reporting of suicide). The Committee noted that it was reassured by the publication's response to the complaint; the steps it had taken indicated that it appreciated the severity of the breach to the Code in this instance.
>
> *(www.ipso.co.uk/rulings-and-resolution-statements/ruling/?id=04394-18 accessed May 2019)*

Many suicides seem to present good storylines, either because of the emotional baggage that may come with such a death or because of the youth of the suicide or their celebrity. But the NUJ guidelines caution about glorifying the suicide:

> While journalists want their audience to identify with the people in their stories, glorifying or romanticising suicide by including exaggerated

community expressions of grief, regret or other comments that suggest the local community are honouring the act rather than mourning the person's death are best avoided. Reports that idealise a person who has died by suicide might encourage others to identify with them and emulate their behaviour. It is important to balance statements that praise the deceased with a more accurate picture of their situation by acknowledging that they may have been experiencing difficulties in their life. If this is left out of the story then suicidal behaviour may seem attractive to others who are at risk, especially if they rarely receive positive reinforcement.

(Ibid.)

The NUJ Code of Conduct states a journalist "does nothing to intrude into anybody's private life, grief or distress unless justified by overriding consideration of the public interest" and this needs to be considered at all points of a suicide, whether dealing with youthful friends, close family or people in a school or workplace.

The BBC's editorial guidelines discuss the handling of suicide in news and drama:

- Suicide, attempted suicide and self-harm should be portrayed with great sensitivity, whether in drama or in factual programmes. Factual reporting and fictional portrayal of suicide, attempted suicide and self-harm have the potential to make such actions appear possible, and even appropriate, to the vulnerable.
- Any proposal to broadcast a hanging scene, portray suicide, attempted suicide or self-harm must be referred to a senior editorial figure or, for independents, to the commissioning editor.
- Care must be taken to avoid describing or showing suicide or self-harming methods in explicit detail, unless there is a clear editorial justification.
- The sensitive use of language is also important. Suicide was decriminalised in 1961 and since then the use of the term "commit" is considered offensive by some people. "Take one's life" or "kill oneself" are preferable alternatives.

Murder-suicides, where a parent murders their children and/or partner and then kills themselves are mercifully rare in the UK, with only about five incidents a year in England and Wales and two in Scotland. However, they do attract a lot of interest as people grapple with the complex motivation for such acts. It's notable for instance that there is probably a far higher incidence in fiction and TV drama than in real life. Consequently such an incident will attract journalists from far and wide. I was once involved in covering a suicided murder where a man came to work with his shot gun and as his four colleagues arrived for work on Valentine's day killed each of them with a single shot and then killed himself. We never discovered if the Valentine's day line was significant, although it did help the headline. Following up such a story meant dealing with traumatised police officers and devastated families. I am far from certain that, as an inexperienced twenty-something dealing with the most exciting story of his career so far, I handled it as sensitively as I should have and I'm certain I did not handle as well as I would now.

Violent death

Violent death of any sort is a certain news story, whether by accident, natural disaster or at the hand of another. In all cases it will involve interfering with the privacy of those close to the person.

The death of a celebrity will add an additional element to such a story. A celebrity with regard to death would be anyone who is known to the community that the newspaper or website serves.

Another area of interest with regard to death includes so-called mercy killings or other deaths where the focus is the method or reason for the death rather than the person who has died. The ability to determine when one will die is presently being debated in the UK, with some calling for the right to euthanasia or elective suicide when faced with an incurable and debilitating illness. At the moment this is illegal, obliging those who can manage it to seek release at a clinic abroad. Unusual or strange deaths also make for good stories but ones that require sensitivity and care.

IPSO, Impress and Ofcom all have strong elements in their codes advising journalists. IPSO has upheld a couple of complaints in its short history against newspapers that did not fully check that families were aware of the death before reporting killings that took place abroad, in one instance when a wife in Malaysia stabbed her husband to death and in another case where a woman was the victim of a terrorist outrage in Tunisia. In the Malaysian case, the publication of a video of the crime scene was deeply upsetting to the family.

Door stepping and the death knock

Door stepping is the practice of attempting to get an interview with people at the centre of a major story, while the death knock is the practice of visiting the recently bereaved in order to get information and pictures of the person who has died. Usually this will be someone who has died unexpectedly and in newsworthy circumstances and may often be a young person, requiring the journalist to visit their parents. The IPSO has guidance on its website for the public about how the press should handle a death. It says that:

> The press has a right to report the fact that someone has died, even if friends and family of the person who has died are unhappy with this. However, journalists must follow the rules in the Code.

Journalists must make sure that:

- they approach members of the public with sympathy and discretion
- they do not publish information that might cause any unnecessary upset to friends and family of the person who has died
- they do not break the news of a death to the immediate family
- reports about a death are accurate
- they do not harass people
- in cases where someone has died by suicide, they do not publish too much information about how they died.

(www.ipso.co.uk/media/1535/reporting-on-deaths-public-18.pdf
accessed May 2019)

There is some controversy about the death knock in that it is often as an unreasonable intrusion into the bereaved's privacy. However, that is not how it is always seen by the bereaved themselves. Early and unexpected death is not as common as it was decades ago and we generally are not good at coping with it. This means that often families do not get the opportunity to talk about their loss. Despite the negative elements of journalistic contact (Tulloch, 2006; Walsh-Childers, Lewis and Neely, 2011) the ethical decision not to intrude and leave the family alone may seem the appropriate one but this to fail to involve the family in the story of their loved one's death and many families actually welcome the opportunity to talk about the person they have lost and how their death has affected them. Duncan and Newton explain:

> The "exclusion" as opposed to intrusion issue has implications for the way stories are told and the impact they have on the families themselves and the wider community. Perversely in our view, this situation is sometimes seen as an ethical one, in which the bereaved are respected by the media and left alone in their grief. It is easy to see how avoiding the family can be seen to be a virtuous and respectful act when even an inquiry about coverage can be seen as intrusive. But the story does not stop there. The family may be left alone, but the tale of their loved one's death will still be told … giving centre-stage in the story to sources with no knowledge of the deceased. In other words the family are excluded from the story of their relative's death.
>
> *(Duncan and Newton, 2017: 112)*

They go on to describe a comparative survey published by Newton and Brennodden (2015), the results of which seemed to show that, in such circumstances, where families were approached for their comment, British press coverage produced more sensitive reporting than Norwegian reporting that relied on official accounts and did not approach the family.

Names, addresses and pictures

When reporting a story, details of the person, including their name, age, address, occupation and often a picture are often considered important. But it needs to be remembered that these are personal details and their collection, storage and publication will need to be considered. It may be perfectly right to run a story about a named person, but does adding a picture interfere with their privacy? Whilst it might often be right to add someone's age, occupation or picture to ensure there is no confusion with another person of the same name, it might also not be appropriate. The supermodel Naomi Campbell sued for privacy in 2004 and eventually won when the *Mirror* published a story with pictures of her attendance at a narcotics anonymous meeting shortly after she had denied to newspapers that she had taken drugs (see Chapter 13). Had the newspaper published the story without pictures of her at the treatment centre, then the story itself was not an intrusion into her privacy, the court said, since exposing her hypocrisy was in the public interest. However, the journalists involved need to remember that it was the hypocrisy that triggered the public interest defence, not the drug-taking.

Anonymity in court

Privacy for victims of a crime is also important, particularly when the crime is personally invasive as in a sexual offence. UK law generally requires that in the reporting of sexual offences the alleged victim is kept anonymous in order to protect the sensibilities and privacy of the victim. The accused do not get anonymity, in line with the rules of privacy for all others accused of crimes. Justice should be done in public for several reasons:

- So that the public can be assured justice is being properly delivered;
- So that those who might be able to provide evidence might come forward;
- So that those who might be able to provide an alibi or other defence can come forward; and
- So that the public can learn who has been found guilty of crime.

However, the guarantee for the public, that those who have been victims of crime have received justice, cannot be provided if the victim has been personally violated in an area of their life that we normally keep private and so anonymity is an important protection of personal autonomy.

Children and young people are also particularly vulnerable and so whilst it may not be appropriate to award them their own autonomy because they require the protection of their parents and other adults, it is also appropriate to set a higher threshold on their privacy in order to ensure those adults responsible for them respect that responsibility.

The right to tell one's story

An important element of privacy is the right to tell one's story. Often called "kiss and tell", where a celebrity has a relationship with someone, that someone may well be free to talk about it. In the Campbell case, for instance, had she decided to talk openly about her drug problem, then that story could not be an intrusion into her privacy.

Similarly, if someone had an affair with a celebrity and then decided later to reveal the details to the press, perhaps for money, then they are entitled to tell their story. Only if there is a real or implied obligation of confidence would that not be acceptable. Usually marriage or employment or perhaps a close family relationship would normally be considered a confidential relationship barring "kiss and tell". In one of its last stories before it closed the *News of the World* reported on its front page in September 2010 how "Cheating Roo beds hooker." Complete with pictures of her in skimpy underwear, "hooker" Jenny Thompson told of her romps with Wayne Rooney while his wife was pregnant with his son Kai. Thompson had no obligation of confidence to Rooney, although she presumably did not expect him to pay her £1,200 again for sex, and was perfectly entitled to tell her story of the details of their liaison.

Police raids, emergency calls, public cameras

It is becoming more and more common for video to be used as part of a TV programme arising from police body cams, CCTV or ride along cameras. TV companies will have their own protocols to deal with these issues where there is a clear risk of privacy intrusion but usually the main requirement is the subject's written permission to use the film, usually with their faces pixelated, to prevent recognition by all except those very close to them. The difficulty often comes in deciding when permission is required. A close frame shot of a police officer interviewing a member of the public clearly requires permission of them both unless there is a good public interest reason not to; an arrest in the middle of a large public demonstration, for instance, or other fast-moving news event. Similarly, taking a picture of a large number of people in a public place taking part in a demonstration or as part of a football terrace crowd or some other major gathering would not require permission from every member of the crowd.

A film crew or photographer and journalist on what's known as "a ride along" or "tag-along" needs plenty of thought beforehand. Not only are there the pictures of the subjects of the raid, but also the filming of their home. Joining an early dawn police raid of an alleged drug den, for instance, requires serious consideration of several issues. Can one film the raid without identifying the occupants or their home and property? It's very difficult to exclude everything. Is it acceptable to show exterior and interior shots of the property but to pixelate the people? There are some difficult decisions to consider, balancing between both gaining permission and deciding for what it is felt permission is required. The BBC in its editorial guidelines says:

> We should only go on tag-along raids when there is a public interest and after careful consideration of editorial and legal issues including privacy, consent and trespass.
>
> When we go on a tag-along raid on private property we should normally:
>
> • ensure people understand we are recording for the BBC;
> • obtain consent from the legal occupier and stop recording if asked to do so;
> • leave immediately if asked to do so by the owner, legal occupier or person acting with their authority.
>
> Exceptions may include where we have reason to believe illegal or anti-social behaviour is being exposed, or another public interest will justify our continued recording or presence.
>
> *(www.bbc.co.uk/editorialguidelines/guidelines/privacy/tagalong-raids*
> *accessed June 2019)*

These also raise other issues. If a ride along leads to an arrest, then court reporting restrictions and contempt of courts laws means a journalist can often not use the film or photographs before a trial for fear it would taint a jury and the fair trial process. This means that the video or photographs might be pretty worthless by the time they can be used.

It is in the middle ground of intrusion between the crowd shot of hundreds or more and the close-up film that clearly identifies people that problems often lie. Morrison et al. (2007) discussed the issue with many of their subjects. One 30-to-45-year-old Leeds woman told them:

> We were actually filmed in Whitby years ago. When the kids were really young and we'd been to Whitby and the kids were on the donkeys – we saw them filming on the beach and about six months later this programme called One Summer in Whitby came on and there we all were. On the beach, on the donkeys. The phone never stopped ringing all night – everybody had seen it – it was amazing … it felt weird …
>
> I was really embarrassed. It was awful. People even shouted in the supermarket "We saw you on TV" and everyone's looking to see who it is. It was awful. I was just so embarrassed.
>
> *(Morrison et al., 2007: 300)*

These shots were obviously fairly broad, taking in the beach and the donkey rides but also focusing in closely enough on the donkeys to allow identification of the family. The filming was in public, the family were aware of the filming and even if they had been asked for their permission they would have probably given it gladly, but they were totally unprepared for their few moments of fame months later and found it an "awful" and "embarrassing" experience. It is a comment that was repeated by others and that journalists should remember in their dealings with the public.

Shame and shaming

Shame and shaming are concepts that many tabloid newspapers take seriously. The tabloids have long taken the view that part of their role is as moral arbiters for the public, despite the public itself going through a long period of gradual liberalisation where it has become largely accepted that in order to do whatever we choose we must turn something of a blind eye to the practices of others, whether this lies in the area of hobbies, family life or sexual relations. The law has become the defining line for most people and, whilst wavy in some areas such as recreational drug use and motoring, is the now the only serious social convention to which people adhere.

The tabloids though, led by the *Daily Mail*, have long found a rich and profitable seam in exposing and shaming those it feels breach a standard of public morality more at home in the 1950s than the 2020s. Most people feel happy in knowing where the general boundaries of acceptable behaviour lie by using gossip – a social interaction that can come close to shaming but generally manages to stay short of pointing fingers even if disapprobation is obvious. The tabloids however need to make the act they are exposing one that is beyond the pale if they are to entice people to buy the newspaper.

Petley (2013) calls on Melanie Phillips writing in the *Daily Mail* to lead the charge of self-righteous indignation:

> Scorn or shaming are important in reaffirming the boundaries of what is considered acceptable behaviour and helping ensure that people adhere to them. Centuries ago, this function was performed very effectively by the stocks. Today's Press fulfils much the same function. It allows individuals to identify those who they feel have wronged them and hold them up to public ridicule and contempt.
>
> *(Phillips, 2016 cited in Petley, 2013: 33)*

Of course part of the problem with Phillips's claim is that it ignores that the stocks were set up under the law of the time and those suffering the shaming had been found guilty by a court and also that the press is hardly an acceptable replacement for the courts, with their requirement to adhere to democratically decided laws and protocols, no matter how much we might criticise both institutions.

Paul Dacre, the former editor of the *Daily Mail* and now editor-in-chief of Associated Newspapers and Chairman of Associated Newspapers, is a serious enthusiast for the newspaper as a tool of public morality. Following several of Justice Eady's decisions on important privacy cases he ranted against the judge at a speech to the Society of Editors, accusing him of being amoral because he said in court that when it came to morality, the law in Britain is now effectively neutral, and attacked the judge for imposing a privacy law: "The law is not coming from Parliament – no, that would smack of democracy – but from the arrogant and amoral judgements – words I use very deliberately – of one man" (www.pressgazette.co.uk/society-of-editors-paul-dacres-speech-in-full/ accessed June 2019).

Dacre's speech is worth reading if only for the sheer arrogance and hubris contained within it alongside a complete lack of self-awareness. Dacre may attack Justice Eady, who at least is paid to interpret the law, but he is as guilty of the same arrogance of which he accuses the judge and sets himself up as judge and jury of public morality at a time when the concept of a shared set of public standards and ideals outside of those controlled by law barely exists:

> Since time immemorial public shaming has been a vital element in defending the parameters of what are considered acceptable standards of social behaviour, helping ensure that citizens – rich and poor – adhere to them for the good of the greater community. For hundreds of years, the press has played a role in that process. It has the freedom to identify those who have offended public standards of decency – the very standards its readers believe in – and hold the transgressors up to public condemnation. If their readers don't agree with the defence of such values, they would not buy those papers in such huge numbers.
>
> *(Ibid.)*

Shaming of course involves intruding on the privacy of those being shamed. Whilst there is a strong interest from the public in such things that does not mean there is always a public interest. Many have pointed out that, without interesting the public, newspapers will die and of course that is self-evidently true. But that doesn't mean that newspapers must be filled with tasty titbits of gossip designed to shame celebrities and the like. Of course it is much easier for a newspaper to continue to boost its sales and therefore its profits by exposing areas of the private lives of celebrities and the general public, as Dacre (a man very careful with his own privacy) himself admits in his speech and evidence to Leveson, but that doesn't mean it is ethical or that it's continued use will leave future press freedom unscathed in a time of online media. It's also not a method that seems to work especially well, as a look at national newspaper circulation figures in Figure 5.2 in the previous chapter shows all too clearly.

7

PUBLIC INTEREST

If journalists considered privacy in its ethical setting as a human right and therefore not something to be invaded, then many important stories would remain uncovered as they might involve some element of privacy invasion, either at the point of researching the story or at publication or broadcast. Most, if not all, journalism codes carry an element protecting the privacy of the home and family life. The BBC opening line is as good as any other as a reminder: "The BBC respects privacy and does not infringe it without good reason, wherever in the world it is operating. The Human Rights Act 1998 gives protection to the privacy of individuals, and private information about them …" (www.bbc.co.uk/editorialguidelines/guidelines/privacy accessed March 2019).

We all have a right to privacy as has already been explained; so how can journalists write stories about people, exposing elements of their private life, family or correspondence if they have a right to privacy? The easy answer, and certainly the starting point for this conundrum is that there is also a universal right to free expression and a right to receive information of public interest. In other words, journalists have the right to write stories and the public has a right to be informed about what is being done in their name, by those people who are operating in the name of the public and are therefore answerable to the public.

The most important starting point is to identify the difference between journalists and some other professionals. I will ignore the debate about whether journalism is a trade or profession and use professional in the sense that journalists are (or should be) professional about their work, relying on codes and the law to control and guide their work. Various other professionals have a duty to protect their client's privacy. Whether they are lawyers, doctors or other health professionals, the law and their professional codes of practice require them to keep information about their patients or clients entirely confidential. Only if the subject themselves gives them permission to tell others, whether that is a court or fellow professional, can they reveal information for the treatment or assistance of the subject. Journalists also have this duty to sources, to people they interview as part of a story, but this is done on the basis that the evidence is being gathered with a view to publication. This is essentially the reverse of other professionals who keep information about or given by a person confidential, but will reveal the identity of that person, whilst a journalist is releasing the information about or given by the person but may well be obliged to keep their identity confidential.

Normal journalistic practice means that this needs to be made clear from the very beginning of dealing with a source or witness. The person being interviewed must be made aware that the interview is taking place in order to gather information to publish a story about the issue. The contact, witness or source of the story needs to be aware that the information they are providing will be published unless an agreement is made with the journalist *beforehand* to keep their identity or certain information confidential. This needs to be arranged at the start of the evidence-gathering process. A source needs to know that anything revealed including their identity and the information they give is likely to be used in the story and, if that's a problem, that needs to be discussed before they give the information. If there are good reasons for keeping their identity confidential or for withholding some of the information they provide then both sides need to be sure that is agreed before the source gives the information. There may well be circumstances where it would not be appropriate for a journalist to agree to keep an identity confidential and certainly there may be no good reason to withhold information simply to protect the source. Without evidence and a credible source to support it, the story may well be unusable and journalists should be aware that information given under promise of confidentiality without the journalist knowing what it is can lead to extremely difficult ethical situations. Journalists should always start off with the assumption (and inform the source of this assumption) that nothing they say is out of bounds for publication. Unlike doctors and lawyers, journalists do not assume confidentiality unless otherwise agreed but that they assume openness unless there is a very good reason to keep an identity confidential.

Giving source confidentiality can mean that a story is not credible to publish or broadcast and so it may be better to simply refuse to give that promise even if it means the source won't talk. Occasionally confidentiality can be agreed because, although a credible source is required, this can be found elsewhere once the details of the story and supporting evidence are known.

Since the Data Protection Act 1989, confidentiality has become even stricter for some professions and this can make the journalist's job more difficult. Hospitals routinely refuse to give out condition reports, often not even being prepared to confirm whether they have that patient. Other professionals follow suit. Whilst this has made the journalist's job harder initially, it is now part of the working pattern. The journalist's biggest problem is not to get confused between their early research and data collection that will be controlled by the Data Protection Act 2018, obliging them to maintain records in good and accurate order and also ensure their security, and the special purposes that allow the publication of such information (see Chapter 10).

So how can publication be justified if the law and the codes of ethics require journalists to protect people's privacy? The two-word answer is public interest. There is a public interest defence both under the codes and the law if what a journalist is doing in exposing elements of a person's private life is in the public interest.

The public interest defence for publishing an intrusive story

The public interest is a term that is as difficult to describe as privacy itself. There are elements of it that refer to the public good, to the public benefit. It is information that can help inform and educate the public. Something done in the public interest should not be of sole benefit to the individual or to a corporate body. It is a consequentialist argument. Ethically speaking journalists should not be solely interested in the motive of our actions, but should also be considering their consequences. If journalists discover that a minister of the crown is taking bribes, then it would be in the public interest to expose that to the public. Whilst the journalist would certainly benefit individually from such a tasty story in terms of their reputation, and their news organisation would also benefit corporately in terms of increased audience with its linked potential for financial reward, the main and most important benefit in terms of intruding on the minister's privacy by exposing their financial and business dealings is the public and their knowledge and understanding of the type of person who has been appointed as a minister. Such an expose would almost certainly lead to the minister's resignation and disgrace and call into question the competency of the government. The parliamentary expenses scandal was a good example of this kind of story. MPs' expenses were kept confidential by parliament despite many highly questionable claims. Journalist Heather Brooke fought for five years to force the parliamentary office to reveal expenses under the Freedom of Information Act and was taking the case to the High Court in 2010 for judicial review in the hope of obliging the parliamentary office to reveal the figures when a CD with all the details was leaked to the *Daily Telegraph,* circumventing her struggle. The *Daily Telegraph* ran the story and this was quickly picked up by others, leading to a reworking of the parliamentary expenses system and the jailing of several MPs and the disgrace of a number of others. With all the information out in public, everyone accepted that the story was in the public interest despite the personal details released. It is in the public interest for the public to know how MPs are spending public money – in this case the claims they were making on their expenses; claims that were, in some cases, excessive and even fraudulent.

In another important case, in 2003, Mark Daly, a BBC TV journalist, managed to gain a place on a Greater Manchester police training programme and took a hidden camera with him. He filmed officers making racist comments and one, a North Wales police officer, dressing in a Ku Klux Klan mask and making violent racist remarks. The officer resigned after the documentary was aired. Daly stuck with the training programme for seven months before being exposed after an anonymous tip off. He was arrested on suspicion of obtaining a pecuniary advantage by deception. The BBC said later that it had set his salary aside in a special bank account to be repaid after transmission. The BBC claimed the documentary was in the public interest and the Crown Prosecution Service later dropped charges saying there was insufficient evidence for conviction. Twelve police officers were suspended and six later resigned. The Home Office initially wrote to the BBC protesting about the "deceit" used in gathering film for the documentary but later accepted that its use was justified. A spokeswoman told the *Independent* at the time: "This letter was … before the programme was broadcast and before journalists knew what was in the programme." She confirmed that the Home Office "absolutely refuted" reports the letter was an attempt to get the programme pulled.

This was a classic undercover investigation that breached the privacy of a number of individuals at both the time of researching the story and on broadcast. The issues are serious as they led to six officers being obliged to resign and several others being disciplined. Although Daly invaded the privacy of officers on the training course by filming them in a place where they had a reasonable expectation of privacy, and also invaded their privacy by broadcasting selected clips of their actions in the documentary, these were police officers with a duty to treat all members of the public equally and fairly, something the documentary proved was unlikely to happen because of their racism. Several of the officers admitted treating black and Asian motoring offenders more harshly than white offenders and one even said he would murder Asians if he could. Because of that, the story was very much in the public interest.

Daly rightly received much praise for his work and was properly supported by the BBC. However, it is worth dissecting the issues carefully to fully understand the privacy issues involved. Daly needed to infiltrate the police training programme, thereby potentially invading the privacy of a number of officers, on what was essentially a fishing expedition. He was not certain that he would get any evidence of wrongdoing, although concerns about police racism were high. He needed to film officers during their periods of relaxation so was not particularly concerned with their on-duty behaviour; in other words, he knew he was intruding on their private lives, the time when they were relaxing with colleagues and friends. However, police officers, like a number of other professions with particular duties and responsibilities to society, can be held to higher standards of integrity than most of us. Many people unfortunately hold and express racist views and provided these do not spread hate or threaten violence, the right to free speech means they can discuss them with friends and family in private without breaking the law. No one should consider intruding on their privacy unless, like those officers, there was some element of their public life that might depend on it. For instance, a butcher working for a supermarket might have racist views that they express in private, but this only becomes a potential matter of public interest if it affects their work – tainting the meat they sell to black customers or refusing to serve black customers for instance.

There is a scale of privacy invasion that has been mentioned before that helps to determine if something is in the public interest. Celebrities, politicians, public figures, authority figures and criminals give up varying degrees of their right to privacy in the areas where they influence public life in return for the power and influence it brings them in society. Those who become involved in public events, often against their will, may also find their privacy on that issue invaded.

Politicians are probably most at risk of having their privacy invaded as their public work drawing up legislation and shaping public policy may well be influenced by elements of their public life and is often information the public needs to know in order to make informed decisions about whether to continue support or vote for a particular politician. The royal family may have slightly more right to privacy as they are not directly involved with policy making but they do have considerable influence on public life and so again it will be of public interest to understand how elements of their private life engage with their public views. Many civil servants, councillors, teachers, professors, doctors, lawyers and other professionals also will have influence within their communities; small amounts of power for which they should be accountable to the public. The American system carries this to the ultimate, with many public offices from local dog catcher to mayor filled by an elected position. The public votes regularly to choose the office holders and so there is a public interest in knowing if they are failing to carry out their duty and obligations. Whilst many of those positions in the UK are filled by employees, journalists still have a right to hold those who employ and discipline them to account and this may mean a public interest in knowing about elements of their private life. It would be appropriate to reveal, for instance, a council officer who used council employees, paid for by taxpayers, to carry out work at their home.

The public interest defence for researching an intrusive story

It is not always possible to gather evidence for a story of wrongdoing without either alerting a subject who may then decide to hide or destroy evidence and possibly threaten others who may have knowledge. Often the only approach that is likely to gather evidence is to use clandestine or non-straightforward methods that are themselves invasive.

Using clandestine or non-straightforward methods to research a story such as hidden cameras, hidden microphones, drones, personation or hacking may often be the only way of getting the evidence required. A journalist's first choice, of course, should always be to talk to a subject or other source openly and on the record, identifying themselves as a journalist seeking a story.

I mentioned the risk of fishing expeditions in regard to the Secret Policeman. A fishing expedition is where a journalist will seek to trap someone into saying something they later regret. Often in order to expose abuse of position, a journalist will use non-straightforward means to gather evidence. This might include secret recording, filming or pretending to be someone they are not as did Mark Daly. If the journalist has reasonable grounds to suspect that someone is abusing their position then they may decide that the only way to gather such evidence is to use non-straightforward means so they will not warn the subject that they are a journalist giving them the chance to consider a more plausible response. For instance, if a contact talks of a famous cricketer who regularly takes bribes to adjust their play and affect the results of games, the cricketer can hardly be asked outright if this is true so the journalist might set up a meeting pretending to be someone else. They could then arrange to meet in a hotel room and would fit hidden cameras in order to record proceedings. If after discussions, a bribe to throw a game was offered and this was accepted, it would be in the public interest for you to use the recording as evidence for a story about bribery. This happened in 2010 when the *News of the World* secretly videotaped Mazhar Majeed accepting money in return for arranging for bowlers Mohammed Asif and Salman Butt to deliberately bowl no balls to affect the game and allow gamblers to benefit. Four people were later jailed for offences related to the matter. In this instance, the decision to set the trap and film Majeed was justified. The tip off received, suggesting that they were open to bribes, was tested and found to be justified. The later publication of the story was also justified. However, if the tip off had been proved to be wrong then it would have been wrong to invade Majeed's privacy by using the video. The problem with using non-straightforward means to investigate a story is that it is often invasive, requiring filming or recording of activities, places or times when a person can reasonably expect privacy and consideration to such invasion should only be given if there is a sufficient evidence to reasonably suppose that there is something to be exposed.

Daly spent more than seven months on his investigation; a very significant investment of time and effort and he would have needed strong evidence of potential wrongdoing in order to convince his editors to allow him to do the story. Modern technology, especially social media, can lead to short cuts that potentially invade privacy but without the protection of public interest. In one case, very early in the genesis of IPSO, a *Sunday Mirror* reporter tweeted a number of Tory MPs pretending to be a "Tory PR girl" in her 20s called Sophie Wittams, and possibly other names. The reporter created a Twitter account using pictures of a Swedish model. He got responses from Brooks Newman, who was Minister for Civil Society at the time, and was one of several MPs who responded but he was the only one who continued to correspond, exchanging increasingly raunchy sexts and pictures. On Saturday 27 September 2014, Newman was approached by the paper and shortly after resigned saying he had been a complete fool and had no one to blame but himself. (https://hackinginquiry.org/brooks-newmark-public-interest-and-the-editors-code-will-ipso-act/ March 2019). Whilst he had certainly behaved unwisely, there is no evidence he would have behaved in that way had he not been sent a message in the first place.

IPSO Chairman Alan Moses said shortly after publication that the story was a matter of "urgent public concern" and that IPSO would investigate, as subterfuge should only be used as a "last resort". The IPSO investigation found that Alex Wickham, the reporter who set up the fake accounts, had well-placed sources – not identified to the regulator – who were not willing to go on the record, obliging the reporter to set up the sting to gather supporting evidence. However, this evidence came from the *Sunday Mirror*, who assured IPSO that they had been assured about its authenticity by Wickham and IPSO did not see the evidence. Nevertheless, IPSO agreed on that basis that the story was in the public interest, as the *Sunday Mirror* had claimed, and exonerated the publication. It was an inauspicious start for the new regulator born in difficult circumstances against a background of considerable criticism of the press. For those who remembered the similarly difficult start for IPSO's predecessor the PCC it was not a moment for optimism. It certainly had an impact on IPSO's decisions for future investigations. One of the main differences between IPSO and the PCC, a difference that Leveson had made much of in his report, was the ability to investigate without receiving a complaint. IPSO has not made any significant investigations since the Brooks Newman case.

Despite Wickham's claims of previous evidence, this story has all the hallmarks of a fishing expedition, pure and simple, and whilst it exposed the fact that even ministers can be tempted to do foolish things it leaves the debate wide open about whether this was a legitimate intrusion of his privacy. I doubt that any journalist would welcome a world where they were constantly tempted through private communications in order to see if they would succumb to a bribe or sexual invitation.

The public interest is an important tool that allows journalists to contrast privacy with freedom of expression and determine whether to continue with the story. It allows them to move beyond the strict requirements of a code, based in duty ethics, that requires them to act in a certain way. In the case of privacy the duty element of the various codes says that journalists should not invade privacy, but the codes are then obliged to accept that there may be times when journalists should break that restriction and invade privacy in order to produce a story. That caveat is the public interest and so journalists should consider carefully whether and why they believe the story is in the public interest before intruding into someone's privacy. The decision process is made more difficult by codes that identify differing classes of invasion. The IPSO code identifies a public interest caveat to code clauses by marking them with an asterisk. This applies to Clauses 2 – privacy, 3 – harassment, 5 – reporting suicide, 6 – children, 7 – children in sex cases, 8 – hospitals, 9 – reporting of crime, 10 – clandestine devices and subterfuge and 16 – payments to criminals.

The Ofcom broadcast code deals with this in Section 8 and says any infringement of privacy must be warranted.

> In this section "warranted" has a particular meaning. It means that where broadcasters wish to justify an infringement of privacy as warranted, they should be able to demonstrate why in the particular circumstances of the case, it is warranted. If the reason is that it is in the public interest, then the broadcaster should be able to demonstrate that the public interest outweighs the right to privacy. Examples of public interest would include revealing or detecting crime, protecting public health or safety, exposing misleading claims made by individuals or organisations or disclosing incompetence that affects the public.
>
> *(www.ofcom.org.uk/tv-radio-and-on-demand/broadcast-codes/*
> *broadcast-code/section-eight-privacy accessed March 2019)*

All organisations also accept that children and vulnerable adults require a higher threshold when considering the public interest.

Because all codes make it clear that intrusion must be justified it is probably a very good idea to record discussions with editors about why it would be in the public interest to use clandestine means to invade privacy and why using such methods to access the story were acceptable, as this would be useful evidence in the case of a complaint to IPSO, Impress or Ofcom or if the matter came to the courts.

Leveson inquiry view

The Leveson Inquiry investigated the concept of public interest fairly thoroughly coming to the conclusion – a conclusion reached by many before, but usefully and thoroughly confirmed by Leveson – that free media (Leveson talks about a free press because that limitation was one of the terms of his commission, but what he says applies to all media) are vital to the public interest for several reasons. The first is the democratic purpose of the media, allowing for the free flow of information and debate about its meaning and application. Leveson relied on the evidence from a number of academics, journalists and politicians who had given evidence to the inquiry in support of his thesis that a free press:

> serves democracy by enabling public deliberation. Citizens need information to make intelligent public political choices. To this end the press serves both as a conduit for the dissemination of information as well as a forum for public debate. It is therefore unsurprising that the proliferation of newspapers which followed the abolition of the stamp duty in the nineteenth century was accompanied by one of the most active periods of political reform in modern history.
>
> *(Leveson, 2012: 64)*

He quoted several witnesses to support this view including Rowan Cruft:

> a free press serves the public interest instrumentally in two key respects: –
> Constraining power: A free press is an important check on political and
> other forms of social power (corporate, individual) ... – Enabling demo-
> cratic deliberation and decision-making; educating and enabling under-
> standing. A free press – especially a diverse press in which many views are
> represented – is an important forum for public deliberation and education,
> a means for enabling the public to engage in informed democratic deci-
> sion-making.
>
> *pp. 1–2, www.levesoninquiry.org.uk/wp-content/uploads/2012/07/*
> *Witness-Statement-of-Dr-Rowan-Cruft.pdf*

Another, Prof. Susan Mendus, said:

> The public interest in a free press lies largely in the character of our soci-
> ety as a liberal democracy. It is in the public interest that there be a free
> press because and insofar as such a press serves as a necessary bulwark
> against government duplicity or tyranny. A free press serves also to inform
> people about the principles under which they live and the policies which
> government adopts and pursues in their name
>
> *pp. 4–5, www.levesoninquiry.org.uk/wp-content/uploads/2012/07/*
> *Witness-Statement-of-Professor-SusanMendus.pdf*

Neil Manson, another academic, went further in starting to discuss the extent to
which the public have a legitimate interest in being told of information that
might be of significance to their lives and decision making even if that information is something others might wish to conceal.

> A free press can communicate important facts that the public have
> a legitimate interest in knowing (and which others might want to con-
> ceal). ... there is a public interest in learning of dangers and risks, even
> where others may wish to conceal them ... A free press, free of the censor-
> ship and restrictions imposed by the powerful, ... serves the public interest
> by its investigative and communicative role. Both roles are necessary.
>
> *p. 2, www.levesoninquiry.org.uk/wp-content/uploads/2012/07/*
> *Witness-Statement-of-Dr-Neil-Manson.pdf*

The second way Leveson identified in which a free press serves the interests of
democracy is through its public watchdog role, acting as a check on politicians
and other holders of power. The press is able to perform this function, he said,
because of its hard-won position as a powerful institution independent of the
state, a position which earned it the nickname or sobriquet of the Fourth Estate
amongst 19th-century writers.

A third importance of public interest was raised in 2002 by the Lord Chief Justice, Justice Woolf, when considering the claim by married footballer Garry Flitcroft that his right to privacy was breached by *The People* newspaper when they planned to run a story about his affairs with two women. An injunction preventing the paper from publishing had been granted by the courts but was finally lifted by the Court of Appeal. Justice Woolf said that Flitcroft could not prevent publication as the stories being published were those of the young women and that they owed Flitcroft no duty of confidentiality. Justice Woolf went on to say that:

> The courts must not ignore the fact that if newspapers do not publish information which the public are interested in, there will be fewer newspapers published, which will not be in the public interest. The same is true in relation to other parts of the media.
>
> *(cited in Frost, 2016: 50)*

This idea that a free press means that interesting the public is in itself a potential public interest was one that was picked up with alacrity by the Press Complaints Commission, even though this caution is itself often challenged with the view that public interest is not the same as interesting the public. The IPSO code of practice now includes the phrase: "There is a public interest in freedom of expression itself" (www.ipso.co.uk/editors-code-of-practice/#ThePublicInterest accessed Mar. 2019). Editors would need to justify such a broad defence by demonstrating "that they reasonably believed publication – or journalistic activity taken with a view to publication – would both serve, and be proportionate to, the public, the public interest and explain how they reached that decision at that time" (ibid.). However, Leveson goes on to recognise that these public interest powers must be used consistently with other democratic powers including the law and the personal and public rights of others.

The IPSO code of practice as amended in 2016 also identifies the public interest as including:

- Detecting or exposing crime, or the threat of crime, or serious impropriety.
- Protecting public health or safety.
- Protecting the public from being misled by an action or statement of an individual or organisation.
- Disclosing a person or organisation's failure or likely failure to comply with any obligation to which they are subject.
- Disclosing a miscarriage of justice.
- Raising or contributing to a matter of public debate, including serious cases of impropriety, unethical conduct or incompetence concerning the public.
- Disclosing concealment, or likely concealment, of any of the above. (Ibid.)

Ofcom, in its broadcasting code, outlines a range of circumstances in which privacy can only be invaded if warranted. This has a particular meaning in that broadcasters should be able to demonstrate why intrusion in that instance is

warranted. One of the reasons could be that the coverage is in the public interest and that the public interest outweighs the right to privacy. Ofcom gives
examples of public interest as: "revealing or detecting crime, protecting public
health or safety, exposing misleading claims made by individuals or organisations
or disclosing incompetence that affects the public" (www.ofcom.org.uk/tv-
radio-and-on-demand/broadcast-codes/broadcast-code/section-eight-privacy
accessed March 2019).

Live by exposure, die by exposure

Many people believe that the more you live your life in the public eye, profiting
from public engagement in terms of financial or reputation value, the more closely
the public is entitled to scrutinise the reality of that life. Many celebrities, as previously discussed, build their reputations on a public image. The more that public
image diverges from reality, the more that learning about that hypocrisy is in the
public interest and the more entitled the public is to learn about the reality.

People's position in society affects the level of privacy the public believes they
should receive. Research by Kieran, Morrison and Svennevig in 2000 asked
a group of people to rank the different levels of privacy requirements of various
groups in society. The results are identified in Table 7.1. These results have

TABLE 7.1 The reaction of a group of people to different levels of privacy requirement

| Type | *More < Control > Less* | | | | | |
	A	B	C	D	E	F
Child	54	19	10	6	3	3
Patient with Alzheimer's	54	20	12	4	3	2
Parent of murder victim	54	24	13	4	3	2
Person with disability	49	23	14	6	3	2
Witness to a crime	48	28	11	6	3	2
A victim of crime	47	26	12	5	4	4
A lottery winner	46	31	10	5	4	3
Member of the royal family	16	19	22	22	12	6
A schoolteacher	13	24	17	20	17	5
A senior policeman	11	18	15	23	21	9
A senior civil servant	10	15	16	27	21	7
A businessman	9	17	21	28	17	4
A film star	8	13	21	21	10	3
A religious leader	8	12	18	23	21	11
A politician	6	10	14	28	29	11
A shoplifter	4	8	9	24	26	25
A drug dealer	3	3	5	9	20	57
A rapist	3	3	3	8	19	60

Source: Kieran, Morrison and Svennevig (2000).

been confirmed as largely right by numerous students and others over the years of presenting this table as part of my teaching. Most people accept that children deserve a stronger protection of their privacy than politicians, the royal family or police officers, who in turn deserve stronger protection than serious criminals.

No matter how high up the social ladder one is, then privacy is still desirable.

Paparazzi photos in German magazines of Princess Caroline of Monaco out shopping breached her right to respect for her private life, the European Court of Human Rights ruled in 2004. The court said that:

> The court considers that the public does not have a legitimate interest in knowing where [Princess Caroline] is and how she behaves generally in her private life – even if she appears in places that cannot always be described as secluded and despite the fact that she is well known to the public … Even if such a public interest exists, as does a commercial interest of the magazines in publishing these photos … those interests must, in the court's view, yield to the applicant's right to the effective protection of her private life.
>
> *(www.ippt.eu/files/2004/IPPT20040624_ECHR_Von_*
> *Hannover_v_Germany.pdf accessed Sept. 2019)*

Even the most powerful have some right to privacy and the media always needs to draw an appropriate line.

8

PERSONAL REPUTATION

As one of the key facets of privacy is the right to control information about ourselves and determine who should get to know about it, the right of privacy often becomes confused with the right to reputation. If we wish to control our privacy by determining who has access to information about us then we are doing that in order to maintain control over the image we present to the public and to control how we are seen by others. An important element of that is to determine the image and therefore the reputation we present to the world. If we wish to develop a reputation of being a family-loving upright citizen then our reputation would be damaged if it became known that actually we involved ourselves in drunken roistering at Satan-worshipping orgies. Conversely, a celebrity wishing to develop an image of being a hard-drinking rebel, constantly pushing the boundaries of unacceptable behaviour, would find their reputation just as badly damaged by the discovery that their downtime was spent helping out a soup kitchen on the way home from church with their family. The key to reputation and privacy is not one-size-fits-all; Tommy Robinson (real name Stephen Yaxley-Lennon), the former leader of the English Defence League, would be as insulted to be called a liberal as I would be to be called a fascist.

If one's reputation or public image, as self-controlled, remains pretty close to reality then there can be no damage; to publicise that the artist Grayson Perry often wears women's clothes in public as his alter-ego "Claire" is to merely confirm the truth of the image Perry is happy to present in public. He doesn't always wear women's clothes but he does sometimes and so it could not damage his reputation nor invade his privacy to describe how he dresses. However, to report that a male cabinet minister often dressed as a woman whilst at home, something that the minister did not seek to make public, would be to invade his privacy and might well damage his reputation, especially if he was on the right of the political spectrum and more conservative and authoritarian in the image he wished to project. If a reporter came to learn of this (in itself) harmless activity, then they would need to look carefully at the public interest justification for the intrusion. If the minister had never spoken out about cross-dressing or attacked or condemned those who cross-dress then it might be difficult to find a public interest justification to run the story. Whilst it would doubtless be of interest to a number of people (the "ooh, fancy that" defence) it would be difficult to justify as being in the public interest except in that it would interest the public. However, if the information about cross-dressing turns out after publication to be false, or there is insufficient evidence to prove it, then the minister might well consider he has a case to sue for defamation. He would need to prove that the alleged revelations caused or could have caused serious damage to his reputation. This might be difficult, depending on how much harm it might do him. Whilst such a revelation might well make the minister the butt of jokes from comedians and pundits on television, online and in print for a while, it is unlikely that he could prove serious harm even if he could prove malice. It is doubtful if, in these times, cross-dressing in the privacy of your own home would expose the minister to hatred or contempt, cause him to be shunned or avoided or call into question his competency as a minister. However, in the UK it is possible to sue for false privacy in these circumstances. In this instance the minister would not be challenging the truth or otherwise of the allegation but simply saying that, true or false, it is an unwarranted invasion of his privacy. This would require the publisher to prove the importance of publishing in the public interest, whilst not requiring the claimant to confirm or deny the truth of the allegations, something that might be embarrassing or simply difficult; proving a negative is often impossible. The UK Court of Appeal said in the McKennitt case:

> The question in a case of misuse of private information is whether the information is private not whether it is true or false. The truth or falsity of the information is an irrelevant inquiry in deciding whether the information is entitled to be protected.
>
> *(https://inform.org/2010/12/14/opinion-defamation-and-false-privacy-hugh-tomlinson-qc/ accessed Sept. 2019)*

The law is different in the US and some other jurisdictions. In the US, in order to sue for defamation the claimant would have to prove the allegation was not true and, since the minister is clearly a public figure, he would also have to prove malice – that the false statement was made intentionally or with reckless disregard for the truth. He could sue for false light, which is not the same as false privacy. In a false light suit the claimant must show that the information published showed the claimant in a false or misleading light and that this was highly offensive or embarrassing to a reasonable person of ordinary sensibilities. A perfect example of the conundrum involved is summed up by "Piggate", an uncorroborated anecdote in Lord Ashcroft and Isabel Oakeshott's unofficial biography of former PM David Cameron, *Call Me Dave*, in which they alleged that as a student the PM belonged to the Piers Gaveston Society that required him to take part in an initiation ceremony that involved a dead pig's head. The publication of the book sparked headlines around the world; it was serialised in the *Daily Mail* and provided a field day for satirists and comedians. Cameron, though, held his nerve and did not go to court, and Downing Street merely said it would not "dignify" the claim with a response. Cameron was probably very wise to try to stand above it. With very little evidence, most people probably doubt its provenance and it is one of the oldest tricks in the political book to smear an opponent with a false and disgusting story, hopefully obliging them to deny it and therefore instantly giving it some credence since credibly denying a false claim is almost impossible.

Since privacy is about keeping information about oneself out of the public domain, by protecting its dispersal through data protection law, as will be explained in a later chapter, and by limiting what can be published about one with laws of confidence, privacy and trespass, and the ethical limitations placed on privacy by media regulators, reputation is protected by the laws of defamation and ethical requirements of accuracy. Whilst privacy is about exposing a matter that should remain private, journalists are entitled to trash someone's reputation if the story about that person is true in all its essential parts, or if it is an honest opinion based on true facts and that in both cases, the journalist can prove that the information is essentially true. This means gathering evidence from sources that will stand up in court in case the journalist is sued. Editors are, of course, well aware that the richer the person, the more possible it is that they will sue, because they can easily afford to do so. Even though complainants now have to show a court that the words used were defamatory and are likely to cause serious harm, the fear of a lawsuit might well discourage an editor from publishing – known as the chilling effect – or, if the editor goes ahead with publication, a lawsuit, even one the publication is likely to win, might well oblige an editor to capitulate and publish an apology and pay damages in order to avoid massive legal costs. This was an issue that was identified by the Leveson Inquiry, amongst others. The Inquiry recommended an arbitration scheme that could quickly and cheaply rule out frivolous or vexatious claims whilst being free for complainants to use and cheap for defendants. IPSO did introduce such a scheme in August 2018, but it is compulsory only to those newspapers that sign up to it. The scheme allows complainants to bring claims about defamation, malicious falsehood, breach of confidence, misuse of private information, data protection and harassment. It costs £100 for claimants, which is refundable if the claim is successful, and the scheme can only award to a maximum of £60,000 in damages. Costs to a respondent are a maximum of £9,000 or only £3,500 if the claim is dismissed as frivolous or vexatious at an early stage. (www.ipso.co.uk/media/1582/arbitration-scheme-rules-310718.pdf accessed March 2019). This is considerably cheaper for a publication, even if it loses outright, than going to court. Settling a legal case even at an early stage can lead to legal fees and costs of £10,000–£20,000 and losing a big High Court case can cost hundreds of thousands of pounds. Impress also runs an arbitration scheme that works in much the same way but whilst the Impress scheme is compulsory for all its members, only 19 publications belong to the compulsory IPSO scheme: these are the national publications of Reach PLC, Telegraph Media Group, News UK and Associated Newspapers. IPSO's voluntary scheme includes 13 national magazines in the Condé Nast stable. All other publications, including all local and regional newspapers and most magazines, do not belong to either scheme and so complaints cannot be arbitrated and have to go to law. The compulsory scheme obliges members to go to arbitration if required by a complainant whilst the voluntary scheme allows publications to refuse. It is too early at time of writing to get any useful figures on how the scheme has been operating but information on the website was nearly a year out of date when accessed in March 2019, which is not a good sign of frequent use.

Whilst few local newspapers or websites are sued for privacy or defamation, none have joined the scheme. It's difficult to know why this is the case as no editors I've asked have been able to tell me. Local newspapers claimed from the introduction of IPSO that such a scheme would lead to a massive increase in cases and therefore increase in costs to hard-pressed local newspapers but there is no evidence of that. Only 49 defamation cases were brought in 2017 and only 11 of those were against publications. It's unlikely that more than two of those were local papers. It's a similar picture when looking at privacy. The number of cases vary year on year, but reports in the *Daily Telegraph* and *The Times* put cases in 2014/15 at 58 and that they fell to half that in 2017. A third of those relate to government or public sector and few were complaints against publications. 20% involved celebrities or politicians and its probable that these might be privacy cases against national publications or broadcasters, but that's still only six cases, virtually none of which were against local newspapers so it's difficult to understand why local papers are so concerned when arbitration is likely to favour them in terms of costs, certainly at the early stages of a complaint.

In order to sue for defamation rather than privacy in the UK a complainant first has to show that the words complained of caused serious harm. The complainant doesn't have to prove the words are untrue, just that they would cause serious harm.

Once the case gets to court, and a newspaper can offer an apology and compensation before it gets to court, the complainant has to also prove that the words were published to others, that they were about the complainant or could be considered to be about the complainant, and that they would cause serious harm. A newspaper can defend itself on three main grounds:

- Truth;
- Honest opinion based on true facts; and
- Privilege.

Proving that the story is true is not always easy but it is probably the best defence. Privilege is regularly used. This is where a reporter is publishing the claims of others made in a forum that has privilege. In order to allow public debate and hear evidence at courts, inquiries and tribunals, it is legitimate for those taking part to say things within the rules of the forum without risk of being sued. In order to fulfil the right of the public to be informed, journalists may report what is said without needing to check whether it is true, provided it is an accurate account. There are two types of privilege.

Absolute privilege is granted to those actually involved in public debate – in the courts, parliament, local government or public meetings. Qualified privilege allows the reporting of matters of public concern, including parliamentary debates, council meetings and other public tribunals. Absolute privilege protects debaters and allows reports that are:

- fair;
- accurate; and
- published contemporaneously.

Qualified privilege covers reports that are:

- fair;
- accurate;
- without malice; and
- should be published in the public interest.

It also cannot be defamation to report someone's criminal conviction but there are rules about rehabilitation and some offences are regarded as spent after a certain time. A conditional discharge, for instance, is spent after 12 months.

Case studies

Example 1

Melania Trump filed a defamation action in the New York state commercial court and in the UK High Court against the *Daily Mail* over allegations that she previously worked as an escort. Ms Trump claimed damages in the sum of $150m.

The *Daily Mail* later retracted the statement, published an apology and settled the case for $3m. The case was subject to much media attention, being covered by the BBC, the *Guardian*, *Independent* and ABC News.

Example 2

In a social media defamation claim, food writer Jack Monroe sued blogger Katie Hopkins concerning two tweets made by Hopkins in May 2015 which accused

Monroe of desecrating a war memorial. Monroe was awarded £24,000 in a judgment in March 2017. Notably, damages awarded were exacerbated by the continual harm caused to Monroe's reputation by the Tweets as well as injury to feelings caused by the defendant's reprehensible behaviour throughout the matter.

The case affirmed the Court's approach to social media platforms, including the application of the idea of a reasonable reader on Twitter and how they might construe the innuendo inferable from Tweets.

Example 3

Robert Dee, a professional tennis player, lost 54 matches in straight sets over three years and was named by several newspapers as the "worst tennis player in the world". He threatened to sue and more than 30 news publications settled but the *Daily Telegraph* stood firm and the courts agreed that the description was honest opinion based on true facts. Mrs Justice Sharp said there was no additional obligation on the paper to prove its claim that he is "objectively the worst professional tennis player in the world in terms of his playing skills".

9

LAW OF PRIVACY

This chapter will discuss UK privacy legislation and related legislation, including the law of confidence and its application to human rights, the development of data protection law and the development of a tort of privacy through the Human Rights Act.

There are two main aims of the law in the UK developed around different needs at different times. First this chapter will examine the means complainants have of gaining redress for breaches of privacy or confidence, or potential breaches of privacy, either when an invasive story may be published and they seek to prevent that or when it has been published and they seek to achieve some redress.

The second aim of the law is data protection and Chapter 10 will examine how the law is designed to protect personal data collected by government agencies, commercial organisations or individuals rather than offer redress for an intrusion.

Prior restraint

The only method of prior restraint, the prevention of publication or broadcast of a story, in the UK and most western democracies, is to go through the courts to prevent publication with an injunction. Many injunctions are ex-parte, that is they are heard without the defendant being there. The newspaper or broadcaster will only learn of it when they are served with the order preventing publication. The newspaper can fight the injunction but courts will tend to allow the injunction initially as the balance of convenience will lie with the person seeking the injunction in that, if they don't get the injunction, the story will be published defeating the object of seeking the injunction. This lies at the heart of all injunctions because they are sought to prevent someone doing something until the courts can hear the arguments about why they should or should not be able to do it.

Injunctions are not too common in the UK. The number granted dropped in early 2012, reaching an all-time low in 2013 and 2014, and that might have been connected with the Leveson Inquiry. The number has risen steadily since then to return to approximately 20 a year. Many of these are either anonymous, that is where the person at the centre of the case cannot be named, or so-called super-injunctions. These are sometimes applied to prevent the newspaper even reporting that an injunction has been granted. Largely these are asked for by celebrities who do not even want a mention that they are attempting to prevent publication because even the story that they are seeking to prevent publication suggests they have something to hide and that might damage their image.

Mr Justice Tugendhat identified the principles in anonymity cases in the case of JIH, a well-known sportsman who obtained an injunction to restrain publication of details of his private life. The judge said that the general rule should be that names of the parties to an action are included in orders and judgments of courts, including privacy cases. To grant anonymity is a derogation from open justice and so a court needs to closely scrutinise the application and consider if a less restrictive alternative is available. The judge went on to say that the court also needs to consider if there is a public interest in publishing the names and details that over-rides the applicant's right to privacy. Because of this consent of both parties is irrelevant as parties cannot waive the public's right to know.

Despite this care in ensuring that injunctions are only granted if justice will be served, newspapers hate the idea of them. Julian Petley points out that, around the time of Leveson, much of the national press had been obsessed with injunctions:

> In one week alone in April (2011) there were over 200 stories about injunctions in the national press. Typically the majority of these stories generated a great deal more heat than light. Most British newspapers are not exactly renowned for their accuracy, and stories which concern their own interests are particularly prone to distortion, if not outright fantasy. In this instance, certain newspapers repeatedly conflated super-injunctions … and anonymised injunctions … often wildly exaggerating the numbers of both.
>
> *(Petley, 2013: 19)*

Petley went on to report that the parliamentary Committee on Super-Injunctions could only identify two super-injunctions in 2010. It recommended that some system of recording the frequency of such injunctions would be helpful. A system has since been introduced (see Figure 9.1).

Another favourite way for someone to attempt to prevent publication of an unwanted story is to send a solicitor's letter threatening action unless the story is spiked. These usually come direct to the editor so discussion needs to take place

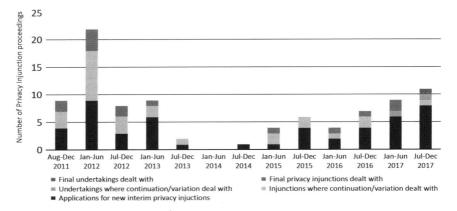

FIGURE 9.1 Privacy injunctions and undertakings in the UK courts (https://assets.pub lishing.service.gov.uk/government/uploads/system/uploads/attachment_data/file/ 684410/civil-justice-statistics-quarterly-oct-dec-2017.pdf accessed April 2019)

about whether there is a breach of Data Protection Act or some other potential problem but solicitors' letters can usually be ignored provided the editor and journalist are confident that the legal threats have been considered and have been dismissed as groundless or are something sufficiently important to be pre- pared to fight for. Such letters are often just an attempt to intimidate the publi- cation and oblige its editor to withdraw or publish an apology. The same applies to other threats or attempted bribes to prevent publication. Inform the editor and let him or her deal with it.

Privacy law

There are no laws providing a direct tort of privacy in the UK although there are a number of laws against privacy invasions such as harassment, trespass, phone hacking, computer hacking and data protection. The courts, however, have long accepted there needs to be some protection of privacy for citizens in their daily lives. Complaints about neighbours spying or eavesdropping led to detailed planning legislation to protect people's priv- acy, for instance, limiting rights of access, determining rules for the placing of windows and distances between boundaries. The key protections have arisen out of common law and been developed and refined by the courts. Breach of confidence as a tort for which a judicial remedy could be sought developed through the late 19th century and 20th century from *Prince Albert v Strange* through to the Human Rights Act. Breach of confidence takes a very particular approach to privacy in that its concern is about confi- dential information and this tends to be information that has a commercially sensitive element to it. One of the key cases is *Saltman Engineering v Campbell*

Engineering (1948) in which a company contracted to produce plans for a new process and assist with its development took over the innovation for itself. The Appeal Court found that there had been a breach of confidence and that Campbell Engineering owed a duty of confidence to Saltman Engineering. Lord Greene MR said:

> The information, to be confidential, must, I apprehend, apart from contract, have the necessary quality of confidence about it, namely, it must not be something which is public property and public knowledge. On the other hand, it is perfectly possible to have a confidential document be it a formula, a plan, a sketch, or something of that kind, which is the result of work done by the maker upon materials which may be available for the use of anybody; but what makes it confidential is the fact that the maker of the document has used his brain and thus produced a result which can only be produced by somebody who goes through the same process.
>
> What the defendants did in this case was to dispense in certain material respects with the necessity of going through the process which had been gone through in compiling these drawings, and thereby to save themselves a great deal of labour and calculation and careful draftsmanship ... That, in my opinion, was a breach of confidence.
>
> *(https://swarb.co.uk/saltman-engineering-co-v-campbell-engineering-co-ltd-ca-1948/ accessed April 2019)*

Forty years later, in *Attorney-General v Observer Ltd* (1990) – the Spycatcher case – Lord Goff of Chieveley refined the limitations to common law breach of confidentiality:

> The first limiting principle ... is that the principle of confidentiality only applies to information to the extent that it is confidential ... once it has entered what is usually called the public domain ... then, as a general rule, the principle of confidentiality can have no application to it ... The second limiting principle is that the duty of confidence applies neither to useless information, nor to trivia ... The third limiting principle is of far greater importance. It is that, although the basis of the law's protection of confidence is that there is a public interest that confidences should be preserved and protected by the law, nevertheless that public interest may be outweighed by some other countervailing public interest which favours disclosure.
>
> *(www.casemine.com/judgement/uk/5a8ff8cb60d03e7f57ecd7d2 accessed April 2019)*

Confidence implies a relationship between the person revealing the information and the person the information is about and Lord Denning, Master of the Rolls, said one should not take advantage of information disclosed in confidence. In line with Lord Goff's judgment there are three tests used to determine whether something is confidential and therefore receives protection:

1. The information must be confidential;
2. The circumstances must impose an obligation of confidence;
3. An unauthorised breach must be detrimental.

These points have been developed further and it is now a well accepted point of case law that the circumstances imposing an obligation of confidence need not be contractual. Whilst employees or employers have an obligation of confidence to one another, someone who inadvertently comes into possession of confidential information, say a dropped diary or a confidential paper blown onto the street from a window on a hot day, may still have an obligation of confidence as the unauthorised disclosure could be detrimental. It may also be a breach of confidence to publish information disclosed by a third party in breach of a duty of confidence knowing that it has been disclosed in breach of a duty of confidence. This is a difficult area for journalists. Whistle-blowers often supply information provided to them under a duty of confidence and also often insist on becoming a confidential source in order to protect themselves.

However, it is here again that the public interest rides to the journalist's defence with the courts obliged to weigh the public and individual interest in maintaining confidentiality against the public interest of disclosure of matters of public concern (see Chapter 7).

Breach of confidence has been developed significantly by the courts since the introduction of the Human Rights Act in the UK. Whilst the courts had taken the European Convention of Human Rights into account beforehand, the Human Rights Act emphasised the need for the courts to consider this element of law and a number of the key cases of privacy intrusion brought by complainants against media companies concern elements of breach of confidence. In the *Max Mosley v News of the World* case the newspaper publicised a report and pictures, including video online, about a sadomasochistic orgy with Mosley and five women. The newspaper claimed that the orgy was "Nazi-themed", linking it to Mosley's father, the former leader of the British Union of Fascists. Much of the court's findings hinged on whether there was a public interest, but also whether there was a duty of confidence between Mosley and the five women he had paid to join him in the party. The judge said in his judgment that the law of confidence, "well-established for many years", had recently been extended by the Human Rights Act and the European Convention on Human Rights itself to "afford protection to information" even when there was no pre-existing relationship giving rise to an enforceable duty of confidence. Justice Eady did not find there was sufficient public interest in the event to warrant over-riding the duty of confidence and several other elements of privacy (see Chapter 13 for the full details of the Mosley case).

There have been a number of inquiries over the years into whether there should be a law covering a tort of privacy, including the Younger Committee and the Calcutt Committee which both concluded that there was a need to ban some forms of intrusion including long lenses and bugging with hidden microphones or recording devices. Whilst the law was developed around the issue of bugging and computer and phone hacking, the issue of long lens photography is still in the hands of IPSO.

Human Rights Act 1998

The introduction of the Human Rights Act, ensuring that the European Convention on Human Rights is something the British parliament and courts needed to take into consideration when both making and interpreting the law, brought about the most significant change in recent years. Developments through the courts such as the Mosley case and the McKennit case (see Chapter 13 for full details) have helped firm up the judiciary's take on privacy, bringing improved clarity for editors, parliament and the public.

Article 8 of the HRA introduced a right to respect for privacy. This means that, unlike most other rights, government has some obligation to protect our right to privacy and that the courts can use the Human Rights Act and other laws to protect the right to privacy in home and family life, health and correspondence.

Article 10 confirms the right to freedom of expression which government must also protect. The HRA identifies the balancing act to be played out from any gathering of a story through to any court case consequent on publication in S12 of the Act. This says that courts must have a particular regard to "the importance of the Convention right to freedom of expression" www.legisla tion.gov.uk/ukpga/1998/42/section/12 accessed April 2019). Where the proceedings relate to journalistic, literary or artistic material, the court should consider the extent to which the material has become available to the public; or if it is in the public interest for the material to be published alongside any relevant privacy code.

Broadcasting Acts

Whilst privacy as it affects the press is largely bound up with the laws of confidence and the Human Rights Act, the situation is entirely different for broadcasters. Broadcasters and broadcasts are controlled under the Broadcasting Act 1996 and the Communications Act 2003. The Broadcasting Act 1996 introduced the concept of digital broadcasting and laid down the framework for the move from analogue to digital broadcasting, now largely complete in the UK. It also set the funding systems for Channel 4 and identified sporting and other events of national interest, preventing exclusive broadcasting of events of national importance. Group A listed events must allow full live coverage to all qualifying broadcasters whose channels are available without payment. Group B events may have live coverage on subscription-only channels, provided secondary coverage is offered to qualifying broadcasters. Group A events include the Olympic Games, World Cup tournaments, the Grand National and the Wimbledon Tennis Finals, whilst Group B includes the six nations rugby matches, the Commonwealth Games and the Ryder Cup (see https://researchbriefings.files.parliament.uk/documents/SN00802/SN00802.pdf for full details).

The Broadcasting Act does not of itself contain significant elements of regulation and privacy but is the basis for the newer Communications Act 2003. Amongst other things, the Communications Act sets up Ofcom with a jurisdiction that spans TV, radio, internet, broadband, telephones, mobile telephony and any other form of electronic communication. Ofcom's aim is to further the interests of citizens in relation to communications matters and further the interests of consumers in relevant markets by promoting competition.

As far as broadcasting is concerned, these two, often conflicting, aims identify the need to understand that people are both consumers, interested in a wide choice of material at sensible prices and citizens needing to be informed and educated as well as being entertained. The consumer element aims to give a wider choice of entertainment whilst the citizenship test ensures that the needs of minority groups are catered for and that news and other educative areas are covered.

Ofcom is obliged by the Act to consider the vulnerability of children and of others who are need of special protection such as those with disabilities, the elderly and those on low incomes. Account should be taken of the opinions of consumers in relevant markets and of members of the public generally; the different interests of persons in the different parts of the country, of different ethnic communities and of persons living in rural and in urban areas. Ofcom also has a duty to consider the desirability of preventing crime and disorder.

However, two particular areas are identified when it comes to regulating broadcasts. Section 3.2(f) obliges Ofcom to uphold standards that provide adequate protection to members of the public and all other persons from both unfair treatment in programmes, and from unwarranted infringements of privacy. These statutory duties provide protections in programmes radio and TV and their linked websites that have no equivalent for press or World Wide Web. It obliges Ofcom to draw up a code (see Chapter 13) that is legally enforceable with penalties that can fine a broadcaster found to be in breach of the Broadcasting Code or even withdraw a licence to broadcast.

This statutory protection is one of the main differences between press regulation and broadcast regulation and may explain why (the Cliff Richard case excepting – see Chapter 13) TV and radio have far less history of press intrusion than newspapers or magazines.

Harassment

The Protection from Harassment Act was introduced in 1997 largely to protect people from stalkers. This makes it illegal to "pursue a course of conduct" which amounts to harassment of another and which the person knows or ought to know amounts to harassment of the other. The maximum penalty is six months in prison. The only defence is that the harassment was to prevent or detect crime, or that the pursuit was reasonable under the circumstances.

Police forces will issue "Prevention of Harassment Letters" on occasions and Gareth Davies, a journalist working for the *Croydon Advertiser,* was issued with such a letter in 2014 whilst making legitimate enquiries with a convicted fraudster. The Metropolitan Police later rescinded the notice after a two-year battle. At the same time Northumbria police issued Police Information Notices warning journalists they risked harassment prosecution if they contacted any victims of the Newcastle sex grooming ring trial. A Northumbria Police spokesperson told journalists:

> Any victim may choose to speak to the media, however where the victim has informed police they have been contacted by the media and this contact is not wanted it is appropriate for us to issue an harassment warning if that contact persists.
>
> Media directly contacting victims in Operation Sanctuary has had a damaging effect on them, causing distress and harm to their well-being. Despite issuing two notices asking media not to contact victims directly journalists continued to make direct contact.
>
> It was decided due to the damaging effect the actions of the media were having on the victims that an harassment warning would be issued where appropriate in order to protect these very vulnerable women and girls – none of who wish to speak to the media.
>
> We know media have requested, through us, to speak to victims and these have not been ignored. If and when a victim does wish to tell their story we will facilitate this.
>
> We understand the benefits of victims speaking to the media, however, this will be done in a managed way to ensure the victim is fully supported and any further unnecessary distress is minimised.
>
> *www.pressgazette.co.uk/journalists-told-by-police-they-will-receive-harass*
> *ment-notices-if-they-contact-newcastle-grooming-network-victims/*
> *accessed April 2019)*

Whilst such PINs are rare, they are concerning as there is no right of appeal regardless of the circumstances and can remain on someone's record indefinitely. This means that, if the police decide they need to issue such a warning, based on the untested claims of the complainant, it is not possible or at least is extremely difficult to prove, as Gareth Davies discovered, that the journalist is merely carrying out his or her job of fulfilling the public's right to information according to the codes of practice and in line with standard ethical practice.

Trespass

Trespassing on private land is an offence if you refuse to leave when asked. Going up to someone's front door or elsewhere in their property in order to speak to them is not strictly an offence but if you refuse to leave, the police may be called and they do have the power to ask you to leave. A refusal could be treated as aggravated trespass.

Aggravated trespass is where someone trespasses on land and does anything which is intended to have the effect of intimidating persons there to deter them from engaging in any legal activity, obstructing that activity or disrupting that activity. This is an arrestable offence that can lead to a fine or three months in prison. It should also be remembered that behaviour likely to lead to such an arrest is also likely to be considered harassment by IPSO or Ofcom and lead to a finding of breach of the code of practice. Whilst it may be important to speak to the person on the private land, if you are asked to leave you should do so.

Malicious access: phone tapping, hacking and accessing communications

Phone tapping and hacking is illegal under the Regulation of Investigatory Powers Act 2000 introduced before the phone-hacking scandal of 2011 and the Investigatory Powers Act 2016. The Acts regulate the investigatory powers of government agencies, the police, Revenue and Customs and various intelligence agencies. It also set up the office of the Interception of Communications now called, since 2018, the Investigatory Powers Commissioner's Office (IPCO). The commissioner, Lord Justice Fulford, and his judicial commissioners are responsible for overseeing the use of investigatory powers by public authorities which include law enforcement, the intelligence agencies, prisons, local authorities and other government agencies (e.g. regulators). In total over 600 public authorities and institutions have investigatory powers.

RIPA regulates the interception of communications by the various agencies and details how and under what circumstances interceptions can be authorised. The Human Rights Act gives people a right to privacy and RIPA provides a statutory framework to identify covert surveillance activity. The Act also gives the authorities the power to demand passwords to encrypted data, whether on a computer or smartphone, with a penalty of up to two years in prison for refusal or five years in a national security or child indecency case.

RIPA has many critics from human rights campaign groups to MPs and charities. They complain that there was insufficient debate of the Act in parliament and that it was rushed through. There are also complaints that its use is oppressive and that permission for surveillance is too easy to obtain using the fear of

terrorist activity. Local councils came in for particular criticism about using surveillance to confirm (or otherwise) claims about such relatively trivial matters as
to whether people do live in the popular school catchment areas that they are
claiming.

Of more concern to journalists is the use of RIPA to circumvent protections
of journalist sources present in other legislation. The Police and Criminal Evidence Act covers powers of search and seizure of goods by the police and was
introduced in 1984, well before mobile phones and computers became significant everyday items. PACE takes the view that journalistic confidential sources
require some protection and the Act consequently defines journalistic material
and provides for rules of access to journalistic material that are stricter than for
ordinary material. Under S8 of the Act police officers who are investigating an
indictable offence and may wish to search a home or office for material of substantial value in that investigation must apply to a magistrate for a warrant.
However, a magistrate must be satisfied that the material does not consist of
"excluded material" or "special procedure material", both of which can include,
under S11, journalistic material. PACE identifies "journalistic material" as material held in confidence that was acquired or created for the purposes of journalism and is in the possession of a person who acquired or created it for the
purposes of journalism. If a constable wishes to search premises for journalistic
material then they must seek a warrant from a circuit judge and not
a magistrate. Applying to a judge allows the person holding the material to be in
court and put their argument to the judge.

Whilst this was a reasonably strong protection of confidential source material
the Regulation of Investigatory Powers Act has recently been used by police to
circumvent PACE and access details of confidential sources by accessing journalists' phone records from the mobile phone company. Whereas, before RIPA,
police would have needed to apply to a judge for a warrant to search for journalistic material or to tap phones to identify sources, using RIPA, the police
used its own internal authority to access phone records of journalists from telephone companies who do not, themselves, have confidential source protection.
A warrant can be quickly signed by a senior officer and the phone company is
obliged to give up the phone records of journalists, allowing the police to identify sources.

The Plebgate inquiry (where then Conservative chief Whip Andrew Mitchell
was accused of calling police officers at Downing Street "plebs") and the prosecution of Chris Huhne for perversion of the course of justice were two cases
where confidential sources were accessed through phone records but the Interception of Communications Commissioner's Office in 2015 identified a further
82 cases where journalists phone records had been obtained by 19 different
police forces over the previous three years.

The Sun's political editor, Tom Newton Dunn, had his records accessed in
order to identify his source. *The Sun* later made a complaint about the matter to
the Investigatory Powers Tribunal. Around the same time the news editor of

the *Mail on Sunday* and one of its freelance journalists also had their phone records accessed by police. Using RIPA allowed officers to access confidential sources with just the approval of a senior officer with no right of the journalist to contest it and, indeed, often without their knowledge.

The then Interception of Communications Commissioner, Sir Paul Kennedy, launched a full inquiry and urged Home Office ministers to accelerate the introduction of promised protections. Although the government at the time said that they would reform RIPA to protect journalistic sources, the 2015 election meant the government ran out of time to do anything but introduce interim guidelines.

The Interception of Communications Code of Practice was published in January 2016 (https://assets.publishing.service.gov.uk/government/uploads/system/uploads/attachment_data/file/496064/53659_CoP_Communications_Accessible.pdf accessed April 2019). It gives guidance to various authorities, including the police, on how to apply RIPA and could be used by a complainant in civil or even possibly criminal proceedings if and when it is breached.

Whilst the code confirms the definition of confidential journalistic material as spelt out in RIPA, it does nothing to block the loophole of accessing phone records from the phone company. The NUJ claimed that the proposed reforms were not enough to ensure press freedom.

> The campaign against RIPA was always about its misuse by the authorities to spy on journalists. In response we demanded urgent action to prevent RIPA being used to secretly obtain the phone records of journalists. We have been campaigning to change the law so that the authorities should be required to make a public request to a journalist or news organisation to access communications data that could identify their sources.
>
> Andy Smith, NUJ president, said: "The bottom line is that no journalist can attempt to protect their source if the authorities can identify them using phone records without any notification or the ability to challenge the authority's actions."
>
> *(www.nuj.org.uk/news/ripa-reforms-will-not-go-far-enough/ accessed*
> *April 2019)*

The government introduced a new Investigatory Powers Act in 2016, defining the process for intercepting communications and the authorities entitled to intercept communications but it made no attempt to clear up the loophole of accessing call records, leaving journalists with little option but to consider other methods to protect sources such as burner phones (phones with numbers unregistered to the journalist) or old style communication methods such as letters or notes that would clearly be journalistic material as defined by PACE.

Nor is the police force the only authority using RIPA. *Press Gazette* revealed in early April 2019 that it had made a freedom of information request to the Financial Conduct Authority about its use of RIPA to access journalists' call records. This followed its report the previous year that the FCA had grabbed six years of call records of *Daily Mail* journalists Geoff Foster at the request of its French counterpart the Autorité des Marchés Financier.

Computer Misuse Act 1990

The Computer Misuse Act makes it an offence to perform any function aimed at securing access to any program or data held on any computer if the access is unauthorised. The aim of the Act is to prevent computer hacking, something the Information Commissioner's Office identified in its report *What Price Privacy* as still fairly widely practiced by a range of commercial operations including a number of newspapers and magazines.

Hacking computers is clearly unethical and can get you up to 12 months in jail.

10

DATA PROTECTION

This chapter looks at the concept of data protection and the limitations it places on journalists working in the UK and the EU on access to information about individuals.

Protecting personal data and its conflict with publication

Journalists working as reporters in news or feature-based editorial collect and process personal data and need to fully understand the need to protect personal data and the restrictions that are often placed on the journalist's ability to access information.

The widespread introduction of computers into government and then business through the 1970s and 1980s led to considerable concerns about the sharing of personal data and the invasion of privacy this could cause. Whilst data had regularly been collected before this time by various agencies and businesses in order to run their operations efficiently it had not been easy to share data between agencies as all data was kept in paper files. Tax office records could not be easily linked to records held by agencies such as social security or the NHS but the growing introduction of mainframe computers into government departments during the 1970s and the later development of personal computers in the late 1970s and early 1980s meant that such sharing became a real possibility and this led to significant concerns about the need to protect the privacy of people's data and so to the introduction of the Data Protection Act 1984. This was designed to protect personal data and laid down data protection principles. It spelt out rights of access to personal data and remedies and penalties for misuse.

Computers continued to be more common and by the mid-1990s, not only were they ubiquitous in business environments but they were also common in homes, with portable versions becoming more widely used, whilst most businesses and organisations now stored all records on computer. The internet and the World Wide Web were taking off and e-mail had started to become a useful communication method. The European Union introduced the Data Protection Directive in 1995 and this required the UK to introduce this into UK law and the 1984 Act was replaced by the Data Protection Act 1998 that introduced the concept not only of personal data – that is any data that could lead to the identification or a person such as name, address, place of employment or education – but of sensitive personal data. This could include race, religion or trade union membership.

This Act changed the way journalists worked quite considerably. Before the Act it was possible to ring a hospital and seek a condition report on someone who had been injured in a crime or a road accident and stories identifying someone and saying they were in a stable or critical condition in hospital were common. Similarly the police would give information about people involved in incidents. Following the introduction of the 1998 Act this stopped. A person's health or criminal offences became sensitive personal data under the 1998 Act and hospitals and other medical establishments were obliged to refuse to give condition reports or even confirm they had the patient unless the patient had given permission to release details. Similarly the police stopped giving information unless the person involved agreed or a senior officer considered the release of such information to be in the public interest, a verdict often taken against different criteria to those used by journalists. For a while this made what had been routine inquiries more difficult, increasing the number of contacts with family members of people involved in incidents.

Data protection

Whilst there is little in law preventing publication of someone's private affairs, there is strong legislation protecting the privacy of personal data. The rise of computers in the 1980s to manage data for government and private companies brought with them serious concerns about the privacy of data collected. No longer would one's data on different issues be kept on paper in dusty filing rooms but in modern computers capable of storing that data and worse still (for the data subject), sharing it with other computers to give a fuller picture of the person behind the data. In pre-computer days, the DVLA might know about your car and driving record, but only the NHS knew about your health and your social security record was a closed book to all but the DSS. Enter the computer age and suddenly government departments can share information easily by electronic communication, giving government and others a much more detailed picture and removing a person's control of information that should be private. This sharing of course also increased the risk that someone who could hack into a computer could get all your personal information instead of having to visit a number of different departments to blag information or hack into a computer. The development of security equipment such as CCTV (now misnamed as it is rarely Closed Circuit TV but video surveillance that is widely available as it is run over the internet) has led to its inclusion in the GDPR and the DPA, allowing people to put security cameras around their property without risk of being prosecuted for intruding into the privacy of another.

The urgency to protect this privacy has increased over the years with the development of the World Wide Web, broadband communication, surveillance cameras, other security devices, spy technology and personal computers. We can all now access more information from home than there has ever been available in any system before, including some private information. If we are to keep our information private, protected from both those with legal and necessary access and those who might wish to access our data illegitimately and with malicious purpose, we need various legal protections for our data protection and against malicious access.

The latest legislation is the EU General Data Protection Regulation (GDPR) in 2018 and the Data Protection Act 2018, introduced to reinforce the GDPR in the UK and to replace it should Brexit go ahead and the GDPR became no longer applicable in the UK. The GDPR and the DPA have seven principles that should be maintained by data controllers: These are:

- Lawfulness, fairness and transparency;
- Purpose limitation;
- Data minimisation;
- Accuracy;
- Storage limitation;
- Integrity and confidentiality (security);
- Accountability.
- Access to data

As the DPA and GDPR are introduced to protect the privacy of personal data, they have a massive impact on journalists. Journalists collect data about people in order to their jobs and as such are data controllers and need to apply the seven principles. That means they should only collect the data they need with a view to publication, they should ensure its accuracy, they should determine how long they need to keep the data and they should ensure it is kept safely and confidentially pending publication, probably on an encrypted flash drive or hard drive on an encrypted laptop. Whilst staff journalists will be covered by their employer's registration with the Information Commissioner's Office as a data controller, freelance journalists, whether writers, photographers or videographers, will need to register in their own name and pay an annual fee to the ICO. This easy to do at https://ico.org.uk/for-organisations/data-protection-fee/self-assessment/. Collecting data and processing it without registration is an offence. Photographers are considered data collectors as the data required for digital photography is considered by the ICO to be personal data to be processed by a computer.

Journalists do get some special protection under various elements of the GDPR/Act both in terms of what are known as the special purposes that include processing personal data for literary, journalistic and academic purposes. The government says that the aim is to "strike the right balance between freedom of expression of the media and the right to privacy of individuals" (https:// assets.publishing.service.gov.uk/government/uploads/system/uploads/attach ment_data/file/711181/2018-05-23_Factsheet_2_-_General_processing.pdf accessed April 2019). And this is done through both the special purposes and the public interest defence.

The Act is designed to protect privacy but also allow fulfilment of legal obligations on employment law, to allow scientific research and to allow the processing of data necessary for the administration of justice, or for an activity that supports or promotes democratic engagement.

The Act gives people the right to receive clear information about what their data will be used for; the right to access their own personal information and request that their data be revised if out of date or erased. These are known as the right to rectification and the right to erasure. Whilst in many cases a data subject will be aware that a journalist carries a limited amount of personal data about them (name, address, phone number, job title, email address and maybe some other limited personal details) they will usually have consented to giving the journalist that information. Occasionally the journalist will have gathered the information without their knowledge. Should a data subject contact the journalist to question the data held, then it should be remembered that they have rights under the Act but so do the journalists. The data subject has the right to ask what personal data are held. They can then ask to amend the information if it is incorrect. Correcting inaccurate information is not a problem as information should always be accurate. However, things can get more complicated if they ask for data to be erased. Even if the journalist is not working on a story right now about that person, they may wish to hold the information for potential future use. If they are working on a story then they will not want to erase the data and they may not at that stage wish to discuss the information with the data subject.

The ICO is obliged by the DPA to draw up a code of practice for journalists and guidance in the processing of data for journalism. In fact the ICO drew up such guidance in 2014 following the Leveson Inquiry and is still relying on this guidance, pending the update process obliged by the DPA. The code makes it clear that as a general rule, a journalist will comply with DPA if they are "fair, open, honest, handle information responsibly and don't cause unnecessary harm" (https://ico.org.uk/media/for-organisations/documents/1552/data-protection-and-journalism-media-guidance.pdf accessed April 2019). That is unlikely to change with the introduction of GDPR.

The ICO's key advice in the code of practice is

- Be open and honest wherever possible. People should know if you are collecting information about them where it is practicable to tell them. We accept that it will not generally be practicable for journalists to make contact with everyone they collect information about.

- You do not need to notify individuals if this would undermine the journalistic activity. This will be a trigger to consider the Section 32 exemption.
- Only use covert methods if you are confident that this is justified in the public interest.
- Only collect information about someone's health, sex life or criminal behaviour if you are confident it is relevant and the public interest in doing so sufficiently justifies the intrusion into their privacy.

Much of the information you collect will include some personal data. The act of obtaining it counts as "processing" and is therefore covered by the DPA.

The DPA expects you to collect information in a fair way. In practice, this means:

- a journalistic justification for collecting the information,
- where practical, telling the person you are collecting the information from, and the person the information is about (if different), who you are, and what you are doing with their information, only using someone's information as they would reasonably expect.

(Ibid.)

Journalists need to remember that it is personal data that are involved. Whilst the journalist might be working on story about, say, council corruption, the personal data about the person suspected of being involved can be kept separately to the other, non-personal, information, notes, interviews and other details concerning the corruption allegations. The GDPR and the DPA only concern information about personal details or special category personal data. Information that cannot identify a person is not covered as this Act is about privacy, not confidentiality (although of course other Acts concerning secrecy may be applied). Provided any notes about a particular story are collected separately without a link to any personal details, except, perhaps, a separate contact book file reference, then if asked what data is being stored about that person the journalist can give the personal data and check that they are accurate, correcting them if not, without referring to the story for which the information was gathered.

As well as personal data, the GDPR and Data Protection Act also identify special category data, that is data that are particularly sensitive and could lead to unlawful discrimination or other detrimental effects. Special category data include:

- racial or ethnic origin;
- political opinions;

- religious beliefs or other beliefs of a similar nature;
- trade union membership;
- physical or mental health or condition;
- sex life and sexual orientation;
- genetic data and biometric data.

As these data are particularly sensitive, data controllers must have a legitimate reason for collecting such data. Those that concern journalists are:

- Explicit consent, often given as a matter of course by politicians and trade unionists;
- Processing related to personal data made public by the data subject;
- Processing is necessary for the defence of legal claims;
- Processing is for reasons of substantial public interest.

Normally a journalist would use the defence of substantial public interest in collecting, storing and publishing special category data but could use the need to hold such data for the defence of any potential future legal claims.

Special purposes

Special purposes cover journalism. However, they are not a get-out-of-jail-free card, they merely give some protection for gathering data for journalism. The 2018 DPA says that to claim special purpose protection:

> Processing must be undertaken with a view to publication by a person of journalistic, academic, artistic or literary material which has not previously been published by the controller. The Data controller must believe the information is in the public interest; this was previously identified by The Data Protection (Processing of Sensitive Personal Data) Order 2000 as the disclosure of personal data that must be in the public interest and connected with any unlawful act; dishonesty, malpractice, or other improper conduct; unfitness or incompetence of any person; mismanagement in the administration of, or failures in services provided by, any body or association.
>
> The Data controller must also believe that compliance with the provision in question is incompatible with the special purposes. Both the public interest defence and the belief that compliance would be incompatible needs to be supported by evidence and argument but is about the Data Controller's honest belief and would not be measured against the ICO's belief.

(Ibid.)

Registration

Journalists need to register with the ICO as data controllers. Staff journalists will be covered by their employer's registration but freelances will need to register and a pay an annual fee in their own right.

The ICO has a website that checks whether you need to register and pay a fee that leads you to the payment form. The questionnaire is simple and quick to access and is available at: https://ico.org.uk/for-organisations/data-protection-fee/self-assessment/.

Right to be forgotten

The so-called right to be forgotten, included in the EU Data Protection Direct-ive and subsequently updated in the General Data Protection Directive was recently considered by the European Court, which confirmed the usage right to be forgotten. The Data Protection regulations and the DPA protect our individ-ual privacy by requiring data collectors to delete data that are wrong or no longer relevant to the purpose for which they were collected. Whilst this does not require journalists to remove material as their data may always be relevant, it can oblige search engines to remove links to data that are inaccurate or no longer relevant. Google was found to be a data collector by the European Courts when a Spanish resident applied to have searches that led to items in a newspaper about his home being repossessed. The Court ruled that the data laws applied to Google and that Google should remove the ability to access the information. The courts only required that searches on Google should be pre-vented. Those who searched the newspaper's archive could still access the item. Newspaper articles are matters of public record and there has been no suggestion they should be removed or be made inaccessible. However, some newspapers do occasionally limit the meta-tags that allow people to make searches online. This would apply to stories concerning minors or other vulnerable people.

11

NEW TECHNOLOGY AND PRIVACY

Social media is arguably the most significant revolution so far this century, allowing billions of people to become publishers in their own right whether they merely tweet what they just had for dinner, send photos to their friends on Instagram, contact groups of friends or family on WhatsApp or manage a busy Facebook page. Social media has taken the huge advantages of previous communication technological advances such as letter writing and phone calls and made them easier and faster to apply. Now, instead of the relatively laborious process of sitting down to write a weekly letter to each friend and relative, or individually phoning friends and family in order to catch up and pass on news, we can pass on snippets of gossip, news about family or thoughts on the world in general to individuals or groups at the push of a few buttons, often as they are actually happening.

Social media has quickly become ubiquitous and is so enjoyed by many that they become sleep deprived, addicted and find it difficult to be parted from their phones. It should be no surprise that a device that allows one to keep in close immediate contact with friends and family, sharing thoughts and events almost as they happen, has become so popular. We are social animals and we all want to keep in touch with those close to us. Social media has been shown to strengthen those relationships, allowing us to better keep in touch with those who live away and even those who live nearby. Social media has been shown to help the elderly feel less isolated, to benefit those with chronic illnesses who find it difficult to go out of the house or hospital. It is also advantageous in professional relationships, helping doctors, academics and others to improve their professional practice by keeping them in touch with colleagues, sharing the latest information.

But nothing good ever comes without a downside. People started to complain about their fear of addiction, their anxiety about missing something – an anxiety so real that Fomo (fear of missing out) is now listed in dictionaries – and the sheer amount of time they were spending on social media. The fragmentation threat to your concentration can also affect your ability to be successful at work or at physical relationships. There are also some real threats in terms of criminals, conmen and inappropriate marketing of goods and political ideologies. It is this last area that should be concerning journalists. The invasion of personal privacy, by criminals and those hoping to access our data to focus marketing information at us, is a serious concern for journalists as we need to ensure that journalistic research activities in this are not confused with criminal or marketing behaviour.

Social media is a totally new way of researching and sourcing stories as well as being a new way of publishing, not so much because it is a publishing method but because it can be a very useful auxiliary publishing method. Think how often your social media of choice is used to alert you to stories, documentaries, films or TV programmes. Often social media takes the place of the old-fashioned newspaper seller's billboard trumpeting the teasing headline that will get you to buy the paper.

I need to say upfront that none of this changes the journalist's basic ethics. We still need to consider invasion of privacy in researching stories, and accuracy and intrusion into privacy when publishing. However, it can make it more diffi-cult to identify when journalists are being intrusive as they become used to using social media with friends and relatives and may find it more difficult to separate professional use of social media from personal use.

Smartphones have become the standard journalistic tool for accessing data and sources. Only a few years ago, the idea that a journalist could have a device that would enable them to access data on practically anything in an instant as well as track sources and be able to talk to them either in real time or sequentially through messaging apps would have seemed like a dream. Social media is the icing on the cake. It's a great way of contacting people that you know and want to follow, it allows you to see what's trending, what people are interested in and what they want to know. It's incredibly useful to contact witnesses and other sources. Want to know why all the traffic is unusually backed up? Put out a message on Twitter and Facebook asking your followers if there's something going on that is likely to cause the traffic jam. The chances are someone will have seen the accident or whatever it is causing the delay, allowing the journalist to decide if there's a story there. The plotline of one TV favourite programme, *NCIS*, involved trying to track the destination of a low–flying terrorist aircraft. A well-followed social media user's page was used to ask people to report if they spotted the plane. Of course, following the laws of TV, scores of social media users tweeted in to thwart the bad guy.

Other information can be gathered using social media and it's a great way to contact people for comment or witness statements. Picking up tweeted com-ments has become so common place that some journalists seem to forget that others read those tweets from the original source and that the journalist has to add some originality by providing detail of the underlying story or other witnesses or opinions. It's no good essentially retweeting the wisdom of others. Twitter is doing that already.

When it comes to concerns about privacy though, social media can be a real problem. Not everyone is as careful with their privacy online as they ought to be or, often, as they really want to be. Privacy fundamentalists – people whom Westin defines as being very concerned with their privacy and highly suspicious of the motives of government and corporations – are unlikely to be on social media. These are people who are well aware of the risks of social media, almost to the point of paranoia, and are therefore not likely to even use smartphones. Privacy pragmatists –those Westin defines as being more relaxed about their privacy but still with some concerns – are more likely to be on social media but are also more likely to be careful about their data. However, even though they may be well aware that they need to take care whilst on line, both they and those who are privacy unconcerned are likely to allow more data onto social media than may be wise. Although they may be concerned to protect data, especially the pragmatists, they may not realise the ease with which their social media can be accessed nor fully understand the motivation of those who would want to do so.

The analogy could be a group of friends in a pub. There are about 15 of them gathered around a large table drinking. As the evening wears on they will become louder and possibly franker with their comments and observations about friends. They would assume that no one else in the pub would be particularly interested in their gossip, having their own friends to talk to, nor would they imagine that this gossip would be taken and presented to the world. But anyone could listen in and could possibly gain a lot of data that would put one or more of those people or their friends at risk: a burglary, a robbery on the way home, relationship problems with others not at the table or the transmission of private gossip to others.

The friends would assume their conversation was private, but that may not be the case. The same is true of social media, with the additional problem that technological ineptitude could also hamper their ability to protect their data.

We need to be careful about privacy. The recent scandal involving Cambridge Analytica and Facebook shows just how significant privacy can be. Mark Zuckerberg, CEO and co-founder of Facebook, told the Cruncie Awards in San Francisco in 2010 that: "people have really gotten comfortable not only sharing more information and different kinds, but more openly and with more people". He identified this as reflecting changing attitudes among the general public and a shift in the general view on privacy but just a couple of months into 2010, Zuckerberg had to admit that Facebook had "missed the mark" with its privacy controls and new privacy controls were added at the end of May. Following his 2018 appearances before a House of Representatives hearing in the US, Zuckerberg still seems to believe that it is users' responsibility to control what they put on Facebook and not Facebook's duty to protect that data. Manually scraping data from Facebook pages is widely practised in order to gather information about the subject of a story, but the ethics of this practice are more complicated. Many people put information about themselves on Facebook and other social media, largely on the assumption that only those who know them can access it and that certainly only those who know them would want to access it. We can liken it to that group of friends gossiping around a table in a pub who do not expect eavesdroppers on their conversation and certainly do not expect to see it repeated later in a news story. However, that is not always the case. A person dying in bizarre circumstances on holiday or involved in a major disaster may suddenly become very newsworthy and accessing their Facebook page will bring pictures, data and potential contacts to further the story. Is it appropriate to access such pages despite high privacy settings or because the subject did not fully understand how to set high privacy settings?

The Independent Press Standards Organisation (IPSO) has dealt with a number of such complaints. The *Herne Bay Gazette* carried a story about a young woman jailed for causing death by dangerous driving and drink driving. They used a photograph taken from her Facebook page showing her holding up a full wine glass saying she had enjoyed a "booze-fuelled Christmas trip just days before she was jailed". In fact the picture was taken on a family outing and the glass contained cola. She said that her Facebook page was set to family and friends but the newspaper said it was publicly accessible. The IPSO upheld the complaint (www.ipso.co.uk/rulings-and-resolution-statements/ruling/?id=03139-14 accessed May 2019).

In another case, the *Lancashire Evening Post* reported that photographs of children from Lancashire had been found on a file sharing website which the newspaper described variously as a "Russian pervert website" and a "paedophile website". The article was illustrated with five pixelated photographs of local children which had been hosted on the Russian site. The complainant said that two of these images were of her young child. They had originally been published on her Facebook profile, and recognised from the newspaper by friends who had alerted her to the article. The IPSO upheld her complaint (www.ipso.co.uk/rulings-and-resolution-statements/ruling/?id=00256-15 accessed May 2019).

The *Edinburgh Evening News* published a story about a teenager who died from brain cancer. The article was based on copy by a news agency and was published in a number of media outlets. It was largely based on information from social media including information from the teenager's Facebook page, and expressions of condolences from her classmates. The complaint, made by an uncle of the teenager who was concerned about the article being based on social media, was upheld (www.ipso.co.uk/rulings-and-resolution-statements/ruling/?id=03856-15 accessed May 2019).

Twitter brings its own problems. A woman complained to IPSO after a photo of her daughter was published on the front page of the *Daily Star* identifying her as one of the people missing or dead following the terror attack in Manchester Arena; the caption identified her as "missing" and referred to her by an incorrect name (www.ipso.co.uk/rulings-and-resolution-statements/ruling/?id=12629-17 accessed May 2019).

IPSO upheld the complaint and required the publication of an adjudication after hearing that the complainant's daughter's details had been appropriated and used by a hoax Twitter account. The newspaper had taken no further steps to establish the accuracy of the claims on the Twitter account.

These cases give some idea of different types of usage. When accessing Facebook pages for a publication, make sure to record confirmation of the privacy settings. Fully private settings should only be breached if there is a significant public interest, and that public interest has been formally agreed.

Other issues to consider are:

- Is the subject a minor? If so the public interest needs to be overwhelming.
- Is it appropriate to publish pictures? Remember about copyright; it may well be owned by the subject, a family member or a commercial photographer.
- Think about the nature of all the material. Just because, for instance, a road accident concerning the subject is in the public interest, it does not mean that other details of the subject are appropriate to publish.
- Take a screenshot of the page with privacy settings to confirm what was there.
- Should images of other people in any pictures you intend to use be pixelated?
- Who placed the material on the page and is it therefore still appropriate to use it?
- When was a picture or item published by the user? Is it still current and appropriate to use?
- Is the material likely to intrude on anyone's private life, grief or distress without an over-riding consideration of the public interest?

Twitter

Twitter is an extremely useful tool for publishing and for finding sources for stories allowing quick and easy access to readers and contacts. However, journalists need to remember:

- Using it as a source is fine but take care when publishing;
- Tweets need to be able to stand alone;
- Avoid personal opinions.

Facebook

Facebook is also good for contacting sources but some rules apply here as well:

- Publishing on Facebook is controlled by the same rules as Twitter. Avoid personal views that can be mistaken as professional views.

- Privacy is an issue that requires care:

  - Lifting material from Facebook can be equated to eavesdropping, in that the material might be available for the public but was not intended for the public. Is there a public interest? What about copyright considerations?
  - Using it as a contact book brings the risk of being perceived as a "friend" of contact.

- Accessing information and pictures on public sites or private sites:

  - Remember pictures are someone's copyright and we should seek permission before use.
  - Can we use pictures taken from private pages? If there is an overwhelming public interest then many publications will use such pictures first and argue copyright later. However, copyright approval should be sought first where possible.

Case study 1

Ms Laura Clegg complained to the Press Complaints Commission that a *Sun* article falsely quoted her, and that the newspaper had invaded her privacy by obtaining a photograph of her from her Facebook page. Resolution: The complaint was resolved when the PCC negotiated the removal of the article from the newspaper's website.

- Be careful of stories on social media that could be hoaxes. Checking with additional sources is just good journalism.

Case study 2

Mr Ash Choudry complained to the Press Complaints Commission about an online article in the *Daily Mail* which reported on a Facebook campaign urging Saudi men to whip women who planned to defy a ban on women driving. The complainant believed that the Facebook campaign was in fact a hoax. While the newspaper did not accept that its article was in breach of the Editors' Code, the matter was resolved when it agreed to remove the piece from its website.

Witness contributors will become more and more a feature of future newsgathering operations. The consumer can supply her or his own slant on the news directly to the supplier faster and more efficiently than ever before. Journalists now tend to be alerted to stories by readers using social media or e-mail, particularly on breaking stories. This developing interactive element is seen by many as the most important facet of the internet when it comes to journalism. Properly used, it should allow more input from a vast range of sources, but it is crucial to remember that most of this information may be opinion rather than fact, pushing personal viewpoints and prejudices. With this wider range of available material, the filtering process, if only in terms of time available to read all this information, will become more difficult.

Much material on the internet comes from unofficial or commercial sources and needs to be treated with suspicion. The rise in conspiracy theories can probably be laid at the door of the internet as anyone with a campaign, no matter how ridiculous, can not only find an audience of potentially millions but also sufficient people to take the idea seriously to give it some authority. Credibility and balance is difficult to measure on the internet without seeking additional sources.

Instagram

This is a photo app allowing friends to share photos. The usual concerns about copyright and privacy are the same as for other social media.

WhatsApp

WhatsApp is an encrypted message system that allows groups of people to communicate, send pictures and video and chat live by voice or video. An invitation is needed to join a group so unless you already have a group of people for sourcing or publication use this is not the most likely social media tool for breaking news but might be something you use all the time. If so, the privacy and copyright elements need to be made clear with each member of each group from the start. This can be done in the group description and with each invitation to join the group.

Flickr

Flickr is a photo management and sharing application that is widely used by photographers, both professional and amateur. It allows photographers to manage photographs in different ways:

> In Flickr, you can give your friends, family, and other contacts permission to organize your stuff – not just to add comments, but also notes and tags. People like to ooh and ahh, laugh and cry, make wisecracks when sharing photos and videos. Why not give them the ability to do this when they look at them over the internet? And as all this info accretes as metadata, you can find things so much easier later on, since all this info is also searchable.
>
> *(www.flickr.com/about.)*

If you wish to publish a picture from a professional member, then a fee-paying system is available to facilitate that. If you wish to use a picture from an amateur then their privacy settings will say whether they allow that or you can message them. It would be a breach of their copyright to use a picture if their privacy settings prevent that. IPSO offers guidance on social media use (www.Ipso.co.uk/press-standards/guidance-for-journalists-and-editors/social-media-guidance/ accessed June 2018).

Professional use of social media

Social media is now widely used in the everyday lives of journalists as well as their professional lives, but if journalists are to convince readers that their material is accurate, balanced and disinterested they need to be very careful about identifying their personal social media with their professional social media. This has become a big problem for many journalists and their employers. A number of journalists around the world have faced a reprimand or even dismissal for a hasty tweet or Facebook comment. The infamous UK *Mail Online* columnist Katie Hopkins was one following her comments about Muslims. Octavia Nasr lost her job as CNN's senior editor for Middle Eastern affairs for a tweet concerning Israel. The list goes on but more than a dozen journalists, many of them in senior positions, were reprimanded or sacked over the past couple of years for ill-advised tweets. Most companies now have social media policies for employees. For instance, the BBC says:

> when someone clearly identifies their association with the BBC and/or discusses their work, they are expected to behave appropriately when on the Internet, and in ways that are consistent with the BBC's editorial values and policies …
>
> Our audiences need to be confident that the outside activities of our presenters, programme makers and other staff do not undermine the BBC's impartiality or reputation and that editorial decisions are not perceived to be influenced by any commercial or personal interests.
>
> *(www.bbc.co.uk/editorialguidelines/guidance/social-networking-personal/*
> *guidance-full accessed May 2018)*

This often leads to a debate about whether journalists are allowed personal lives that may lead to accusations of partiality. Some US journalists carry this to extremes, refusing to play any part in their local communities for fear they will be seen as being partial. However, it seems to me appropriate to belong to your local community even if you are a local journalist. If a journalist is reporting on that local community, then it may be appropriate to be careful about taking sides over issues of major local significance, but that doesn't mean they can't support the local PTA where their kids go to school or more general community groups of a social or cultural nature. Even political or campaign groups may be OK provided the journalist is up front about them with their editor and news editor.

This can apply equally to a personal social media page. Whilst journalists can write more or less what they want on their personal social media (remembering the law still applies) they should always remember that they may be recognised as working for the news media and that might affect how their writing is perceived by others. It might also get them into unnecessary trouble with employers and sources if they were to write about them in a disparaging way. Always be upfront with news editors if hobbies, beliefs or pastimes risk coming into conflict with work.

Intrusive technology

Technology is increasingly intrusive as further developments are introduced to "improve" our lives. Many are extremely useful and supportive in our everyday lives but bring with them the risk of privacy intrusion. When I get up in the morning I can ask my Echo device to read me the news and tell me the weather. I can start my coffee brewing with a yelled instruction from my shower and start warming up my car on a cold morning from my breakfast table. I can tell my car to follow the route of my morning commute, whilst asking the radio to play the news. Should I get a caller while I'm out, I can answer the doorbell from my phone. And so it goes on throughout the day ending with asking Echo to turn off the bedroom lights. Wearable technologies such as Google Glass are on the market and following the pattern of other technologies are likely to become common usage in around ten years. Augmented reality, the ability to apply additional information to your normal vision in terms of descriptions, explanations, directions and other support will soon be common place. Of course these devices also bring with them the risk of privacy invasion in terms of knowing where you are, where you have been, who you were with, who else was nearby, what you have bought, listening in to your conversations and what you have been doing. They make the concerns about computer data storage that sparked the Data Protection Acts seem like paranoia. This is real Big Brother stuff, with police, security forces and presumably those with malicious intent having virtually total access to our lives. It would be a real test of faith to share your password for access to this data with your nearest and dearest.

CCTV and video surveillance

So-called CCTV or Closed Circuit Television is now widely available in the UK. This form of surveillance technology is not strictly closed circuit anymore as most transmit not on a fixed, closed circuit line to a screen, but through the internet. This allows the signal to be picked up from anywhere. The term Camera Surveillance System is the phrase now widely used by the police and security industry.

Caughtoncamera.net, suppliers of CCTV systems, estimates there are around 500,000 public CCTV cameras in London alone, in streets, tube and rail stations, and businesses. There are 15,516 just in tube stations (www.caughtonca mera.net accessed April 2019). Most commentators estimate that there are between 4m and 5m cameras monitoring public spaces throughout the UK but many of these studies are based on relatively small samples in places that would have a particularly high density of cameras. Whatever the real figure, we can say that there are a lot of cameras in the UK and that we have a high percentage of the estimated 25m cameras globally (ibid.).

Not only are there a lot of public space surveillance cameras whether run by various authorities or private businesses or individuals, but many of them are able to run automated number plate recognition (APNR). This recognises a car and is widely used to check for motoring offences such as no insurance and failure to pay road vehicle duty. It is also use to alert police to a vehicle that is wanted for being involved in crime in some way. Some police forces are also experimenting with automated facial recognition (AFR). Whilst this technology is so far falling well short of the desired aim of the authorities of being able to track known criminals and is also a long way from the usefulness of AFR, as seen on many popular US federal agency TV dramas, like most technology, we are simply talking about time. The police and some others now also wear body cameras, recording their everyday interactions with the public.

The real problem for the media in all this Big Brother technology is the use to which CCTV footage is often put. More and more TV programmes rely on footage bought from or supplied by local authorities or the police to prove real-life dramas. Watching the police in a high speed chase, or pulling over a suspicious vehicle has a level of drama to which we have normally become desensitised. Clips taken from CCTV are now regular options either as whole TV programmes or as clips for use in news programmes. Generally speaking such clips are filmed in public places where there is no legitimate expectation of privacy however there can be times when this is not the case. A complaint by Ms K to Ofcom concerned CCTV footage of her performing oral sex on a man in a lift that was broadcast in a Channel 4 programme: *CCTV: Caught on Camera*. Her face, and that of the man, were obscured and their voices were not heard. Ofcom found that, although she had a limited legitimate expectation of privacy, "the public interest in broadcasting footage showing the role of CCTV cameras in monitoring anti-social behaviour outweighed Ms Ks expectation of privacy". Therefore the complaint was not upheld (www.ofcom.org.uk/__data/assets/pdf_file/0017/45440/issue275.pdf, p. 57 accessed April 2019).

Drones

Drones are another fairly recent development and one that has revolutionised film and video practice. No longer need a director hire a stunningly expensive helicopter and crew that has massive Civil Aviation Authority (CAA) limitations on where it can go and what it can do. Now a professional quality drone can be bought for a couple of thousand pounds (or hired from a specialist hire company) that will hover motionless at a range of heights and swoop in and out on the action as required. From filming wild life and wild country to scenes of mayhem and violent disruption, the drone has made filming quality footage safe, relatively cheap and easy to do.

If you do not have your own drone then you might wish to hire someone to operate one for you. This is considered a commercial operation by the CAA, which defines it as:

> any flight by a small unmanned aircraft except a flight for public transport, or any operation of any other aircraft except an operation for public transport–
>
> (a) which is available to the public;
>   or
> (b) which, when not made available to the public,
>
>> (i)   in the case of a flight by a small unmanned aircraft, is performed under a contract between the SUA operator and a customer, where the latter has no control over the remote pilot;or
>> (ii) in any other case, is performed under a contract between an operator and a customer, where the latter has no control over the operator,in return for remuneration or other valuable consideration.

> *(www.caa.co.uk/Commercial-industry/Aircraft/Unmanned-aircraft/*
> *Small-drones/Guidance-on-using-small-drones-for-commercial-work/*
> *accessed April 2019)*

However, you do not need to hire a commercial operator if you have your own drone, provided you can show you are competent in its use by passing the CAA's online safety testing. It is a requirement from November 2019 for the owners of all drones weighing more than 250g to register them with the CAA.

Drones of use to journalists are fitted with cameras and, if these are of sufficient quality, they add to the weight. The Air Navigation Order (2016) introduced new rules for Small Unmanned Aircraft (SUAs, commonly called drones) weighing less than 20kg. The CAA has published the new rules as a Dronecode:

- Don't fly near airports or airfields;
- Remember to stay below 400ft (120m);
- Observe your drone at all times; stay 150ft (50m) from people and property;
- Never fly near aircraft;
- Enjoy responsibly.

(https://dronesafe.uk/wp–content/uploads/2019/02/Drone-Code_March19.pdf accessed April 2019).

SUAs that weigh more than 7kg, which few top-quality camera platform drones likely to be of use to journalists do, have additional rules that apply within certain airspace. Additional rules also apply for cameras on drones (and I can't imagine a journalist flying a drone professionally without a camera). If you wish to fly your camera-fitted drone:

- within 150m of either a congested area or an organised open air crowd of more than 1,000 persons, and/or
- within 50m of people or properties/objects that are not under your control

then you will need permission from the CAA in order to do so legally.

The CAA ensures you are safe to reduce these safety limits by asking:

- about your drone and how it works;
- how you intend to conduct the flight in a safe manner;
- for evidence of your competency to fly your drone.

Essentially this is the same process the CAA uses that must be followed by drone operators who wish to conduct commercial operations and the CAA will require a:

- demonstration of "piloting competence";
- evidence of sufficient understanding of aviation theory (airmanship, airspace, aviation law and good flying practice);
- practical flight assessment (flight test).

The limitations on flying close to people and property could be a problem for journalists hoping to film over crowds for sporting events, charity events and political campaigning but at the time of writing there is little suggestion that journalists have hit problems.

Archives

Stories published on the web that risk intrusion into privacy are a conundrum. If they have been published should they be taken down? Should information current 30 years ago still be readily available for all to read? This is a particular issue with people who may well have done something foolish in their childhood or as young adults – should that blight them for the rest of their lives?

Stories on the web form a superb archive of material published by the news provider over the years that can easily be mined for specific information. While it has always been possible to research newspaper archives for data, this has been cumbersome and time consuming, requiring the researcher to attend the newspaper office or a library to search the past issues on paper or microfiche. This meant that such research was normally only carried out for very good reason and with a purpose in mind. No one would casually go to a library and search newspaper records to find out if someone had been named in a story. Now Google searches are quick and easy. This means that any error in the archive, or any invasion of privacy, will easily be discovered and so newspapers and websites are having to reconsider their policies about archive material.

For instance, say a person was arrested in connection with a series of serious crimes. A report appears in the local paper and in the website. A few weeks later the charges are withdrawn as the person arrested is found to have no involvement at all. Yet every time someone searches that person's name, the arrests could come up on Google or Yahoo. Of course this emphasises the importance of news organisations following through with stories and publishing the withdrawal of the charges so those would also show up on the search. But this is not the only reason why people want to revisit website reports that may show them in a bad light, many may seek to protect their privacy that might have been legitimately breached in the first place but is, the complainant believes, no longer appropriate. Newspapers and broadcasters are being increasingly bombarded with requests to "unpublish": to remove references to people involved in stories. This is not about errors; most news organisations now accept that errors on websites need to be either deleted or tagged with the correction. The main concern now is legitimate, accurate stories that may make life very difficult for the person in an age when searching is so easy.

The main options for a website are:

- delete or edit the item;
- take the whole page down;
- block search engines from accessing the page; or
- tag the page with a correction.

Google explains how to block access to search engines on http://googlepublicpo licy.blogspot.com/2009/07/working-with-news-publishers.html. This can be done either at the time of loading or at a predetermined specific date so that the search engine will remove the page from the index on a certain date.

Publishers sometimes tag outdated web pages or limit search potential or both. Pages are rarely deleted. This is building into a major ethical issue contrasting a publisher's right to maintain an archive of published material that is easily available to the public with an individual's desire to forget a troubled past and remove details of it from the web. The General Data Protection Regulation and the Data Protection Act 2018 both provide for a right to be forgotten. This allows people to seek to have their data removed if it is no longer relevant or accurate. This does not directly concern published stories on the web as they constitute an archive but it might concern a search engine and Google lost a major case in Europe obliging it to remove data from its search engine. In the test case, the original data could remain on the newspaper's site, but Google was obliged to remove meta-data that allowed for the story to be searched. If you knew the story was published in the newspaper then you could access the information but if you searched for it, you would not find it.

According to Kathy English, public editor of the *Toronto Star*, requests to unpublish are becoming more frequent (cited in Frost, 2006: 218). The problem with unpublishing is that archives are a matter of public record and to remove or to delete them would be a form of censorship. This has led to considerable reluctance by some editors to even consider it. The Rehabilitation of Offenders Act in the UK requires that minor criminal charges are not mentioned after a certain amount of time has passed and it is this issue of how long misdemeanours are available to read online that is troubling some editors as it perhaps presents the most difficult balance between public interest and potential personal harm. According to English, Gatehouse Media, which owns hundreds of weeklies in the United States, is piloting a policy where minor misdemeanours are removed from the website six months after initial publication.

There is guidance available concerning rehabilitation with regards to past offences on www.gov.uk/government/publications/new-guidance-on-the-rehabilitation-of-offenders-act-1974 (accessed April 2019) and also on the national social justice charity, Nacro's website at https://3bx16p38bchl32s0e12 di03h-wpengine.netdna-ssl.com/wp-content/uploads/2018/07/Rehabilitation-of-Offenders-Act-1974-Guide-2018.pdf (accessed April 2019).

Pranks and revenge porn

Whilst hoaxes and pranks are common, with people trying to convince newsrooms about things that might well invade people's privacy, revenge porn is less common and also unlikely to be used by a publisher in a way intended by the perpetrator. Stories from sources concerning privacy should be investigated to ensure they are not pranks in the same way as all potential stories. Revenge porn can become a story in its own right but needs to be handled very carefully. Image-based sexual abuse or revenge porn is about sharing intimate or sexually explicit pictures or video without consent. It was made illegal in the UK under the Criminal Justice Act 2015.

This type of abuse can be from a former partner, hence the term revenge porn, or can also be from online criminals who lure people into providing explicit images and then use the threat of wider exposure to blackmail their victims. Whilst it is unlikely that any reputable publisher would use such material if sent it, it is important to be aware of this type of privacy intrusion and the importance of gaining consent from the person pictured if it were important to use the picture to support a story for some reason. In one case considered by the Press Complaints Commission in 2007 before the Criminal Justice Act, a couple complained about a picture of their daughter published in *FHM Magazine*. The magazine had published a gallery of mobile phone "snapshots" of readers' girlfriends, many of them topless or in lingerie. The topless picture of the daughter had been taken two years before when she was only 15 and sent in by a former boyfriend. In its adjudication that upheld the complaint the PCC said:

> The magazine said that it received approximately 1,200 photographs for publication each week from or on behalf of women posing topless or in lingerie … It had no reason to believe that the image was taken without her consent. The magazine had been informed that the complainants' daughter was in a cohabiting relationship with the person who submitted the photograph and, in those circumstances, no further enquiries about the image were made.
>
> *(www.pcc.org.uk/cases/adjudicated.html?article=NDcxNA==*
> *accessed April 2019)*

The Criminal Justice Act 2015 S33 makes it an offence disclose a private, sexual photograph or film without the consent of an individual who appears in it with the intention of causing that individual distress. The Act identifies "private" as showing something that is not "of a kind ordinarily seen in public" and "sexual" as any image showing exposed genitals or pubic area or anything a reasonable person would consider to be sexual.

There is little doubt the pictures published by the magazine were intended to titillate and would potentially breach the CJA2015. The only defence a magazine could have for publishing such pictures would be consent of the person pictured.

Other cases also outline the dangers of publishing pictures of this sort. In 1991, *The People* published a picture of the Duke of York's young daughter naked in a garden. This case was upheld by the PCC, but *The People* did not take it too seriously, rerunning the picture with a mocked-up picture of the Duke of York running into a stream saying, "Where's your sense of fun?" The Protection of Children Act 1978 makes it an offence to take or distribute any indecent picture of a child. The Criminal Justice Act 1988 also makes it an offence to possess such pictures. The law does not specify what constitutes "indecent" in this context and the Act does allow a defence of having a legitimate reason for distributing such photographs. Prosecutions can only be brought with the consent of the Director of Public Prosecutions, but it is probably wise not to publish pictures of children that might be seen as indecent. The updated law also included pseudo-pictures in this definition.

12

MEDIA REGULATORS

Whilst the law has a clear part to play in regulating the media, ensuring that important individual rights are protected, it would be foolish to invoke the law for every element of media behaviour. This is particularly true with regard to privacy. Providing legislative protection for every potential or actual breach of privacy by the media and legal debate about the public interest defence in each instance, would lead to a timorous news media. It would be unable to question or criticise those with power and influence and unable to fulfil its primary duty of informing the public about events and the society in which they lived. In order to deal quickly and efficiently with everyday minor concerns about privacy intrusion, a regulator, with expertise in the field, is much better suited to monitor performance, identify standards and take complaints. Regulatory bodies vary around the world but tend to follow one of several patterns of regulator, including independent, self-regulatory bodies, bodies run independently but underpinned by statute in some way, statutory bodies set up with strict legal duties and powers or tribunals that are part of the judiciary system.

Types of regulators can also be identified by the range of their regulatory duties. Some regulators cover all media, including news media, in their geographic jurisdiction whilst other regulators control either traditional press, broadcasting or electronic media. Those countries with a long history of various media are more likely to split regulation between press and broadcasting. Until recently, the technology for broadcasting meant that limited access to the broadcasting frequencies meant stricter control was felt necessary over both the allocation of broadcasting frequencies and the material that could be broadcast, whilst newspapers and magazines were allowed a freer hand as, in theory, anyone could set up a newspaper or magazine. With the advent of the internet and web browsers, plus the move to digital transmission of broadcasts, the limitations on broadcasting were largely, removed putting them on an even footing with the press with both media able to access the internet to support their publications or even supersede them. This historic framework has meant that the US, UK and most of Western Europe still tends to have separate press and broadcasting regulation. In the UK, for instance, the change in technology has not led to a significant change in the regulatory landscape. Broadcasters and their associated websites are still controlled by the Communications Act and the regulators it provides, whilst the press is still regulated by a voluntary industry-run body. Internet media meanwhile are still largely unregulated, although changes in law and desire by government to apply significant regulation may change that dramatically over the next few years.

It is also important at this stage to draw a distinction between a regulator and a complaints body as it is an issue that has caused much confusion, particularly during the life of the Press Complaints Commission (1991–2014). A complaints body takes and adjudicates complaints, usually from the public, judging them against a code of practice to determine whether the complaints should be upheld. A regulator has a much broader remit in that, whilst it will take complaints, it is also able to identify standards for those that it regulates and monitor and initiate investigations into breaches of those standards. It is then able to apply sanctions against those that it regulates that breach the identified standards. It is an important distinction that has dogged UK regulation.

Leveson, the government and the press

The Leveson Inquiry was a major game changer for the press in the UK. The Inquiry started work in the summer of 2011 and reported in November 2012 after hearing evidence from numerous people including politicians, industry spokespersons and the public. Full reports and videos of evidence are available on the website https://webarchive.nationalarchives.gov.uk/20140122144906/http://www.levesoninquiry.org.uk/ (accessed April 2019).

Leveson recommended the PCC should be disbanded and be replaced with an independent self-regulator. Leveson identified that any future regulator taking over from the PCC would need a number of qualities. The key criteria identified by the report were:

- the need to verify a regulator as satisfactory;
- the importance of all major media being included;
- full independence from industry and government;
- penalties of up to £1m fines for breaching code;
- third party complaints;
- no power to prevent publication;
- ability to launch investigations and monitor coverage;
- an arbitration panel for civil suits.

Following lengthy debates in parliament and considerable pressure being placed on the government, a royal charter was enacted by the Privy Council in October 2013 to:

- identify conditions for a satisfactory regulator as advised by Leveson;
- set up an independent Press Recognition Panel.

The royal charter as agreed by the Privy Council cannot be amended without a vote of at least 60% of both Houses of Parliament and the Scottish Parliament.

Press Recognition Panel

The Press Recognition Panel was set up under the Charter in November 2014. Funded by the Treasury to the tune of £3m it is chaired by David Wolfe QC. The PRP started its work consulting widely about regulation and started taking applications from regulators in 2015. To be recognised as charter-compliant, a regulator must:

- Have an independent board with no serving editors or MPs and a majority independent of the press but including sufficient with experience (former editors or journalism academics);
- Be industry funded;
- Offer advice to the public;
- Provide guidance on the public interest;
- Establish a whistle-blowing hotline for journalists.

The PRP was not overwhelmed with applications for recognition, with only Impress applying. IPSO refused to consider applying, claiming that the PRP was evidence of statutory control. Since the industry had attempted to apply for its own royal charter to do pretty much the same thing this was not an easy argument to advance convincingly.

The Independent Press Standards Organisation

Despite Leveson's recommendations and parliaments attempts to put them into practice through a royal charter, the industry went ahead with the Hunt plan and set up a new self-regulatory body, the Independent Press Standards Organisation (IPSO). This new body took over the work of the PCC but failed to pick up a number of the Leveson recommendations on independence, investigation and arbitration.

The industry employer associations and major publishers set up a Regulatory Funding Company that raised the money to fund IPSO's operations. It agreed to set up IPSO to:

- carry on activities which benefit the community;
- promote and uphold the highest professional standards of journalism in the UK;
- have regard at all times to the importance of freedom of expression;
- have the power to take complaints about subscribers and adjudicate on them.

The Funding Company has a board of nine directors, all of them executives of major publishers in the UK including editors-in-chief, MDs, CFOs, CEOs, COOs and legal directors. It convenes an Editors' Code of Practice Committee to draw up and maintain the code as "the appropriate benchmark for the ethical standards of journalism expected of such publishers." (www.regulatoryfunding.co.uk/accessed April 2019).

The IPSO itself has a board of 12 directors, seven of whom, including the chair, are independent and five of whom are industry directors, none of whom shall be serving editors or politicians. The views of the RFC should be taken into consideration when appointing the industry directors and the following sectors, national mass market newspapers, national broadsheet newspapers, Scottish newspapers, regional newspapers and magazines, should each be represented.

The IPSO deals with editorial content included in a traditional printed newspaper or magazine and editorial content on electronic services operated by regulated entities such as websites and apps, including text, pictures, video, audio/visual and interactive content but does not deal with complaints about:

- TV and radio services;
- advertising;
- matters of taste/decency and due impartiality;
- legal or contractual matters which are dealt with more appropriately by the arbitration service or the courts;
- books; and
- unmoderated user generated content.

IPSO has no power to prevent publication of a story, no matter what the complaint might be, although it does offer advice to members of the public on issues such as harassment and it will offer advice to newspapers about the line it might take over a complaint on a particular story.

Members of the public can make complaints about articles to IPSO if they are named in the story or if the complaint concerns accuracy. The majority of complaints made to IPSO concern accuracy or privacy, often both (see Table 12.2).

Should IPSO find the publisher has breached the code then it can oblige the publisher to publish the adjudication in full and can identify where in the publication that should be published. IPSO can impose fines or costs if the code breach or other conduct is sufficiently serious. The regulator can fine a publisher up to £1m or 1% of its UK annual turnover if a systemic failure is found following a standards investigation.

The IPSO has been receiving a growing number of complaints as more people learn of its existence and purpose. Table 12.1 and Figure 12.1 show the level of growth over its first five years.

An average of 3.75% of the complaints made are taken on for investigation, the remainder drop out for a number of reasons, including readers' comments that have not been moderated, complaints about publications that are not IPSO members, complaints not made in time, complaints about matters of taste and the two big ones: multiple complaints about the same article (only one complaint is taken forward) and complaints that did not raise a potential breach of the code.

TABLE 12.1 Complaints to IPSO broken down by complaints upheld or rejected

	2014	2015	2016	2017	2018
Complaints within remit	394	4,560	8,660	1,1978	3,389
Not pursued	305	673	1,203	1,235	859
Breach	7	60	47	68	68
No breach	14	183	171	147	129
Resolved	71	387	334	381	85
Rejected	302	3,157	4,069	7,758	2,924
Total complaints	2,401	12,278	14,455	20,903	6,765

Source: www.ipso.co.uk/monitoring/annual-reports (accessed May 2019). Details for 2014 and 2018 not available at 2 May 2019 and extracted from rulings data.

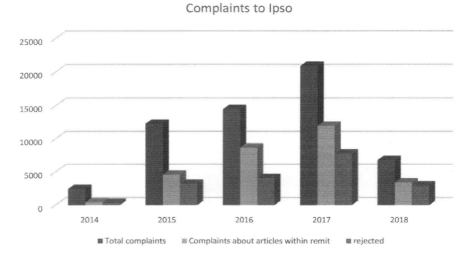

FIGURE 12.1 Number of complaints made to IPSO by year

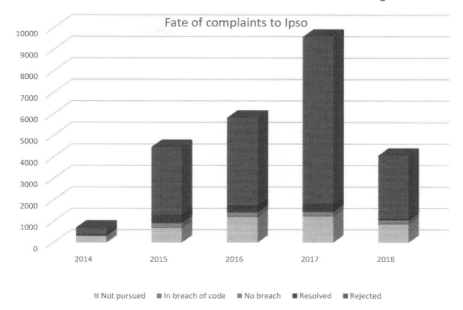

FIGURE 12.2   Fate of complaints made to IPSO that are investigated

The complaints that are accepted as a potential breach of the code are examined by standards officers and referred to the publication concerned for comment. Some papers take up the issue then, making a sufficient apology or other form of making amends for the complaint to lapse. If that does not happen then the IPSO complaints panel examines the issue. They do this by examining the written complaint, the publication's response and any other written evidence provided. The complaints panel does not hear evidence from people in person nor is there an opportunity to cross-examine and challenge claims or defences made on either side. Of the cases taken on for investigation, on average nearly 13% are upheld, although that percentage has been increasing steadily over the years and it is probably too early to draw any conclusions.

Of the complaints that are investigated, as well as the 12–15% that are upheld, 56% are resolved on average and 30.5% are rejected (Figure 12.2). This rejection rate is far lower than the PCC before it but this may be because IPSO is more likely to seek a resolution to the issue. The PCC was able to oblige a complainant to accept a resolution by threatening to refuse to take the complaint further. IPSO is obliged to adjudicate and so is more likely to arbitrate a more acceptable resolution (Figure 12.3).

IPSO receives most of its complaints about accuracy or privacy matters as Table 12.2 shows. 85% of complaints adjudicated concern accuracy, with privacy, harassment and intrusion into private grief accounting for more than 50%. This totals more than 100 because people can complain about privacy and

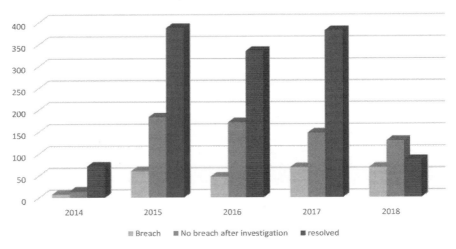

FIGURE 12.3 Fate of adjudicated complaints to IPSO

TABLE 12.2 Adjudications by IPSO to April 2019 by type

Total IPSO adjudications by type				
From Sept 2014 to April 2019				
Total individual complaints against a newspaper: 1485			Total upheld: 299	20.1%
Total of all code categories of complaint made: 2606			Uph as off: 182	12.3%
			Uph corr/adj: 117	7.9%
			Resolved: 357	24.0%
	Total complaints	Total as % of all complaints	% of total upheld	% of category upheld
Accuracy:	1266	85.2	273.0	21.6
Opportunity to reply:	82	5.5	25.0	30.5
Privacy	519	34.9	69.0	13.3
Harassment:	198	13.3	26.0	13.3
Intrusion:	160	10.8	20.0	12.5
Children:	82	5.5	9.0	11.0
Children sex cases:	13	0.9	5.0	38.5
Hospitals	8	0.5	0.0	0.0
Innocent relatives:	25	1.7	3.0	12.0
Listening devices:	82	5.5	9.0	11.0
Victim of sexual assault:	23	1.5	10.0	0.0
Financial journalism:	3	0.2	1.0	33.3
Confidential sources:	22	1.5	5.0	22.7
Discrimination:	116	7.8	22.0	19.0

(Continued)

TABLE 12.2 (Cont).

Payments to witnesses:	3	0.2	0.0	0.0
Suicide:	17	1.1	2.0	11.8
Reporting of crime	4	3.8	3.0	5.4

Note: many individual complaints cover several clauses of the code so the percentage of complaints may not total 100. *Uph (corr)* are breaches required to publish the adjudication or a correction, *uph (as off)* are breaches where IPSO required the publication of the amends offered by the publication.

TABLE 12.3 Publication adjudications by publication type: as of 3 May 2019

IPSO adjudications by type of publication

Type	Upheld	Uph as %	Uph (corr)	Uph (as off)	Resolved	Rejected	Total
Daily	35	18.6	19	16	28	123	188
Magazine	14	34.1	5	9	11	16	41
Magazine website	1	100.0	1	0	0	0	1
National	137	21.4	56	81	145	352	639
National website	54	21.3	15	39	94	101	253
Sunday	0	0.0	0	0	0	3	3
Website	7	9.2	2	5	32	35	76
Weekly	51	18.0	19	32	47	185	284

TABLE 12.4 Privacy adjudications by publication type as at 3 May 2019

IPSO privacy adjudications by publication

Type	Upheld	Uph as %	Uph (corr)	Uph (as off)	Resolved	Rejected	Total
Daily	13	12.6	11	2	10	77	103
Magazine	6	33.3	2	3	5	7	18
Magazine Website	1	100.0	1	0	0	0	1
National	39	16.3	22	17	41	156	239
National website	11	9.5	6	5	41	60	116
Sunday	0	0.0	0	0	0	2	2
Website	1	2.4	0	1	18	21	42
Weekly	18	13.1	10	8	16	103	137

accuracy in the same complaint. The tables further on (Tables 12.3 to 12.5) show the league tables for complaints against individual publications and types of publications. There is not enough room to put the full league table but very few publications following on have more than one complaint and many have no complaints at all or certainly none that were upheld.

TABLE 12.5 League table of publications by adjudications

Outcome of IPSO adjudications by publication

September 2014 to April 2019

Newspaper	Total complaints	Uph off	Uph corr/ adj	Resolved	Uph as %	Rejected
Mail online	119	11	8	56	16	41
The Sun	91	12	9	25	23	44
The Times	82	11	8	11	23	52
Daily Mail	82	9	3	27	15	43
Daily Telegraph	59	6	8	14	24	31
Express.co.uk	55	17	3	20	36	15
mirror.co.uk	53	7	2	11	17	32
Daily Express	45	10	5	6	33	24
Daily Record	43	6	4	10	23	22
The Sunday Times	37	8	5	9	35	15
Mail on Sunday	32	4	4	6	25	18
Daily Mirror	29	1	1	6	7	21
The Sun.co.uk	27	0	1	15	4	11
The Sunday Telegraph	22	0	0	5	0	16
The Scottish Sun	20	3	1	3	20	12
Daily Star	16	1	3	5	25	7
The Belfast Telegraph	15	2	2	3	27	9
Metro.co.uk	14	2	0	8	14	2
The Herald	14	2	1	2	21	8
The Sun on Sunday	14	1	1	4	14	8
Daily Star on Sunday	13	4	1	4	38	4
The Argus (Brighton)	13	0	4	1	31	8
Telegraph.co.uk	12	3	0	3	25	6
That's Life	11	1	1	6	18	3
Bristol Post	11	2	0	2	18	7
Sunday Life	11	2	0	0	18	9
The Spectator	10	3	0	2	30	5
Manchester Evening News	9	1	0	0	11	8
Sunday Mirror	9	0	1	0	11	8
Metro	9	1	0	3	11	5
Birmingham Mail	8	1	1	0	25	6
Liverpool Echo (Daily and Extra)	8	0	0	2	0	6
Daily Record.co.uk	7	0	1	3	14	3
DailyStar.co.uk	7	1	1	1	29	4
Sunday Express	7	1	1	3	29	2
Coventry Telegraph	7	2	0	1	29	4
Sunday Mail	7	0	0	2	0	5

TABLE 12.6 League table of publications by privacy adjudications

Outcome of IPSO adjudications concerning privacy harassment and intrusion

September 2014 to April 2019

Newspaper	Total complaints	Uph off	Uph corr/ adj	Resolved	Uph as %	Rejected
Mail online	67	2	4	32	9	26
The Sun	42	4	2	10	14	25
Daily Mail	34	2	2	9	12	21
mirror.co.uk	29	0	0	7	0	21
The Times	25	3	3	3	24	16
Daily Record	24	1	2	6	13	14
The Sun.co.uk	16	0	0	8	0	8
Daily Mirror	12	0	0	2	0	10
The Daily Telegraph	12	0	3	1	25	8
The Sunday Times	11	2	2	0	36	7
Express.co.uk	10	3	1	1	40	5
Mail on Sunday	9	1	1	1	22	6
Metro.co.uk	9	0	0	5	0	2
The Belfast Telegraph	9	0	1	1	11	7
The Sun on Sunday	9	1	1	2	22	5
The Scottish Sun	8	0	0	2	0	6
Sunday Life	8	0	0	0	0	8
The Argus (Brighton)	8	0	2	1	25	5
Liverpool Echo (Daily and Extra)	8	0	0	2	0	6
Daily Express	8	1	0	2	13	5
Daily Star	8	0	3	1	38	4
That's Life	7	0	0	4	0	3
The Herald	6	0	1	0	17	5
Bristol Post	6	0	0	1	0	5
Daily Star on Sunday	6	1	1	0	33	4
Sunday Mirror	6	0	1	0	17	5
Edinburgh Evening News	6	1	1	0	0	4
The Sunday Telegraph	6	0	0	1	33	4
Telegraph.co.uk	5	0	0	1	0	4
Bucks Free Telegraph	4	0	0	0	0	4
Nottingham Post	4	0	0	0	0	3
Evening Telegraph	4	0	0	0	0	4
Conventry Telegraph	4	0	0	0	0	4
Brimingham Mail	4	0	0	0	0	4
Scottish Daily Mail	4	0	0	0	0	4

An examination of the privacy complaints made that were upheld by IPSO is useful in the context of this book (Table 12.6). The numbers are a small subset of the total upheld complaints, despite the number of privacy complaints being more than 43% of complaints dealt with by the complaints committee (Table 12.7).

This gives a total number of upheld privacy related complaints of 89 or 14% of all the privacy complaints and 6% of all complaints heard. We can see that, whilst quite a few privacy complaints are made, very few privacy complaints are upheld. Privacy complaints are difficult for complainants. Having had a private area of your life disclosed in a newspaper, many are unwilling to pursue their complaints. The IPSO does not reveal how many of the complaints that are not pursued are about privacy but it is reasonable to assume that many of them will be. If someone has taken the trouble to complain about accuracy, they are unlikely to lose interest but someone complaining about privacy might well feel that it is best to go with the motto "least said, soonest mended".

IPSO continues to be controversial as a press regulator. It takes similar numbers of complaints to its predecessor, the PCC, but adjudicates more of them, taking a slightly firmer line than the PCC. It is able to insist on what should be published in response to a code breach and where in the publication it should be placed. However its code still has most of the flaws of those in the PCC code and this is reflected in the judgments it reaches. Any analysis of IPSO's judgments would lead one to suppose that publications, especially national newspapers, are pretty accurate, are not racist or discriminatory to any particular extent and rarely invade anyone's privacy unnecessarily. Anyone doing a detailed examination of the national press might well take a very different view. Hacked Off, the media campaign group set up around the Leveson Inquiry to support victims of press abuse, is deeply critical of the national press and IPSO:

> In March 2013, the three main political parties supported the implementation of Leveson's reforms, and so did the public. In fact more than 175,000 people signed our petition calling for immediate implementation. 6 years later however, this has still not happened. Press abuse continues

TABLE 12.7 The number of complaints about privacy, intrusion, harassment or concealed devices or recorders

2014 (three months only)	9
2015	27
2016	19
2017	26
2018	8

and in the place of the PCC, the majority of newspapers in the UK are regulated by another toothless complaints-handling body, IPSO.

(https://hackinginquiry.org/about/accessed May 2019)

Various parliamentary Select Committees including the Home Affairs Select Committee and the Digital, Cultural, Media and Sport Select Committee have heard highly critical evidence regarding IPSO's performance (see for instance www.byline.com/column/68/article/2059 accessed May 2019).

Many critics believe that the publishers behind the Regulatory Funding Company stepped in to set up IPSO when it became clear that parliament was intent on setting up a regulator that would clamp down on privacy invasions and require arbitration.

Looking through the privacy cases adjudicated by IPSO does give a feel for how IPSO judges the issue of privacy and allows a comparison with the kind of privacy protection envisioned by Leveson. One of the first cases dealt with in 2015 concerned a report in the *Mail Online* about divorce proceedings between a man and his Ukrainian wife. The website headlined the story: "'My Ukrainian internet bride asked me to have sex within hours of meeting her while her eight-year-old son was in the room … so I did': Astonishing story of husband suing his wife for share of fortune". The complainant described how his stepfather had claimed he had sex with his mother within hours whilst he was in the room. The stepfather also gave details about his wife's sexual preferences. The story was based on an interview with the stepfather yet the IPSO felt that the stepfather was entitled to talk about matters that are normally considered to be confidential between married partners:

> The complainant's step-father was entitled to speak publicly about his experiences, in accordance with his right to freedom of expression, and the publication was entitled to reproduce his comments. In addition, details of the complainant's mother's relationship with his step-father, and indeed information about the complainant himself, had already been placed in the public domain through court proceedings. However, the article had included intimate details of the complainant's mother's sexual relationship with his step-father, including information about her sexual preferences. These have not been included in this decision. While the Committee recognised that the publication sought to defend these references as a means of showing the pitfalls of internet marriage, the Committee was not, on balance, satisfied that the publication of this sensitive personal information was justified. The public interest was not proportionate to the level of intrusion posed by the publication of intimate details. While it welcomed the publication's willingness to remove the online article following receipt of the complaint, and its offer to seek to ensure that it did not appear

elsewhere on the internet, this aspect of the complaint under Clause 3 was upheld.

(www.ipso.co.uk/rulings-and-resolution-statements/ ruling/?id=02466–14 accessed May 2019)

Whilst there were 519 complaints to IPSO that include privacy at time of writing, in fact few of these were upheld for privacy reasons. The complaints were either rejected (about 430) or upheld for accuracy. Very few of the privacy complaints were upheld.

Arbitration

Leveson had identified arbitration as an important part of the work of a regulator, allowing ordinary people of limited means a way to seek redress for torts of defamation and privacy. The industry had been opposed to this as regional papers in particular feared it would increase the number actions for defamation and privacy and so cost them money they could ill afford. There was little evidence this was likely to happen. Actions for defamation or privacy against regional papers are rare, despite Conditional Fee Agreements (no-win, no-fee) and After the Event insurance arrangements that meant complainants suing a newspaper who lost would not face ruinous costs. The government removed the success fee uplift that was an important element of CFAs in S44 of the Legal Aid, Sentencing and Punishment of Offenders Act 2012. This meant that After the Event insurance premiums were no longer recoverable from defendants should they lose. The purpose of ATE insurance was that, should the complainant win, the premium was paid by the defendant and should the complainant lose, the insurance paid the costs. The CFA ensured that lawyers took on the case for free on the understanding that, if they won, there would be a success fee uplift of up to 100% of the normal fee. The press had been strongly opposed to CFAs and ATE so had lobbied strongly for their removal. The government had implemented S44 for CFAs in personal injury cases in 2013 but had maintained them for defamation and privacy pending consultation on S40 of the Crime and Courts Act 2013 that allocated costs for defamation and privacy suits for publishers that were not members of a recognised regulator.

The government decided not to implement S40 in 2018, removing the threat of additional legal costs to publishers who did not belong to a recognised regulator. IPSO introduced an arbitration scheme in 2018 that allowed the public to take cases against participating publishers. This scheme is low cost, with a fee of £100, and can lead to awards of damages of up to £60,000 and costs of £25,000, significantly cheaper in terms of costs than going to law. The scheme was initially voluntary but became compulsory for most participating publishers after a few months. A few months later the government finally implemented S44 of the LASPO 2012, removing the right to CFAs and ATE in defamation and privacy cases.

This means that complainants can bring cases to the IPSO arbitration scheme against participating publishers. These are essentially all the national newspapers regulated by IPSO. Compulsory arbitration covers: *Daily Mirror, Sunday Mirror, Sunday People, Daily Telegraph, Sunday Telegraph, Weekly Telegraph, Daily Express, Sunday Express, Daily Star, New!, OK!, Star Magazine, The Sun, The Times, The Sunday Times, The Times Literary Supplement, Daily Mail, Mail on Sunday, Metro.*

Condé Nast Publications are in a voluntary scheme in that they are not obliged to agree to arbitration: *Brides, Condé Nast Johansens, Condé Nast Traveller, Glamour, GQ, GQ Style, House and Garden, Love, Tatler, The World of Interiors, Vanity Fair, Vogue, Wired.*

No regional papers belong to the scheme as they are still concerned that it would open the doors to complainants bringing ruinous costs. There is little evidence this would be the case. Whilst the removal of CFAs and ATE insurance would reduce the number of lawsuits, the numbers against regional papers were not high in any case. Privacy suits in the UK only number around 30 or fewer a year, only half of which are against newspapers, the majority if not all against national newspapers.

Defamation suit numbers are a little higher. According to *Press Gazette*, There were 49 defamation cases in the UK to the end of June 2017 that made it to a court hearing down from previous years, possibly because of the changes brought in the Defamation Act 2013. Newspapers were defendants in only 22% of those – 11 cases. (www.pressgazette.co.uk/higher-defamation-threshold-has-seen-number-of-uk-cases-drop-as-celebs-look-to-privacy-actions-to-fight-libel/ accessed April 2019). The total number of cases lodged with the High Court in London is shown in Table 12.8. Whilst these numbers are more than double those quoted by *Press Gazette*, many of them will not have made it to court, being settled or abandoned.

TABLE 12.8 Royal Courts of Justice Annual Tables – 2017

Year	Value £15,000–£50,000	Value £50,000	Value unspecified	Total
2017	37	113	6	156
2016	42	60	10	112
2015	40	71	24	135
2014	52	11	56	227
2013	37	56	49	142
2012	65	60	61	186
2011	28	61	76	165
2010	27	47	84	158

Social media will be at the centre of a number of these claims, with very few of the cases likely to be regional papers. Regional papers are now largely protected as there will not be many people seeking to take a case against a regional paper if they have to bear the full costs whilst national newspapers will face a relatively cheap arbitration regime.

Impress

Impress is another new regulator set up in 2015 with the aim of providing a Leveson compliant regulator. It was set up by a group of concerned citizens, academics, journalists and celebrity victims of press abuse, with the celebrated former *Sunday Times* editor Harold Evans as its patron.

Impress is charter compliant and gained recognition from the PRP in late Oct 2016. This means that Impress needs to inform the PRP of its work in order to show that it is fulfilling its agreed role under the charter. The charter merely sets out what Leveson recommended a decent regulator should be and which parliament put into the royal charter. It has no connection with or control over the press and only determines whether a regulator, Impress in this case, maintains recognition as a press regulator. This recognition brings some limited advantages to publications that agree to be regulated by Impress, although not as many as was initially envisaged by parliament in S40 of the Crime and Courts Act 2013.

While Impress has the general support of many media campaigners and the NUJ it does not regulate any of the major media blocks in the UK who have combined to support IPSO, or have gone independent like the *Guardian*, *Observer* and *Financial Times*.

A number of independent news websites and local publications have joined, the best known probably being the national political websites The Canary, Sqwawkbox and Byline. But there are a considerable number of local websites that are now bringing news to smaller communities across the country, as advertising moves online, starving the papers of the resources needed to provide that vital local journalism.

Publications regulated by Impress must have their own compliance schemes and only if these fail to provide satisfaction to the complainant will Impress carry out an investigation. Like IPSO it will take evidence from a complainant, seek a response from the publication and then comments on this from the complainant before reaching a decision based on its code. If an adjudication is upheld then the publication must carry the adjudication as outlined by Impress. Impress also has the power to fine publishers for serious breaches or systemic failings (Tables 12.9, 12.10).

Impress provides a whistle-blowing hotline for journalists and other employees at a publication who believe their employer (editor, line manager or other person) is involved in wrongdoing or is encouraging journalists to commit unethical or unlawful practices.

Impress says:

If you work for a news publication and you believe your employer (editor, line manager or other person) is involved in wrongdoing or is encouraging you or others in your workplace to commit unethical or unlawful practices, and you want to report it *confidentially*, you can contact our whistleblowing hotline run by Protect on 0800 221 8548 at any time.

https://impress.press/regulation/whistleblowing.html
accessed May 2019)

Although compliant with the royal charter, Impress is not totally free of controversy. It is funded by donations from the Independent Press Regulation Trust (IPRT) that has guaranteed £3.8m over its first four years. Whilst Impress identifies this as a positive, critics point out that this money has come from the charity which is itself funded by Max Mosley, a victim of press abuse, and therefore seen by many publishers as someone who prefer the press to be silenced. Mosley himself claims he wants a free press, just one that has standards, whilst Impress points out that Mosley has no control over IPRT decisions as it is independent of Mosley.

Impress complaints

Impress has dealt with two cases concerning privacy matters (Table 12.9 and Table 12.10). In one, against Sqwawkbox, the complaint concerned a claimed inaccuracy and harassment. Whilst the complaints committee agreed a correction to the inaccuracy should be published, they did not believe there was a breach of the code concerning harassment:

> The Committee noted that the Complainant had felt intimidated upon receiving a further phone call from the Publisher immediately after directly requesting that the Publisher desist from contacting her. Nevertheless, the Committee considers that, on this occasion, the Publisher was pursuing a legitimate journalistic inquiry by calling back the Complainant to clarify a point arising from his previous call to ensure accuracy. The Committee

TABLE 12.9 Complaints to Impress by code clause

	2017	2018	2019	Total	%
Complaints	4	11	1	16	
Upheld	3	5	1	9	56
Dismissed	1	6	0	7	44
Resolved	0	0	0	0	0
Accuracy	4	10	1	15	94
Privacy		1		1	6
Harassment		2		2	12
Justice		1		1	6

TABLE 12.10 Impress complaints by publication

Publications	
The Canary	2
Sqwawkbox	8
Caerphilly Observer	1
Evolve politics	2
Byline	2
Llanelli online	1

also noted that the Complainant is a person who holds public office and that the Publisher apologised upon making the further phone call. The Committee considered, in this context, that the conduct did not meet the threshold required to breach Code Clause 5.2c (comply immediately with any reasonable request to desist from contacting).

(www.impress.press/downloads/file/impress-mclaughlin-v-skwawkbox-adjudi cation-final-complaint-adjudication.pdf accessed May 2019)

In the other case dealt with that concerned privacy and harassment, the complainant complained about intimidation, invasion of privacy and a breach of the code on justice. The complainant, the victim of a sexual offence, claimed that Byline had:

failed to preserve the Complainant's anonymity as a vulnerable witness; publishing of the Complainant's name was an act of malice and intimidation and unacceptable conduct by a journalist; and publishing of intimidatory reference to the Complainant was done in an invasive manner.

(www.impress.press/downloads/file/148–2018-a-person-and-byline-final-adjudication.pdf accessed May 2019)

The complaints committee decided that as the complainant had already voluntarily allowed their identity to be made public, naming them was neither malicious nor an act of intimidation and so the complaint was dismissed.

Arbitration

Impress runs an arbitration scheme that is compulsory for all members and free to access for complainants. This covers:

- defamation,
- breach of confidence,

- misuse of private information,
- malicious falsehood,
- harassment,
- or breach of the Data Protection Act.

The arbitrators are appointed by the Chartered Institute of Arbitrators and claims can be made by any individual or organisations against any regulated publisher. The scheme does not cover pre-publication – it is an important element of independent press regulation that publications choose whether to publish or not knowing they may have to justify their decision later. The arbitration is carried out with the minimum of formality, ensuring that legal assistance is not generally required. The scheme is cost free to the complainant, with Impress paying the arbitrator's fee. Where the claimant has succeeded in whole or in part in their claim, the arbitrator may make an award of costs against the publisher up to a ceiling of £3,000, with any legal fees being charged at a "reasonable and proportionate" rate. An award will be decided by the arbitrator in a successful case. No limit is placed on this in the scheme, but the aim of the scheme is to provide quick, but cheap and effective justice for a complainant.

Impress has dealt with two arbitration cases, one for defamation and one for defamation, malicious falsehood and harassment. Evolve Media Ltd was obliged to pay a £900 award in the defamation and publish a retraction and full apology on Twitter, whilst Byline Media Holdings Ltd were ordered not to republish the damaging statements and to pay an award of £2,500.

Ofcom

Ofcom is the regulator for broadcasting in the UK. It gains its powers from the Communications Act 2003 but is constituted by the Office of Communications Act 2002. It is a statutory body made up of the number of members the Secretary of State for Digital, Culture, Media and Sport decides, with a minimum of three members and no more than six. These are made up of:

- a chairman appointed by the Secretary of State;
- other members appointed by the Secretary of State; and
- the executive members: the chief executive and such other persons (if any) as may be appointed to membership of OFCOM from amongst their employees.

When Ofcom started work at the start of the 21st century, digital broadcasting was just coming into being and Ofcom replaced the existing regulators:

- the Broadcasting Standards Commission;
- the Director General of Telecommunications;

- the Independent Television Commission; and
- the Radio Authority.

Its jurisdiction covers England, Wales, Scotland and Northern Ireland where it provides offices. It covers:

- jurisdiction;
- television;
- radio;
- any other broadcast medium;
- internet;
- telephones;
- high speed data links
- the postal service.

Ofcom's duties, as identified in the Act, are to further the interests of citizens in relation to communications matters. It is also charged with furthering the interests of consumers in relevant markets, where appropriate, by promoting competition. This is a difficult role as there are times when the interests of citizens will conflict with the interests of consumers, or at least be incompatible. A public duty to provide religious programmes or children's programmes for instance, may conflict with the desire of consumers to watch sport or celebrity reality shows. Of course the advent and development of digital TV has reduced these conflicts considerably, with channels providing programmes of a religious nature or for children standing entirely separately from channels full of sport or reality shows.

The duties of Ofcom in terms of control include:

- the use for wireless telegraphy of the electro-magnetic spectrum;
- the availability throughout the United Kingdom of a wide range of electronic communications services;
- the availability throughout the United Kingdom of a wide range of television and radio services which are of high quality and calculated to appeal to a variety of tastes and interests;
- the maintenance of a sufficient plurality of providers of different television and radio services; and
- the postal service.

Whilst Ofcom has a duty in terms of restraint to ensure:

- standards to adequately protect members of the public from the inclusion of offensive and harmful material in such services;
- controls of unfair treatment in programmes included in such services; and
- protection from unwarranted infringements of privacy;
- policies to develop media literacy;

- control over spectrum use;
- control of independent radio and television (except S4C) in the UK;
- responsibility for telephone lines including telephone numbers, data links and internet;
- regulation of BBC, C4C and S4C.

The BBC and the Welsh Authority, which controls S4C, are not directly connected to Ofcom, but there are links and it is intended they should work together. Channel 4 is directly linked to Ofcom.

There are a number of Ofcom boards with different responsibilities. These are:

- Content board;
- Community Radio Fund panel;
- Content Sanctions Committee;
- Radio Licensing Committee;
- Fairness Committee;
- Election Committee;
- Audit Committee; and
- Remuneration Committee.

The Content board is the one we are most concerned with here as it is the committee of the main Ofcom Board with delegated and advisory responsibility for a wide range of content issues, predominantly dealing with broadcasting, internet, TV and radio and regulating their standards and quality.

The Content boards work under Ofcom to:

- examine the contents of anything that is broadcast or otherwise transmitted by means of electronic communications networks; and
- promote public understanding or awareness of matters relating to the publication of matter by means of the electronic media.

The Ofcom Board uses the Content board for advice and guidance on content-related aspects of decisions it has reserved for itself. All other content-related decisions are delegated to the Content board. In addition, the Content board:

- regulates television and radio quality and standards;
- champions the voices and interest of the viewer, the listener and citizen; and
- examines issues where the citizen interest extends beyond the consumer interest.

The Content board considers content issues in three categories:

- Tier 1: concerns negative content regulation. Harm and offence, accuracy and impartiality, fairness and privacy.

- Tier 2: quantitative matters, such as quotas for independent television production, regional production and original EU/UK production.
- Tier 3: the public service broadcasters; and in this context Ofcom has particular responsibility for ITV, Channel 4 and Five.

The Ofcom Board delegates its dealings on content sanctions cases to the Broadcasting Sanctions Committee who are members of the Content board chaired by the chair of Ofcom's Content board. This committee decides on penalties (sanctions) to be imposed on companies found to be in breach of the Ofcom code in such a way as requires a sanction. This is usually a fine but can be the suspension of or removal of their licence to broadcast.

Ofcom can take complaints about all broadcasters or their programmes including those from the BBC. They are not able to exercise prior restraint to prevent programmes being broadcast so rely largely on complaints being made by viewers. Viewers can fill in a complaint form online and submit this to Ofcom, who will then investigate. The Sanctions Committee will examine complaints about broadcasters whilst the Content board examines complaints about programmes, uses the Broadcasting Code to determine if the programme is in breach and will then determine whether a penalty is required. All broadcasters are required to keep recordings of radio and TV programmes for a specific time so that Ofcom can request a recording for adjudication.

The key difference between Ofcom and the press regulators is the statutory nature of Ofcom's work. Because it has statutory duties under the Broadcasting Act 1996 and the Communications Act 2003 it is obliged to draw up a Broadcasting Code to which all broadcasters must adhere. The legislation identifies key areas for Ofcom to control with standards objectives that provide:

- protection for those under the age of 18;
- that material likely to encourage or to incite the commission of crime or to lead to disorder is not included;
- news should be presented with due impartiality;
- news included in television and radio services is reported with due accuracy;
- the proper degree of responsibility is exercised with respect to the content of programmes which are religious programmes; and
- that generally accepted standards are applied to provide protection for members of the public from the inclusion of offensive and harmful material.

In setting or revising any standards under this section, OFCOM must have regard to:

- the degree of harm or offence likely to be caused;
- the likely size and composition of the potential audience for programmes of a particular description;

- the likely expectation of the audience as to the nature of a programme's content; and
- the desirability of maintaining the independence of editorial control over programme content.

The elements of the Broadcasting Act 1996 concerning the Broadcasting Standards Commission, whose role transferred to Ofcom, were also included in Ofcom's duties. These included an obligation to draw up a Standards code relating to avoidance of unjust or unfair treatment or unwarranted infringement of privacy in programmes or in connection with obtaining material for such programmes.

Because of this statutory division, and because the privacy and fairness complaints are inevitably different in nature as they involve the broadcaster's treatment of an individual, rather than committing a lapse in standards, Ofcom recognises privacy and fairness complaints as being distinct from standards complaints and lists them separately in their reports. Fairness is covered in Section 7 of the broadcasting code and is designed to ensure that "broadcasters avoid unjust or unfair treatment of individuals or organisations in programmes". www.ofcom.org.uk/tv-radio-and-on-demand/broadcast-codes/broadcast-code/section-seven-fairness (accessed May 2019). The privacy code clause is Section 8 (see appendix) of the broadcasting code and is designed "To ensure that broadcasters avoid any unwarranted infringement of privacy in programmes and in connection with obtaining material included in programmes" www.ofcom.org.uk/tv-radio-and-on-demand/broadcast-codes/broadcast-code/section-eight-privacy (accessed May 2019). Essentially the clause says that any infringement of privacy should be with consent or be warranted. The code states:

> "warranted" has a particular meaning. It means that where broadcasters wish to justify an infringement of privacy as warranted, they should be able to demonstrate why in the particular circumstances of the case, it is warranted. If the reason is that it is in the public interest, then the broadcaster should be able to demonstrate that the public interest outweighs the right to privacy. Examples of public interest would include revealing or detecting crime, protecting public health or safety, exposing misleading claims made by individuals or organisations or disclosing incompetence that affects the public.
>
> *(Ibid.)*

The Ofcom code has some particular advice for broadcasters that takes the concept of intrusion and harassment further than the press regulators. Ofcom gives good advice when it comes to gathering information and dealing with people. The code explains:

> 8.16 Broadcasters should not take or broadcast footage or audio of people caught up in emergencies, victims of accidents or those suffering

a personal tragedy, even in a public place, where that results in an infringement of privacy, unless it is warranted or the people concerned have given consent.

8.17 People in a state of distress should not be put under pressure to take part in a programme or provide interviews, unless it is warranted.

8.18 Broadcasters should take care not to reveal the identity of a person who has died or of victims of accidents or violent crimes, unless and until it is clear that the next of kin have been informed of the event or unless it is warranted.

8.19 Broadcasters should try to reduce the potential distress to victims and/or relatives when making or broadcasting programmes intended to examine past events that involve trauma to individuals (including crime) unless it is warranted to do otherwise. This applies to dramatic reconstructions and factual dramas, as well as factual programmes. In particular, so far as is reasonably practicable, surviving victims and/or the immediate families of those whose experience is to feature in a programme, should be informed of the plans for the programme and its intended broadcast, even if the events or material to be broadcast have been in the public domain in the past.

8.20 Broadcasters should pay particular attention to the privacy of people under sixteen. They do not lose their rights to privacy because, for example, of the fame or notoriety of their parents or because of events in their schools.

(Ibid.)

Ofcom deals with a number of standards complaints each year (see Table 12.11), and a much smaller number of privacy and fairness complaints (Figures 12.4–12.7). It receives on average 14,194 complaints about both standards and privacy and fairness (excludes 2007/8 when three programmes sparked a huge number of complaints launching massive campaigns). Many complaints are duplicated since Ofcom accepts complaints from any member of the public about any programme. Consequently, the number of programmes complained about is significantly smaller than the number of complaints. On the basis of looking at programmes that are potentially in breach of the code, IPSO deals with far more alleged breaches. Privacy and fairness complaints on their own average 199 a year, with approximately half being about privacy, fewer privacy complaints than IPSO receives. Ofcom also levies sanction against broadcasters who recklessly breach the code or breach some other condition of their franchise.

The BBC

The British Broadcasting Corporation is constituted under a royal charter that was renewed in 2016 until 2027 and is funded by licence-fee payers. The BBC is controlled and managed day to day by a Board that has responsibility for

TABLE 12.11 Ofcom complaints received (year runs April to March)

year	Standards Complaints					Privacy and Fairness Complaints					
	Comp	Progs	Uph	Res	Not uph	Comp	Uph	Res	Not uph	Discont	Sanct
2004/5	4184	1146	74	54	1018	190	17	11	50	112	3
2005/6	14,227	1102	63	109	914	202	19	14	51	125	5
2006/7	5575	1483	58	75	3315	170	27	7	53	97	4
2007/8	67,742	12,726	135	25	12,372	194	23	7	51	113	11
2008/9	27,549	13,203	211	43	12,711	238	23	10	15	160	30
2009/10	28,281	10,888	152	13	10,514	209	20	9	58	122	6
2010/11	24,462	9202	168	36	8827	171	9	13	36	113	3
2011/12	21,772	7551	244	34	1221	288	22	6	66	61	10
2012/13	16,151	6141	144	16	106	188	9	6	35	8	6
2013/14	12,774	6337	124	29	88	241	22	7	42	1	9
2014/15	28,551	6912	126	17	74	204	8	3	18	0	2
2015/16	23,420	7080	127	17	61	205	16	2	40	0	4
2016/17	16,093	6157	97	15	50	171	6	4	13	1	2
2017/18	15,293	5774	110	11	58	191	9	1	26	2	6

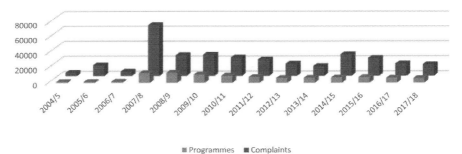

FIGURE 12.4   Number of programmes complained about to Ofcom

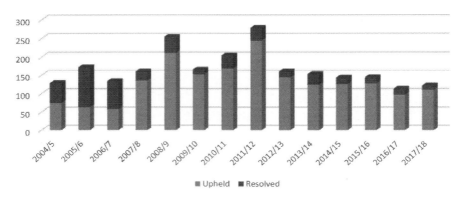

FIGURE 12.5   Ofcom standards adjudications

ensuring the BBC fulfils its mission. The BBC is regulated by Ofcom. It used to have the final say on complaints, but this changed under the latest royal charter as the government felt that firmer external control was required. The BBC still has a complaints body and process and measures complaints against its editorial guidelines and Ofcom insists that standards complaints are fully heard by the BBC before it will consider taking it on, acting essentially as a Court of Appeal. Fairness and privacy complaints can go direct to Ofcom or to the BBC or both. The Editorial Guidelines are available online at www.bbc.co.uk/editorialguide lines/.

The BBC receives 3,000 comments, appreciations and complaints each day from viewers and produces a report of comments and complaints sent in each day to circulate to managers and producers. It aims to deal fairly, quickly and satisfactorily with each complaint. However, it won't waste public money by investigating minor, misconceived, hypothetical, repetitious or otherwise

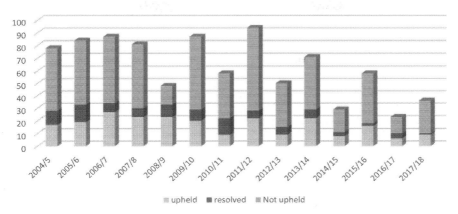

FIGURE 12.6   Ofcom privacy and fairness adjudications

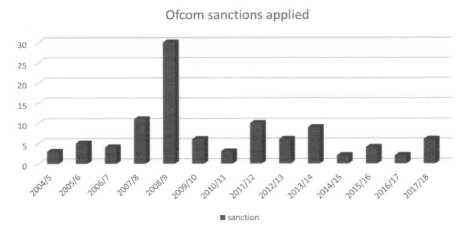

FIGURE 12.7   Ofcom sanctions applied

vexatious complaints which do not suggest a breach of standards. Nor will it investigate gratuitously abusive complaints (www.bbc.co.uk/complaints/handle-complaint/accessed May 2019). The complaint can be appealed to the Executive Complaints Unit if a complainant is unhappy.

Press Council of Ireland

The Press Council of Ireland and its attached office of the Press Ombudsman is the complaints body for the Irish press. The Council is independent of government and the press and has its own code of practice.

Complaints are sent initially to the editor of the publication concerned but if this is not then resolved, the complaint is sent to the ombudsman who will attempt to mediate or conciliate. If that fails, the ombudsman will make a decision to either uphold or reject or refer the complaint to the Press Council of Ireland. This would normally involve a decision of new principle. The ombudsman's decision can be appealed to the Press Council.

Privacy is covered in Clause 5 of the code (see appendices) and aims to protect the human right of privacy as protected under the Irish constitution. The clause includes a requirement for sympathy and discretion over bereavement and suicide.

Broadcasting Authority of Ireland

The Broadcasting Authority of Ireland is the regulator for broadcasting in Ireland, allocating frequencies and controlling standards. Viewers and listeners can complain to the BAI if they feel that a programme or programme maker has breached the law or the BAI codes. Complaints should go initially to the broadcaster and then, if dissatisfied, to the BAI.

The BAI code principle 7 (see appendices) concerns privacy. Intrusions should be warranted and proportionate in protecting the public interest. Participants in broadcasts should be aware of the subject matter and context, nature and format of their contribution. The code also protects the vulnerable, including children, and requires that surreptitious filming is only used when it is warranted.

13
PRIVACY CASE STUDIES

Inaccuracy may be the most common complaint to UK regulators but it is not the area that most concerns the public. Intrusion into privacy is the complaint type that most upsets people. This chapter looks at some of the key cases of intrusion into privacy that have reached the courts or the regulators to give guidance on the decisions of the courts and regulators in the UK on important privacy cases. I start off though with a straightforward case that made the courts but on charges of being drunk on board an aeroplane rather than privacy. It is an interesting case to study and for the amusingly novel way in which *The Sun* handled it. It's sometimes too easy to forget that *The Sun* survives by interesting the public.

Mile-high Mandy – frolics in public

A number of national newspapers ran the story of a man and a woman who, after getting drunk in the business class cabin of an aircraft started a physical relationship. *The Sun* probably handled it best overall and ran a story on its front page headlined "Mile-High Mandy got randy on brandy". It described the incident and then ran a version of its popular Deirdre's Picture Casebook on pages two and three offering advice to the couple. The couple were both married, although not to each other. The incident was described by other passengers in the business class cabin who saw the whole affair and the couple's state of undress and physical closeness and it's for this reason that the couple cannot claim a reasonable expectation to privacy. They were on public view, admittedly to a relatively small number of people, but were still in a position to outrage those who saw them. They were later charged with being drunk on board an aeroplane but charges of outraging public decency were dropped. A court heard that both people had lost their jobs and were deeply sorry for their actions. The judge said that they had already been punished to a great extent by wide-ranging newspaper coverage and also losing their jobs. It's interesting to note as an aside that *The Sun* concentrated far more on the woman, filling the front page with her picture, whilst relegating the man to little more than a passport-sized picture, although there is no reason to believe she was any more to blame for the incident.

The Garry Flitcroft affair

Garry Flitcroft, a premier footballer who was captain of Blackburn Rovers at the time and married, had separate affairs with two young women he met in Manchester nightclubs. These two women decided to sell their stories to *The People*.

Flitcroft sought and was granted an interim injunction to prevent publication on the grounds of confidentiality. The judge refused the newspaper's subsequent application to set aside the injunction, holding that the law of confidentiality should afford the same protection to sexual relationships outside marriage as to sexual relationships within marriage as there was no public interest in the publication of the details relating to the claimant's relationships. The newspaper appealed.

Lord Justice Woolf at the Appeal Court agreed the appeal, saying that where a court was considering whether to grant relief that might interfere with the freedom of the press, that interference had to be justified even if there was no obvious public interest in the story. The court said that whilst the special status of marriage had to be recognised, there had to be appropriate recognition given to the range of other relationships that now existed and the more stable a relationship the more significance it should be awarded.

Lord Justice Woolf also said that there may be a public interest simply in publishing material of interest to the public for to do otherwise was to risk newspapers going out of business despite their importance to the public interest, a comment leapt on by the media.

Schoolboy "father" injunction denied

Alfie P, a schoolboy of only 13, was reported by *The Sun* and others to be the father of 15-year-old Chantelle S's baby, Maisie. A later DNA test showed that Alfie was not the father and several other boys came forward claiming to have had sex with Chantelle, with 15-year-old Tyler B announced as the father.

The local authority sought a court order to ban the media from publishing stories about the DNA test but this was rejected by the court as a "futile gesture". The order sought by the council would have banned the media from reporting anything further about the case, including information and photographs already in the public domain.

News Group Newspapers, the publisher of *The Sun*, argued that that was an attempt to ban the use of material already in the public domain.

In her judgment, Mrs Justice Eleanor King rejected the application, saying that it was too late: "in practical terms there is no longer anything which the law can protect". The judge commented that it was hard to comprehend the amount of publicity the birth of the baby had generated: "Even the time-honoured phrase 'media circus' does not adequately describe what went on in the first week or so after Maisie's birth."

An injunction had already been granted a week after Maisie's birth in order to protect the children from further publicity but then the *Daily Mirror* ran its story about the DNA test as it proved Alfie was not a relative and the injunction only covered relatives. This led Mr Justice Coleridge to amend the injunction to say that it prohibited publication of information likely to lead to the identification of a child as being related to Maisie to add the words "or, for the avoidance of doubt, not related to" her.

Ruling on the local authority's request for an order Mrs Justice Eleanor King rejected an argument by Ruth Kirby, for Chantelle S and Maisie, that the welfare of Alfie P, Chantelle and Maisie should be the court's main consideration. The judge told the court, "I bear in mind that the mere fact that each of the children's rights are engaged does not mean that they have a guarantee of privacy." Mrs Justice Eleanor King said that both Alfie and Chantelle had suffered harm because of the publicity and that Chantelle would find further publicity to be distressing and damaging. The judge said:

> It is accepted that all these articles, photographs and images are in the public domain and may well be unaffected by the proposed reporting restrictions order … Even if the court makes the order sought it is simply unrealistic to imagine that all the website proprietors all over the world will get notice of the injunction and will act upon it … allowing the local authority application to amend the reporting restriction order by preventing publication of the DNA test and/or of photographs and images already in the public domain would represent a disproportionate interference in the Article 10 rights of the press and of Alfie's Article 8 and Article 10 rights to rectify the erroneous information about him. Not only in my judgment would it be disproportionate but it would be futile.
>
> *(www.familylawweek.co.uk/site.aspx?i=ed35695)*

The Blairs and their nanny

An excellent example of the law protecting confidential obligations such as employer/employee confidentiality is the story of the nanny to Prime Minister Tony Blair's three children. She was threatened with a lawsuit by Mrs Cherie

Blair about a book she was writing to illustrate life in an "extraordinary household environment".

Ms Mark had decided to write the book as a social history and had intended to seek the Blair's consent when it was finished and before publication and give any profits to charity. She terminated her agreement with the literary agent but about a week later she was contacted by the *Mail on Sunday*. Ms Mark told the *Guardian* at the time:

> I reluctantly gave them my account of the reasons why I was writing the book. I was subsequently offered by the paper a serialisation contract and fully expensed hotel accommodation which I immediately declined. I contacted Downing Street following my conversation with the Mail on Sunday and they said they were happy with my account. Downing Street were also contacted by the Mail on Sunday and at no stage did the Mail on Sunday reveal to myself or Downing Street that they had extracts from the draft transcript.
>
> *(www.theguardian.com/politics/2000/mar/07/labour.*
> *labour1997to992 accessed June 2019)*

Some of those extracts were published in the *Mail on Sunday* and Cherie Blair immediately sought and was granted an injunction preventing further publication and obliging the newspaper to withdraw the report.

In a statement the newspaper said the privacy of the Blairs' children was not in dispute. The injunction was granted on grounds of breach of confidence, "another matter entirely". The paper had taken "scrupulous care not to intrude on the Blair children's privacy in any way in its article. This would be plainly evident to anyone who has seen one of the 1.5m ungagged copies of the newspaper distributed this weekend."

"Although the terms of the injunction are so wide it is now impossible to spell out what the article did contain, we are convinced the issues it raised are of genuine political and public interest."

Princess Caroline von Hannover of Monaco

The case of Princess Caroline involved two rulings from the European Court and are cases of extreme interest both for their importance as rulings setting the boundaries of private public space for a celebrity but also as an explanation of political and commercial pressures for the British press. The fact that this ruling concerned a member of a foreign royal family and privacy intrusions in another country, but that the effects would be felt in the UK, was just another brick in the wall that much of the UK press was attempting to build along the English Channel.

The European Court of Human Rights (not to be confused with the European Courts of Justice, which are linked to EU law, not the Human Rights

Convention) said that in the first case it believed the public did not have a legitimate interest in knowing where the princess was or how she behaved generally in her private life even if she appeared in places that could not be described as secluded. However, its view was refined in the second case (*von Hannover v Germany 2*).

In the first case, the Princess asked the ECHR to overturn a ruling in the German courts. Whilst the Princess usually lives in France where her permission is required to use photos of her except on official duties, her permission is not required to publish those pictures elsewhere. The Princess has on several occasions unsuccessfully applied to the German courts for an injunction preventing any further publication of a series of photographs that had appeared in the late 1990s in the German magazines *Bunte, Freizeit Revue* and *Neue Post*. She claimed that they infringed her right to privacy and her right to control the use of her image.

In 1999 the German Federal Constitutional Court granted the Princess an injunction regarding some of the photographs – in which she appeared with her children – on the ground that their need for protection of their privacy was greater than that of adults.

At the same time the German court considered that the Princess, who is undeniably a "public figure", had to tolerate the publication of photographs of herself in a public place, even if they showed her in scenes from her daily life rather than engaged in her official duties. The court believed that her right to privacy was overridden by the freedom of the press and the public's legitimate interest in knowing how such a person generally behaved in public.

The Princess took her case to the European Court of Human Rights (ECHR) in Strasbourg, arguing that the decisions of the German courts infringed her right to privacy and her right to respect for her family life. The Court ruled in her favour saying that there was no doubt that the publication fell within the scope of her private life. The Court ruled that, although freedom of expression also extended to the publication of photographs, this was an area in which the protection of the rights and reputation of others took on particular importance, explaining:

> The present case does not concern the dissemination of "ideas", but of images containing very personal or even intimate 'information' about an individual. Furthermore, photos appearing in the tabloid press are often taken in a climate of continual harassment which induces in the person concerned a very strong sense of intrusion into their private life or even of persecution.

The Court considered that the decisive factor in balancing the protection of private life against freedom of expression should lie in the contribution that the published photographs and articles made to a debate of general interest.

Von Hannover 2

The Princess returned to the court in 2013 following a further publication of a picture of the Princess and her husband on holiday while her father, Prince Rainier was ill, that she believed was private. They took the case to Strasbourg after German courts rejected their argument but this time the ECHR upheld the German court's decision.

The ECHR judgment says:

> Since the early 1990s Princess Caroline had sought, often through the courts, to prevent the publication of photographs of her private life in the press. Two series of photographs, published in German magazines in 1993 and 1997, had been the subject of litigation in the German courts that had led to leading judgments of the Federal Court of Justice in 1995 and of the Federal Constitutional Court in 1999 dismissing her claims. Those proceedings were the subject of the European Court's judgment in Von Hannover v. Germany in which the Court found a violation of Princess Caroline's right to respect for her private life.
>
> Following that judgment the applicants brought further proceedings in the domestic courts for an injunction restraining further publication of three photographs which had been taken without their consent during skiing holidays between 2002 and 2004 and had already appeared in two German magazines. The Federal Court of Justice granted an injunction in respect of two of the photographs, which it considered did not contribute to a debate of general interest. However, it refused an injunction in respect of the third photograph, which showed the applicants taking a walk during a skiing holiday in St Moritz and was accompanied by an article reporting on, among other issues, Prince Rainier's poor health. That decision was upheld by the Federal Constitutional Court, which found that the Federal Court of Justice had had valid grounds for considering that the reigning prince's poor health was a subject of general interest and that the press had been entitled to report on the manner in which his children reconciled their obligations of family solidarity with the legitimate needs of their private life, among which was the desire to go on holiday. The Federal Court of Justice's conclusion that the photograph had a sufficiently close link with the event described in the article was constitutionally unobjectionable.
>
> *(https://hudoc.echr.coe.int/eng accessed June 2019)*

The court explained that as far as the law was concerned it was not the court's task to examine whether Germany had satisfied its obligations under the Convention. That was the responsibility of the Committee of Ministers. The present applications thus concerned only the new proceedings.

> In applying its new approach the Federal Court of Justice had granted an injunction in respect of two of the photographs on the grounds that

neither they, nor the articles accompanying them, contributed to a debate of general interest. As regards the third photograph, however, it had found that Prince Rainier's illness and the conduct of the members of his family at the time qualified as an event of contemporary society on which the magazines were entitled to report and to include the photograph to support and illustrate the information being conveyed.

(Ibid.)

The ECHR found that the German court's decision that Prince Rainier's illness was an event of contemporary society was not unreasonable.

Douglas v *Hello*

Film stars Michael Douglas and Catherine Zeta-Jones married in 2000 in a private ceremony attended by many friends.

They entered into an agreement with *OK!* magazine by which *OK!* were given exclusive rights to publish photographs of the wedding. At the wedding and reception photography was prohibited; employees signed agreements not to take photographs and guests were searched for cameras. Shortly after the wedding it became known that *Hello!* magazine planned to publish secretly taken photographs of the wedding. *OK!* brought claims against *Hello!* for breach of confidence and causing loss by unlawful means (the Douglases also brought proceedings but these were no longer in issue).

The initial High Court hearing before Lindsay J held that *Hello! was* liable for breach of confidence. But the Court of Appeal later reversed the judge's decision on the grounds that the obligation of confidence attached only to the photographs which the Douglases had authorised them to publish and not to any others. The magazine then appealed to the House of Lords that held that *Hello!* as liable to *OK!* as *OK!* had paid £1m for the benefit of the obligation of confidence imposed on all those present at the wedding with regard to photographs.

Loreena McKennitt and her "friend" Niema Ash

The Loreena McKennitt privacy case was heard in the High Court, handing judgment to Ms McKennitt. This was appealed by the defence, Ms Ash. The case there found unanimously for McKennitt.

Ms McKennitt is a Canadian folksinger and musician who has a strong following around the world and has produced a number of albums that have sold well.

She sued Ms Ash for intrusion of privacy after Ms Ash published a book called *Travels with Loreena McKennitt: My Life as a Friend*. Ms Ash and her long-term partner, Mr Tim Fowkes, had often socialised with Ms McKennitt and entertained her while she was in England. Moreover, they had sometimes worked closely with her in connection with her business in the UK and abroad. Ms McKennitt is well known for fiercely protecting her privacy, which may be why she is not so well known in the UK.

The judgment of Justice Eady at the High Court and the subsequent judgment of the Court of Appeal outline some important points of law regarding intrusion into privacy.

These are:

1. *Confidential relationship:* A pre-existing relationship of confidence may well mean that the parties to that confidential relationship are not able to reveal information that they know should be confidential.
2. *The role model or public figure argument:* The court decided she was not a role model, nor was she an involuntary role model, a concept the court had serious doubts about, particularly as she is very protective of her privacy.
3. *Public interest:* There was no public interest in communicating and receiving the information. In other words there was no good reason why Ms Ash's right to freedom of expression should over-ride Ms McKennitt's right to privacy.
4. *No anti-social behaviour:* Ms McKennitt had not behaved disreputably or insincerely in any way.
5. *Telling her own story:* Concerns that Ms Ash had been deprived of her right to tell her story were unfounded. The court found that a shared confidence that one wished to tell did undermine the other party's right to maintain the confidence but that in this case, Ms Ash had no story to tell that was her own as opposed to Ms McKennitt's.
6. *False privacy:* The judge threw out the claim that it could not be a breach of confidence as much of it was untrue (an important argument in law – you cannot breach someone's privacy with false information). After discussing whether it should have been a privacy or defamation tort the judge said: "the defendant cannot deprive the claimant of his article 8 protection simply by demonstrating that the matter is untrue".

The Appeal Court judge, Justice Buxton said that the nub of Ms McKennitt's claim was that a substantial part of the book revealed personal and private detail about her which she is entitled to keep private.

> Ms McKennitt has vehemently asserted in these proceedings that she has always sought to keep matters connected with her personal and business life private and confidential. It was confirmed in evidence before me that, whenever a press conference or interview takes place, it is impressed upon those concerned that enquiries about her personal life are very much off limits …
>
> *(www.5rb.com/wp-content/uploads/2013/10/McKennit-v-Ash-QBD-21-Dec-2005.pdf accessed Sept. 2019)*

The judge reminded the court that there is no English domestic law tort of invasion of privacy and that articles 8 and 10 of the HRA have to be "shoehorned" into the law of confidence. However, as the judge went on to point out:

> the complaint here is of what might be called old-fashioned breach of confidence by way of conduct inconsistent with a pre-existing relationship, rather than simply of the purloining of private information.

The judge also discussed the balance identified in the rules laid down by articles 8 and 10 in English domestic law explaining how the courts must support the Human Rights Act.

> Most of the articles of the Convention impose negative obligations on the state and on public bodies ... Article 8 has, however, always been seen as different; as ... article 8 imposes not merely negative but also positive obligations on the state ... More difficulty has been experienced in explaining how that state obligation is articulated and enforced in actions between private individuals. However, judges of the highest authority have concluded that that follows from Section 6 (1) and (3) of the Human Rights Act, placing on the courts the obligations appropriate to a public authority. The court, as a public authority, is required not to act "in a way which is incompatible with a Convention right". The court is able to achieve this by absorbing the rights which articles 8 and 10 protect into the long-established action for breach of confidence.
>
> *(Ibid.)*

Justice Eady, the judge in the High Court, had listed a large number of parts of the book that were said by Ms McKennitt to consist of private information. He refused protection for many of them because he regarded their content as "anodyne", imprecise or already known to the public, however there were a number of matters that both courts believed were of a private matter concerning Ms McKennitt's personal and sexual relationships that included:

- Her personal feelings and, in particular, in relation to her deceased fiancé and the circumstances of his death.
- Matters relating to her health and diet.
- Matters relating to her emotional vulnerability.

The court then turned its gaze to the question of confidentiality and the recipient's perception (in this case Ms Ash) of the confidential nature of material and information received as part of the relationship. The judge said that it was the Ms Ash's perception that imposed the obligation of confidence, remembering that in this instance the recipient was also the person exercising their right to free expression.

The judge said:

> It is also clear from a number of quite explicit passages in the book that Ms Ash realised that substantial parts of it, at least, would fall within the scope of a reasonable expectation of privacy or a duty of confidence ... At the beginning of the book, for example, Ms Ash actually describes an "intimate relationship of almost 20 years with an unfledged small town girl". She also announces to readers that she will be "releasing personality frailties previously concealed in the protective cocoon of anonymity". It is obvious that she was only able to do so by reason of the "intimate relationship.
>
> On page 18, Ms Ash records that Ms McKennitt "confided to me" information about her London friends – which she then proceeds to reveal ... on page 84, she sets out another piece of information which she expressly states was "confided to me". The tit-bit in question may not be of particular significance, but it does illustrate that Ms Ash was well aware that some material was imparted to her in the context of a close friendship and that she is, nevertheless, prepared to reveal it in order to attract readers. The point is again emphasised on page 93, where she states, "She cared for us and we cared for her. We were her closest friends and she knew she could count on our unqualified loyalty". That is, of course, a fundamental aspect of Ms McKennitt's complaint.
>
> *(Ibid.)*

There were further examples in the judgment but they all amounted to satisfying the judge that Ms Ash was well aware she had an obligation of confidence.

The courts had heard that Ms Ash argued that all these matters were not just Ms McKennitt's experience but hers as well, allowing her to tell her own story.

The judge mused that:

> Although we would not go so far as to say there can be no confidentiality where one party to a relationship does not want confidentiality, the fact [talking about the Flitcroft case] that C and D chose to disclose their relationships to B does affect A's right to protection of the information. For the position to be otherwise would not acknowledge C and D's own right to freedom of expression.
>
> By the same token, it was suggested, Ms Ash's decision that her shared relationship with Ms McKennitt should not be treated as confidential undermined Ms McKennitt's contention that it was confidential.
>
> On the facts of our case, as found by the Judge [Judge Eady in the High Court], that argument was wholly misconceived. First, the relationship between Ms McKennitt and Ms Ash, testified to in many places ... was miles away from the relationship between A and C and D. In the preceding paragraph I deliberately and not merely conventionally described the latter as a relationship of casual sex. A could not have thought, and did not say,

that when he picked the women up they realised that they were entering into a relationship of confidence with him.

Second, the judge made a series of factual findings about the relationship that completely destroy this argument.

> It would appear that the fundamental purpose of the book, which Ms Ash has described on its cover as "a must for every Loreena McKennitt fan", was to provide information to her admirers which would not otherwise be available. Much of the content of the book would be of no interest to anyone, I imagine, but for the fact that Ms McKennitt is the central character.
>
> *(Ibid.)*

The full Appeal Court judgement is a masterclass in privacy issues and well worth a read but is far too long to publish here, however it did not satisfy *Daily Mail* editor-in-chief, Paul Dacre, who took it upon himself to critique it to the Society of Editors.

> It was Eady who found in favour of a Canadian folk singer called Loreena McKennitt, who had objected to the publication of a book about her by a former confidante and adviser, Niema Ash. Ms McKennitt did not claim that the book was in any way untrue, merely that it infringed her right to privacy. Never mind Ms Ash's right to freedom of expression.
>
> *(www.pressgazette.co.uk/society-of-editors-paul-dacres-speech-in-full/ accessed April 2019)*

Of course, as I have explained above, the courts, both High Court and the Court of Appeal, spent quite a long time considering Ms Ash's right to freedom of expression.

Following Dacre's speech, Loreena McKennitt, the Canadian folk singer, commented on *Press Gazette*'s website that it was clear Dacre had not read Mr Justice Eady's comments on her case. McKennitt responded:

> The fallacy Dacre would like to propagate is that I did not challenge the contents of Ms Ash's book. Like many, (but not all) of his media colleagues on both sides of the Atlantic, it is clear he has not spent much time reading Eady J's judgment of this trial.
>
> Of the many matters which were challenged in Ms Ash's book, the most interesting was with respect to a property dispute. Central to Ms Ash's "story" and her public interest defence, it was discovered that Ms Ash had "beefed up" 8 witness statements in order to establish a false case against me upon which she would breach my privacy and leverage my reputation through media interest. (A fact yet to be reported by any media) Needless to

say, her public interest defence failed. Mr Justice Eady speaks to this in para 106 to 128 of his judgment.

As the editor of the Daily Mail and editor-in-chief of the Mail group and, if I am correct in understanding, now chairman of the Press Complaints Commission's Editor's Code of Practice Committee, one can only hope Dacre will employ greater veracity of fact and balanced reporting than illustrated in his speech, clearly intended to inform or influence other editors.

(www.pressgazette.co.uk/media-lawyers-hit-back-at-dacres-attack-on-justice-eady/accessed April 2019)

Theakston v MGN ltd

Jamie Theakston, a TV presenter, was photographed without his consent whilst in a brothel in Mayfair. He had been drinking with friends earlier and could not remember much of what happened whilst at the brothel. He refused demands from prostitutes to pay to keep the story quiet and they took their story to the *Sunday People*. He sought an injunction to prevent publication of the story and pictures.

The claimant was well known for publicising certain aspects of his love and sexual life in the press and the courts, as we have learnt, agree that not all relationships of a sexual nature should be afforded the same quality of confidence, nor had Theakston stipulated that his visit to the brothel should be kept confidential. Further, there was a public interest in publishing the prostitutes' story because of his public role as a television presenter of programmes aimed at young people. However, the photographs were a different matter as they were of an intimate, personal and intrusive nature, and consequently the court agreed that Theakston's right to keep them private outweighed the papers' and the prostitutes' rights to publish the pictures.

Naomi Campbell Narcotics Anonymous

The supermodel Naomi Campbell sued Mirror Group Newspapers for breach of privacy in 2004 after the *Mirror* newspaper carried an article about her attending Narcotics Anonymous complete with pictures of her leaving a drug rehabilitation clinic. The model had previously denied having a drug problem.

Campbell did not challenge the disclosure of her addiction, which she had previously denied, but challenged the disclosure of the location of Narcotics Anonymous meetings, and particularly the location of the clinic, as this could be a deterrent to seek further treatment and discourage other patients.

The High Court agreed with her argument and awarded £2,500 in damages and £1,000 in aggravated damages. MGN appealed and was found not liable in the Court of Appeal, with the court agreeing it was "a legitimate, if not essential, part of the journalistic package designed to demonstrate that Ms Campbell had been deceiving the public when she said she did not take drugs". They also said the pictures were peripheral to the story and only showed her in a better light. Campbell appealed to the House of Lords which decided by a majority that MGN *was* liable and that publishing the pictures was a breach of privacy. Lord Carswell told the Law Lords that the *Mirror* went well beyond simply reporting that Campbell was seeking therapy and intruded into some of the details of her treatment, including photographs that included details of where the meetings were held. The court heard this could be a deterrent for some to seek treatment and was an intrusion into the area of her health.

Max Mosley "Nazi" orgy

In *Max Mosley v News of the World* case the newspaper published a story about a sadomasochistic orgy involving Mosley and five women. The newspaper claimed that the orgy was "Nazi-themed", linking it to Mosley's father, the former wartime leader of the British Union of Fascists. The court heard evidence that one of the women involved was paid £25,000 by the paper to film the affair and handed the tape to the *News of the World*. Her husband later had to resign from his job with MI5 as his wife was working as a dominatrix. The court heard there was no evidence that the orgy was Nazi-themed nor that there was any intention that it should be. Mr Justice Eady said in his judgment that:

> It is argued not only that the content of the published material was inherently private in nature, consisting as it did of the portrayal of sadomasochistic ("S and M") and some sexual activities, but that there had also been a pre-existing relationship of confidentiality between the participants. They had all known each other for some time and took part in such activities on the understanding that they would be private and that none of them would reveal what had taken place.
>
> It is alleged against the woman in question (known as "Woman E") that she breached that trust and that the journalist concerned must have appreciated that she was doing so. That could not in reality be disputed, since the whole object of supplying her with a concealed camera, and instructing her how to use it, was to ensure that she could record the events without being suspected by her fellow participants.
>
> *(www.5rb.com/wp-content/uploads/2013/10/Mosley-v-NGN-QBD-24-July-2008.pdf accessed April 2019)*

Mr Justice Eady went on to describe the development of law of privacy and confidentiality since the introduction of the Human Rights Act as outlined in several cases above. Eady went on to weigh the competing Convention rights which included:

- Woman E's right to speak of her experience;
- her right to film it;

- the right of the paper to publish it;
- the public interest in exposing an orgy claimed to be "Nazi themed" by someone holding public office (President of Fédération Internationale de l'Automobile [FIA]); and
- the public interest in exposing criminal acts (actual bodily harm) by such a person:

The judge outlined the significance of the event being exposed:

> The question has to be asked whether it will always be an automatic defence to intrusive journalism that a crime was being committed on private property, however technical or trivial. Would it justify installing a camera in someone's home, for example, in order to catch him or her smoking a spliff? Surely not. There must be some limits and, even in more serious cases, any such intrusion should be no more than is proportionate ... the balancing process which has to be carried out by individual judges on the facts before them necessarily involves an evaluation of the use to which the relevant defendant has put, or intends to put, his or her right to freedom of expression. It has been accepted, for example, in the House of Lords that generally speaking "political speech" would be accorded greater value than gossip or "tittle tattle".
>
> *(Ibid.)*

The significance of visual images was also noted by the judge as:

> This naturally has particular significance in the context of photographs or other visual images. Sometimes there may be a good case for revealing the fact of wrongdoing to the general public; it will not necessarily follow that photographs of "every gory detail" also need to be published to achieve the public interest objective. Nor will it automatically justify clandestine recording, whether visual or audio. So much is acknowledged in the relevant section of the Press Complaints Commission ("PCC") Editors' Code at Clause 10.
>
> Naturally, the very fact of clandestine recording may be regarded as an intrusion and an unacceptable infringement of Article 8 rights. That is one issue. Once such recording has taken place, however, a separate issue may need to be considered as to the appropriateness of onward publication.
>
> When the editor of the newspaper went into the witness-box on 8 July, he went so far as to claim, irrespective of any Nazi element, that the nature of the sexual activities was such that the public had a right to know that the Claimant indulged in them. This was because of his role as President of the FIA.
>
> It would probably have been wise for me to focus in any event on the footage itself, as containing the "proof of the pudding", rather than upon

the evidence of Woman E, whose credibility would naturally be suspect in view of her willingness to betray a trust for money. Moreover, if she had been telling Mr Thurlbeck the truth, one would certainly expect to see the allegation borne out on film. I was now asked to draw the inference that there was in fact a Nazi theme on 28 March from, and only from, the content of the hours of recorded material.

The primary significance of this issue is that the newspaper's original stance was that the intrusion by clandestine filming was justified by the anticipation of a Nazi theme, which was said to be a matter of public interest and relevant to the Claimant's suitability for the responsibilities of his post as President of the FIA. Moreover, the subsequent publication was justified by the "unmistakably" Nazi content. The Nazi theme is no longer the sole basis for the defence case, since allegations of illegality and/or immorality are also relied upon independently of it, but it is nonetheless necessary for me to come to a conclusion about it. The submission is made that, at stage one, it deprives the Claimant of any reasonable expectation of privacy; in any event, any such right would be outweighed at stage two because of the public interest in the quasi-Nazi behaviour.

In his overall conclusions Justice Eady decided that Mosley had a reasonable expectation of privacy in relation to his sexual activities carried out by consenting adults on private property and that there was no public interest as he found no evidence of Nazi behaviour, nor did he consider minor criminal acts carried out with consent (actual bodily harm) a reason for exposure. He saw no public interest justification for a clandestine recording of a private S and M orgy nor for the publication of pictures or video of the event even if such behaviour is regarded by some people with moral disapproval. He came to the conclusion that the right award in all the circumstances was £60,000.

He went on to add that he did not consider this a landmark decision nor that it would be likely to inhibit serious investigative journalism into "crime or wrongdoing, where the public interest is more genuinely engaged" (ibid.).

His judgment was not enough to persuade others that this was nothing more than an attempt by judges to change the law. The *News of the World* editor Colin Myler defended the newspaper's decision to publish, telling a parliamentary committee that:

> We are who we are and I make no apologies for publishing that story … To go to court and have a trial was surprising … Mr Mosley made, I think, quite a case that he never sought publicity. He was, he believed, a private person. I disagree with that fundamentally.
>
> *(www.pressgazette.co.uk/colin-myler-no-apologies-for-printing-*
> *max-mosley-story/ accessed Sept. 2019)*

Prince Harry playing strip billiards

Prince Harry was pictured playing strip billiards with a young woman when one of his entourage took photographs in a Las Vegas hotel room and posted them on the net. The pictures were widely used around the world but no British paper published the pics apart from *The Sun* three days later.

Duchess of Cambridge topless pics

The Duchess of Cambridge was snapped sunbathing topless in a French villa in 2012.

The pictures, taken with such a long lens as to be almost unusable, were published in French *Closer* magazine and later published in a Danish magazine and the Irish *Daily Star*. The *Star* editor was suspended and later quit. The French magazine was sued and settled out of court.

Paul Weller's children in Los Angeles

In 2014, three children of singer Paul Weller were awarded £10,000 damages in the UK High Court after the *Mail Online* ran pictures of them out on a shopping trip with their father in Santa Monica, California. Associated Newspapers told the court they were innocuous pictures taken in a public place. They also argued that the Wellers had previously chosen to open up their private life with their children.

But Paul Weller gave evidence that he never volunteered information about his children when promoting records but was willing to politely answer questions if asked. However he drew the line at allowing his children to be pictured when in public. He said:

> My preference would be just to talk about my music but I can also see that would be a very dull interview. It's just chit-chat. There's a big difference between that and someone following you around and taking photos of babies. That's a distinction that needs to be made.
>
> *(www.theguardian.com/music/2014/apr/16/paul-weller-privacy-damages-children-photos-mail-online accessed Sept. 2019)*

His wife, Mrs Hannah Weller, told the court: "The image of their face should be controlled by their parents and not on a national website. It is part of my job as a mother to control who sees that information."

The Wellers went on to launch a campaign to strengthen privacy rights in public although this failed to gain parliamentary traction.

Cliff Richard police raid

Singer Sir Cliff Richard was accused of child abuse and police searched one of his properties in Sunningdale. The BBC was tipped off about the raid by South

Yorkshire police who carried out the raid. The BBC covered the raid, complete with a helicopter flying around the apartments filming the search. The search found no evidence, Sir Cliff was never arrested and the police later apologised and no charges were ever brought. South Yorkshire police settled the action with Sir Cliff, paying hm £400,000.

The BBC fought the privacy case brought by Sir Cliff after refusing to offer an apology and "reasonable damages" and lost. They decided against appeal. The judge, Mr Justice Mann said the BBC had infringed Sir Cliff's privacy in a "serious" and "sensationalist" way. He went on to tell the court that a suspect in a police investigation "has a reasonable expectation of privacy" and that whilst the search of his home would be of interest to the public there was not a genuine public interest. He accepted that the case would have a significant impact on press reporting but it did not mean the law was changing.

The law in the area of police investigation is complex. A person under suspicion need not be arrested and whether journalists can write about them is confusing. There is no protection against lawsuits for defamation and as Sir Cliff's case shows, no protection against suits for intrusion of privacy. Once someone has been arrested then reporting restrictions come into play, but journalists are able to report the fact of the arrest.

PCC and IPSO cases on privacy

IPSO has only been in operation since September 2014 and the majority of its cases concern accuracy. The IPSO website identifies privacy cases as listed in Table 13.1.

Interestingly most of the privacy complaints also include a complaint about accuracy and it is usually this part of the complaint that is upheld. For instance a woman complained to IPSO in 2015 that the *Daily Star* had published a story under the headline "Too fat to wash! Grubby gran who weighed 27 stone didn't have a bath for 20 years", that this had invaded her privacy and was

TABLE 13.1 IPSO privacy case cases, and privacy cases including harassment, clandestine devices and dealing with bereavement

Type	All privacy clauses	privacy only
Breach – sanction as offered by publication	2	1
Breach – sanction – publication of adjudication	24	20
No breach – after investigation	326	263
Resolved – IPSO mediation	136	109
Resolved directly with publication	316	241
Rejection	6,902	1241
Not pursued	1,476	801
Outside remit	8,830	4745

inaccurate, intrusive and discriminatory. While she had not been able to bath for 20 years, she had washed and was certainly not "grubby". The story was picked up by a news agency who had interviewed the woman after she had lost 16 stone and turned her life around.

The newspaper agreed the headline was inaccurate and apologised for any distress. It amended the article online. IPSO upheld the complaint under Clause 1 of the code (accuracy) after hearing that the complainant had not told the interview she had not washed for 20 years. However, the committee noted that the complainant had freely given the interview to a news agency and agreed it could be published, so the complaint under Clause 3 (privacy) was rejected.

In other cases the police brought the case on behalf of victims. Bearing in mind the reports of police serving warning notices to journalists about approaching victims of high profile crime, this is a matter for some concern. It is the police's responsibility to uphold the peace, prevent disorder and crime and apprehend criminals and their move into social work in order to protect victims, no matter how well intended, is a role they are neither trained for nor fully understand and cannot always be in the best interest of the entire community.

PCC advice

The PCC's "Editor's Codebook" offers advice on privacy and is worth a read:

> Pregnant pause: As with homes, so with health. There are limits on what can be said about celebrities, even though they are constantly in the public eye. Pregnancy, even for non-public figures, can rarely be kept secret for long, but the PCC has ruled that early speculation on whether someone is expecting a baby can be intrusive. The actress Joanna Riding complained that a diary item disclosed that she had withdrawn from a theatre role because she was expecting a baby – before she had even told her family. She subsequently suffered a miscarriage. In a landmark adjudication protecting all mothers-to-be, whether public figures or not, the PCC said that revealing the pregnancy at such an early stage was a serious intrusion (*Riding v The Independent:* Report 73, 2006) (*Ms Dannii Minogue v the Daily Mirror and Daily Record*: 2010)
>
> *(Beales, 2012: 33)*

Child's privacy breached

A woman complained that the *Chester Leader* had carried a court report about her partner and his conviction for charges relating to an incident in which the child's safety had been placed at risk. This report had named the complainant's partner and included his partial address and noted his relationship to the child concerned. The report had gone on to give an account of the incident, including the state in which the child had been found. This allowed the child to be identified, in breach of a reporting restriction, according to the complainant.

The newspaper apologised for the distress caused and wrote a private letter of apology. It also offered to make a donation to a children's charity of her choice. IPSO upheld the complaint saying:

> In general, IPSO upholds the right to report matters heard in open court, both because of the general interest in open justice and because they have entered the public domain through the proceedings. In this instance, however, the existence of a reporting restriction meant that the complainant's child had a reasonable expectation that this material – which related to a distressing incident that raised significant safety concerns – would not be published to the wider public.
>
> *(www.ipso.co.uk/rulings-and-resolution-statements accessed Sept. 2019)*

Photograph of injured child

Children are a regular feature in privacy cases. A woman complained about an article in the *Derby Telegraph* that reported that a teenager was believed to have been knocked down by a car outside a school. A photograph of the scene showed the girl lying on the pavement. Her face had been pixelated. Next to her was another girl in school uniform.

The two girls shown in the picture were 11-year-old daughters of the complainant who said that the photograph depicted a distressing incident for both girls and had been taken at a time when everyone involved had been in shock, and the emergency services were yet to arrive. At the time of publication, the newspaper could not have been aware of the severity of the girl's injuries.

The newspaper had also contacted Derbyshire County Council, as a local campaign by residents made this a matter of public interest.

IPSO said:

> The photograph had been taken while the child had been awaiting medical treatment following what had clearly been a traumatic and distressing incident. Although the photograph had been taken on a public street, in these circumstances – and with regard for the young age of the child involved – the Committee took the view that the injured child had had a reasonable expectation of privacy. The photographing of the child represented a failure to respect her private life. The complaint was upheld under Clause 3.
>
> Although the newspaper had pixelated the face of the injured child and had contacted the ambulance services to try to ascertain the severity of the injury, the publication of the photograph at a time when the newspaper had not been able to verify the identity of the child concerned or establish

whether her parents had been informed of the incident represented a failure to handle publication with appropriate sensitivity. The photograph had been distressing for the family, and risked notifying friends and relatives about the accident. The Committee required that … the newspaper should publish the Committee's ruling upholding the complaint.

(www.ipso.co.uk/rulings-and-resolutions-statements accessed Sept 2019)

Taking care in reporting children

Another complaint also concerned children. A woman complained that photographs of children from Lancashire had been found on a file sharing website which the newspaper described as a "Russian pervert website" and a "paedophile website". The newspaper illustrated the article with five pixelated photographs of local children that had been found on the site.

Two of these images were of her young child from her Facebook profile, that had been recognised from the newspaper by friends. The newspaper said it had used the photographs as an important element of a public-interest story, which made clear the nature of the material on the website. It had been unable to contact the parents of the children involved before publication because it did not know their identities, but it had alerted local schools to give them a chance to implement child protection procedures. It had chosen to pixelate the pictures and carry them in a small size in its print edition only.

The article under complaint had performed a valuable public service leading to the removal of the photographs of local children from the website and new child protection procedures at local schools, and the involvement of a local MP.

The IPSO said:

> The right of the newspaper to publish the story was not in doubt.
>
> The pixelation of the images had evidently been insufficient to prevent the child from being identified by those who were familiar with them.
>
> Notwithstanding the public interest in the story itself, there was no public interest which justified the publication of identifiable photographs of the child in this context. Publication, in this form, represented a failure to respect the child's family life and a breach of Clause 3.
>
> The Committee required the newspaper to publish the Committee's ruling upholding the complaint.

(www.ipso.co.uk/rulings-and-resolutions-statements accessed Jan. 2019)

Privacy invaded by false rumours

In a complaint concerning a report in the *Sunday Life* a Tyrone cleric complained to IPSO the paper had breached Clause 3 (Privacy) and Clause 6 (Children) of the Editors' Code of Practice in an article headlined "Tyrone cleric baffled by false gay rumours".

The complainant said the publication of these rumours was a breach of his privacy. The complainant had confirmed the rumours were untrue when the newspaper had contacted him for comment. The newspaper told IPSO it had become aware of the rumours after being contacted by an unknown source. The newspaper believed the article was in the public interest as the complainant was a prominent local figure.

The committee upheld the complaint and said:

> Details of an individual's sexuality form part of private and family life and as such receive protection under the terms of Clause 3 of the Editors' Code. The complainant had not publicly disclosed the details of the rumours, which were of a personal nature, and the newspaper had become aware of them only after being contacted by an unknown source. The inclusion in the article of his denial was insufficient to justify the intrusion into the complainant's private life caused by publication of the claims, regardless of their inaccuracy. Further, the complainant's rebuttal of the allegations in conversation with the journalist did not constitute consent for publication under Clause 3 (ii). The newspaper breached Clause 3 of the Code.
>
> *(www.ipso.co.uk/rulings-and-resolutions-statements accessed Sept 2019)*

Reporting news of a death abroad

A complaint by Lincolnshire Police, on behalf of the family of Carly Lovett, complained that the *Lincolnshire Echo* intruded into grief or shock by publishing details of the death of a Lincolnshire woman in a Tunisia terrorist attack before it had been confirmed to her family. This had caused enormous upset at an already highly distressing time.

The newspaper denied that it had breached the Code, saying it had waited several hours to publish the information, until it had received confirmation from multiple sources that it considered to be reliable that the family were aware.

The newspaper said the attacks in Tunisia were of international importance and the paper had a responsibility to keep the public informed.

The committee said:

> It was foreseeable, in the aftermath of a terrorist attack that had taken place overseas, that there would be uncertainty among the families of those involved back in the UK as to the fates of their relatives for some

hours, or potentially days. Contradictory and premature reports were highly likely, given the chaos caused by the attack and the difficulties of communicating with overseas survivors and emergency services.

The newspaper was entitled to report on a local connection to the attack, and the Committee acknowledged that it had not intended to cause any distress. However, it had a responsibility to ensure in doing so that its report was accurate and that it was prepared with appropriate regard for the position of those most directly concerned: Ms Lovett's surviving family.

As the newspaper had relied solely on confidential sources, it had been unable to show that it had taken appropriate care before it took the decision to publish … The publication of the information that Ms Lovett had died, so soon after the attack and before it had been confirmed to her immediate family, was a serious failure to handle publication sensitively and a breach of Clause 5.

(www.ipso.co.uk/rulings-and-resolutions-statements accessed Sept 2019)

A royal helicopter ride

A helicopter flight over the home of the Duke of York by the *Daily Mail* to photograph the complainant's daughter's 25th birthday celebrations was an intrusion into the complainant's privacy, the IPSO ruled. The complaint raised two important issues:

1. Whilst aerial photography has a place in news gathering, it can lead to a breach; and
2. The fact the pictures were innocuous and not published is irrelevant.

The IPSO complaints panel said:

> The Code requires editors to show appropriate respect for an individual's private and family life, and specifically cites respect for the home as part of this obligation, reflecting the fact that an individual's home is a particularly private space. This extends to the garden or grounds of a home, although the extent to which an individual will have a reasonable expectation of privacy in relation to the grounds or garden of a home will vary, generally according to their visibility, or potential visibility, to members of the public.
>
> It was irrelevant that the photographs were not in the event published and that they were innocuous. In this case, the flight itself was intrusive because it served to undermine the complainant's reasonable expectation of privacy. It, therefore, required justification.

(www.ipso.co.uk/rulings-and-resolutions-statements accessed Sept 2019)

Sex assault victim named

A report in the *Daily Record* that a woman had been found not guilty of sexual assault by rubbing her breasts against a man's chest at a party had breached the victim's privacy by naming him.

He also claimed that the article had inaccurately reported his initial response in breach of Clause 1. He said that he had not been offered a right to reply to the allegations, and that this breached Clause 2. Lastly, he said that publication of the article constituted harassment, in breach of Clause 4.

The newspaper pointed out that while it is usual practice in Scotland not to name alleged victims of sexual offences, there is no automatic anonymity to victims, or alleged victims, of sexual assault.

At the conclusion of the case the sheriff had said that "against the whole background it's hard to understand the decision making process by which it was found by the Crown to be in the public interest to pursue this case. Although I wasn't convinced by the evidence provided by the accused I'm not going to find beyond reasonable doubt that the accused was guilty of criminal assault, far less a sexual one." The newspaper said that it was clear in this case that the alleged offence should never have been classed as a sexual assault; it had therefore been justified in naming the complainant.

The committee upheld the complaint under Clause 3 (privacy) and Clause 11 (victims of sexual assault) and found that:

> The fact that the complainant considered himself to be a victim of sexual assault was clearly private information. While the Committee acknowledged that the information had been heard in open court, the Editors' Code specifically provides protection to people making allegations of sexual assault, and standard practice is that victims are not identified. The inclusion of the complainant's name in the article represented an unjustified intrusion into the complainant's private life.
>
> *(www.ipso.co.uk/rulings-and-resolutions-statements accessed Sept 2019)*

The Committee required the newspaper to publish the Committee's ruling upholding the complaint in full on page 15, or further forward.

Suicide details

A woman complained that an article in the *Northampton Chronicle & Echo* that was headlined "Northampton woman dies of caffeine overdose, inquest hears" breached article 5 (reporting of suicide) of the code. The article was a report of an inquest and described the substance taken by the woman in detail including quantities and where it had been purchased. It also described the woman's 999 call, expressing regret at her attempt, and the location in which paramedics found her on arrival. The symptoms and treatment she received were described, including the details of the time and ultimate cause of her death. The committee upheld the complaint saying:

> The Committee noted that the purpose of Clause 5 (Reporting of suicide) is to prevent the publication of material which might lead to imitative acts. The article had provided extensive details regarding the method the woman had used ... related to a relatively novel method of suicide, as there was a risk of increasing the awareness of this method among the population.
>
> *(www.ipso.co.uk/rulings-and-resolutions-statements accessed Sept 2019)*

Acknowledgement

I'd like to acknowledge 5RB and its website that I have always found to be very useful in providing confirmation of details on many media cases. 5RB is one of the leading set of London communications and media barristers and the cases section of its website is a must for media and law scholars.

14

PRIVACY IN EUROPE

Even parts of the globe as closely linked as Europe have significant differences in the way their media operate with regard to the protection of personal privacy. Whilst data privacy is protected across the EU and many other European countries have adopted similar legislation, there are still significant differences across different regions. North-western Europe for instance has much in common with the UK whilst the south-eastern countries and those of East Europe, especially those that were formally in the Soviet bloc, often have different approaches driven by their cultures and languages. All European countries subscribe to the general western theory of holding power to account and so need to invade privacy on occasion when justified by the public interest but there is a wide variety of approach throughout the continent.

Scandinavia and the Netherlands

The north-west of Europe including Scandinavia, the Netherlands, and, to a lesser extent, Belgium have a much stronger approach to privacy than the UK. Suspects and victims in court cases, for instance have much stronger protection of their identities in court cases than in the UK. Whilst the UK courts protect the anonymity of minors in most instances – suspects, witnesses and victims – this is much more firmly applied in north-west Europe. In the UK, anonymity is applied mainly because of the obligation applied by law and, were the law to be abolished, it is doubtful if British journalists would consider the concept of anonymity for minors to be much of an impediment to publication. In the case of journalists in north-western Europe such anonymity is ethically very important. This anonymity extends to adults as well and most media tend to refer to suspects only by an initial. Evers, Groenhart and van Groesen carried out a survey of the Netherlands news ombudsman system in the Netherlands in 2010 that helps explain the position of journalism in that country and the picture painted there can be expanded to apply to Sweden, Denmark, Finland, Norway and beyond. Media outlets in the Netherlands tend to rely on self-regulation through the news ombudsman. Each publication has its own ombudsman to examine comments and complaints from readers. Evers et al.'s book identified decisions of the news ombudsman from the *Rotterdam Dagblad*, The *Volkskrant* and the NOS (The Netherlands Broadcasting Company).

The people of the Netherlands take privacy seriously and the report shows that privacy intrusions in the UK that would be treated fairly casually are met with horror in the Netherlands. Because of this, intrusion of privacy is not a huge problem. Evers et al. surveyed ombudsmen and asked about the topic that received the highest number of complaints. In the UK (see Chapter 12) accuracy and intrusion on privacy easily outpace other complaints but in the Netherlands, bias, factual mistakes (accuracy), carelessness (accuracy), unfair actions, language issues and bad taste led the list. Invasion of privacy came well down the list, even below: "Editorial policy: for example publishing the names of juvenile suspects".

The ombudsman of the *Rotterdam Dagblad* writes a weekly column of his findings dealing with complaints. This is a typical approach for ombudsmen. Over several years, only 11 of these columns contained the theme of intrusion into privacy. These concerned complaints about: "initials, black bar across eyes, full first or last names or not" (Evers, Groenhart and van Groesen, 2010: 35). This refers to the Netherlands' newspapers habit of only using initials for suspects and covering pictures of suspects with a black bar across the eyes.

A couple of cases reported by the ombudsman of the *Volkskrant* are very informative. It tells of the case of an abducted girl returned to her home. A picture published on the front page showed the girl and her mother, clearly identifiable, and the girl's full name was published, despite a police warning that press attention would not be appreciated. The report also stated she was sexually abused whilst held hostage. The public was outraged by the publication as was the ombudsman, saying the paper: "Blundered in a terrible way, violating the rules of its own guidelines book beyond a shadow of a doubt." The ombudsman brushed aside the paper's excuse that the TV stations had already covered the event saying that "the paper's own standards must be normative, not the fact that other media keep lowering their norms" (ibid.: 68).

In another instance, the *Volkskrant* in 2006 covered the murder of three children by their mother who subsequently killed herself. The reporter gave the mother's name and age and the names of the children – perfectly normal for the UK. He expected editors to consider their use later in the day, but that never happened. The ombudsman noted that "over recent years the editors have been increasingly sloppy in their consideration for the privacy of perpetrators and victims" (ibid.).

The ombudsman demanded to know, a few months later, "Have the editorial staff gone completely mad?" The cause of his concern was the death of an 8-year-old boy who was murdered at school. The newspaper gave his full first and last name. The paper does not normally print pictures of suspects, nor does it give their full name. This is not unusual practice for north-western Europe.

The broadcast ombudsman is also kept busy. A newsworthy case concerned a Dutch woman who was involved with the Colombian rebel movement Farc. The TV station identified her and this caused some anger. The TV station was unrepentant, pointing out that others had already exposed her name but, from a UK point of view, this is a surprising matter of complaint when compared with, say, the UK media's naming of the young woman who fled to join Isis as a bride while still at school and later had her citizenship removed when she attempted to return to the UK after the fall of the Caliphate.

The *Volkskrant* published a story about an alderman and councillor having sex in a bicycle park. The event was captured on CCTV. This caused much discussion. Using just initials would have labelled them as criminals; in any case the story concerned a particular person. In the end the ombudsman recognised that the story was already global.

France

France is perhaps the strictest country in Europe when it comes to privacy, with the French legal system of privacy protection being perhaps the toughest in the world, involving both the protection of privacy and the protection of personal image, a right that exists in a number of countries.

Respect for privacy is guaranteed by the general principles of civil liability as identified in article 1382 of the Civil Code. Also the European Convention of Human Rights article 8 on privacy is incorporated in the French Civil Code to provide that: "everyone has the right to respect for his or her private life".

The courts have gradually built a definition of private life to include a person's love life, friendships, family circumstances, leisure activities, political opinions, trade union or religious affiliation and state of health. This right applies both during the period of researching a story, even if nothing is published or broadcast, as well as on publication.

The right to privacy also entitles anyone, irrespective of rank, or office, to oppose the dissemination of his or her picture – an attribute of personality – without the express permission of the person concerned.

Various steps such as embargo, confiscation of a publication and others can be directed by the court after trial and in urgent situations they can be the subject of an injunction to suspend publication, prohibit circulation or order the total or partial suppression of a publication.

When it comes to damages the law differs from the UK idea of adjusting the damages punitively to match the degree of fault but are awarded on the extent of the harm which the victim has suffered.

Recording or transmitting words spoken in private or confidentially or taking a picture of a person (living or dead) in a private place without consent are both criminal offences. When a person is at a meeting or openly in a public place, however, consent is presumed. A private place is deemed by the courts to be somewhere that is not open to anyone without the permission of the person who occupies it in a permanent or temporary manner.

The media are obliged by the law to satisfy themselves about the consent of the person photographed when buying photographs from a journalist or through a press agency or risk the consequences.

Prosecutions can only take place with a complaint by the victim or his or her legal representative or successors, however, but a violation of privacy is punishable by up to one year's imprisonment and a fine of around €50,000.

Article 38 of the Act of 29 July 1881 prohibits photographs of any part of a crime scene. This article was used in connection with the publication of photos of the terrorist attack at the RER Saint-Michel station in July 1995. The Paris Court of Major Jurisdiction held that the article contravened the provisions of Article 10 of the European Convention on Human Rights, dealing with freedom of expression, by being too broadly drawn and insufficiently precise for the description of an offence.

An Act of Parliament of 10 July 1991 also made it illegal to intercept communications transmitted by means of radio waves, optical signals, etc., identifying such communication as confidential.

As to the protection of data privacy, the GDPR applies as in the rest of Europe.

Germany

Protection of personal privacy is taken very seriously in Germany. Partly this follows the Second World War when many Germans learnt first-hand of the dangers of state surveillance. Protections are extensive and Facebook and Google have found it difficult to adjust to strict privacy laws and codes that can allow citizens to have their homes pixelated in Google street maps or a law to prevent the like button being placed on Facebook homepages as the data are transferred to the Californian home of Facebook.

Spain

The GDPR applies in Spain but the country's own constitution also guarantees the right to honour and the right to personal and family privacy and the right of self-image.

The right to private and family life covers actions aimed at protecting image, voice, name, honour and private life (including family life) from unauthorised use. Using the image of a public person, such as a celebrity or politician, is excepted and such persons can be recorded and published or broadcast provided pictures were taken and recordings made in public spaces or during public events and the image can be used without consent when recording events of public relevance. The Spanish courts will take into consideration freedom of expression and balance this against the right to privacy.

Italy

Italy is slightly unusual for Europe in that a journalist needs to be registered with the professional body, the Ordine dei Giornalisti, in order to work. This makes controlling ethics easier than in some countries, as a journalist can be "struck off" for serious violations but is opposed by many on the basis that "Journalism is not a profession. It is the exercise by occupation of the right to free expression available to every citizen" (Robertson, 1983: 3). This is an important principle, which is why so few countries insist on registration.

Italy applies the GDPR, of course, but taking pictures for news is generally legal although some Italians do object to having their picture taken in the street. However, taking candid shots in public is not illegal provided they are not for profit and do not damage the dignity of the subject. Of course this can be problematic for a journalist who is taking the pictures professionally but usually it is not a problem provided it is for news use.

15

PRIVACY IN NORTH AMERICA

The United States

The United States of America is one of the largest countries in the world with a relatively free press standing 48th in the Reporters Sans Frontières annual ranking. RSF is critical of the continuing decline of press freedom, with President Trump leading attacks on journalists whom he describes as an "enemy of the American People" that have encouraged others to copy.

The US is a constitutional republic and press freedom is protected by that constitution as is privacy. The first amendment, agreed even before the right to bear arms about which Americans make so much, says that

> Congress shall make no law respecting an establishment of religion, or prohibiting the free exercise thereof; or abridging the freedom of speech, or of the press; or the right of the people peaceably to assemble, and to petition the Government for a redress of grievances
>
> *(https://usconstitution.net/xconst.html accessed May 2019)*

The right to privacy is not announced as such but is contained in the fourth amendment to the constitution that concerns search and seizure:

> The right of the people to be secure in their persons, houses, papers, and effects, against unreasonable searches and seizures, shall not be violated, and no Warrants shall issue, but upon probable cause, supported by Oath or affirmation, and particularly describing the place to be searched, and the persons or things to be seized.
>
> *(Ibid.)*

This clause prevents government agents from entering a place where there is a reasonable expectation of privacy without a warrant that can only be granted upon showing probable cause that a crime has been committed. The idea of personal security in one's home and protection for papers, personal possessions and correspondence means that all have a reasonable expectation of privacy from anyone including journalists.

The developing concerns of the public for protection of their privacy largely mirror those of the UK, with some US citizens, perhaps, being more concerned about privacy invasions by their government than those in the UK.

Some of the key cases in the US follow the development of privacy legislation in the UK. Privacy starts to become a serious issue in the late 1880s with the growth of US newspaper numbers and as circulation rockets. The growth in competition, particularly in big cities, meant the growth of sensationalised so-called yellow journalism (named after a popular comic strip of the time). Yellow journalism went for big headlines, stories that were often invented, or at least factually dubious, and concentrated on crime. It also started to use pictures from the new technology of photography. Privacy intrusion was not far behind as sensationalism mixed with photography and Samuel D. Warren and Louis D. Brandeis, fearing that the development of photography would get ever more invasive, wrote their famous *Harvard Law Review* article 'The Right to Privacy' in 1890 that discussed the need for a remedy to prevent the unauthorised circulation of portraits of private persons:

> The press is overstepping in every direction the obvious bounds of propriety and of decency. Gossip is no longer the resource of the idle and of the vicious, but has become a trade, which is pursued with industry as well as effrontery. To satisfy a prurient taste the details of sexual relations are spread broadcast in the columns of the daily papers. To occupy the indolent, column upon column is filled with idle gossip, which can only be procured by intrusion upon the domestic circle.
>
> *(www.cs.cornell.edu/~shmat/courses/cs5436/*
> *warren-brandeis.pdf accessed May 2019)*

It is a plea that is fully familiar to all these days but was part of a developing concern at the end of the 19th century.

Modern tort law in privacy in the US is now composed of four main elements:

Intrusion of solitude: an actual or electronic intruson into one's private area.

Public disclosure of private facts: the dissemination of truthful private information against the wishes of the subject.

False light: the publication of facts which place a person in a false light, similar to malicious falsehood in the UK.

Appropriation: the unauthorised use of a person's name or likeness to obtain some benefit.

These are not too dissimilar to the torts available in the UK with the exception of appropriation. Using a celebrity's name or likeness is not widely done in the UK, largely because of the global nature of journalism and advertising. Since appropriation is a tort in a number of European countries as well as the US, it is wise not to use a likeness in the UK, but it has not yet become a tort, although there is a tort of passing off that means it may be possible to prevent a company from using a celebrity to endorse a product without the celebrity's permission. Similarly, it may be possible to present a case in court that a celebrity's identity is in fact a trademark. However these protections are not the same as the US right to protect their name or likeness.

There is little evidence that American journalists are more or less intrusive than UK journalists, although interestingly, because of the very different media and regulatory structures between the US and the UK, those journalists relying more on exposure work in different areas to journalists in the UK. In the UK, it is national newspapers, especially the so-called red-tops of the tabloid press, that are most infamous for privacy intrusions (see Chapter 10 and the breakdown of complaints to regulators). In the US there is no real national press, with all the important newspapers being city based, although many sell widely around the world. There are national magazines that cover the same kind of journalism as the UK's tabloids but many of these are working with the celebrities and so are not invading privacy. TV is as likely to take the tabloid line in the US as newspapers.

The usual structure of regulation in the world has little impact in the US. There are no media councils or codes of ethics other than the code of the Society of Professional Journalists, a federal grouping of around 7,600 US journalists and supporters seeking to protect press freedom.

American journalists are too fiercely protective of the amendment rights to concede authority to others and they rely heavily on the protections available to a free press with limited restraints on privacy. Even in defamation cases, following the *Times v Sullivan* case in the Supreme Court that insisted that public figures should have to prove actual malice in order to pursue a case and the Pentagon Papers case in 1971 which confirmed the constitutional ban on prior restraint of publication.

However, all good journalism requires regulation at some level (see Frost, 2016). Journalism is distinct as a style of writing by being accurate, amongst other things, and if ethics are bent too freely the written text becomes not journalism but fiction, PR or fantasy. US journalists are not unaware of this and so while they are proud of their constitutional freedom and look askance at the type of regulation we have in the UK and that exists elsewhere, they do understand the need for care, as Bill Orme, an author representative of the Brussels-based Global Forum on Media Development, explains:

> But the self-image of US journalists as neither self-regulated nor state-regulated is also something of a myth. There are powerful peer-pressure

mechanisms in place – and never more so than today, when the news business is under acute economic pressure and the purportedly "liberal media" is a constant target of conservative grassroots and boardroom hostility.

It is widely recognised in the profession that there are many areas of legitimate concern over media conduct, which remain, properly, outside the jurisdiction of any courtroom. As a result, there are many significant self-regulating mechanisms in American journalism culture, most of them focused on issues of ethics and accuracy. These include the voluntary but influential codes of ethics promulgated by peer groups such as the Society of Professional Journalists, which are mirrored in turn by the codes of ethics adopted by individual news organisations.

Many reputable American news media had to dismiss staff journalists for well-documented cases of plagiarism, or outright fabrication, or failures to disclose clear conflicts of interest – and the editors and producers overseeing those journalists were often collateral damage as well.

> *(https://ethicaljournalismnetwork.org/resources/publications/trust-factor/*
> *united-states accessed May 2019)*

Some US states have attempted light regulation of the media with News Councils. The Minnesota News Council was perhaps the best known, although there were others. It ran from December 1970 until 2011. It brought together publishers and lay people to hear complaints but a steady fall in complaints led to it closing. According to the *MinnPost*, its first case was a complaint from a legislator about the *Union Advocate*. It upheld the complaint that the paper:

> had unfairly described him as being on the take from the liquor lobby. At the hearing, the editor admitted that he had not checked the veracity of the story because it was too good a story to lose. Few of the cases since have proved so easy.
>
> *(www.minnpost.com/braublog/2011/01/after-41-years-minnesota-news-*
> *council-fold/ accessed May 2019)*

The Society of Professional Journalists published a code of ethics that is influential amongst American journalists and is available online at www.spj.org/ethics code.asp. It is a set of guidelines rather than rules and the SPJ makes no attempt to enforce the code on its members or others. It doesn't say much about privacy but under the section headed "Minimize harm" says:

> Journalists should: Balance the public's need for information against potential harm or discomfort. Pursuit of the news is not a license for arrogance or undue intrusiveness.
>
> Realize that private people have a greater right to control information about themselves than public figures and others who seek power, influence

and attention. Weigh the consequences of publishing or broadcasting personal information.

(www.spj.org/ethicscode.asp accessed May 201919)

Broadcasting in the US is regulated by equivalent to the UK's Ofcom, the Federal Communications Commission. This is concerned mainly with the technical and administrative side of regulation and programme content regulation is limited to ensuring "indecent" material in programmes is excluded during the watershed period of 6am to 10pm but outside those times pretty much anything goes. Despite that, TV in the US is nervous about upsetting advertisers with controversial programming.

Canada

Canada lies somewhere between the US and the UK when it comes to media privacy. Like many Commonwealth countries it takes its lead in legal terms from its British colonial past structuring its legal system and common law on Anglo-Saxon norms, strengthened by its connections to the US. It has a constitution that guarantees press freedom and the right to privacy, like the US, is based on the right to life, liberty and the security of the person and the right to be secure against unreasonable search and seizure, but contained in, respectively, S7 and S8 of the Canadian Charter of Rights and Freedoms.

Privacy protection is overseen by the Privacy Commissioner of Canada who is also responsible for overseeing two Federal laws:

* the *Personal Information Protection and Electronic Documents Act* (PIPEDA), which applies to many private-sector businesses operating in Canada; and
* the *Privacy Act*, which applies to federal government departments and agencies.,

The PIPEDA regulates the collection and storage of personal data in private-sector organisations so businesses and private organisations are bound by its rules and protocols in much the same way as the GDPR binds organisations in Europe. It applies ten principles of accountability and protection that are similar in intent to the GDPR.

The Privacy Act governs the personal information handling of Federal government institutions and applies to all personal information collected by and stored by the government in much the same way.

Journalists in Canada apply ethical decisions in line with most other western countries. The Canadian Association of Journalists code of conduct says about privacy:

> We do not manipulate people who are thrust into the spotlight because they are victims of crime or are associated with a tragedy. Nor do we do

voyeuristic stories about them. When we contact them, we are sensitive to their situations, and report only information in which the public has a legitimate interest.

Journalists are increasingly using social networking sites to access information about people and organisations. When individuals post and publish information about themselves on these sites, this information generally becomes public, and can be used. However, journalists should not use subterfuge to gain access to information intended to be private. In addition, even when such information is public, we must rigorously apply ethical considerations including independent confirmation and transparency in identifying the source of information.

(http://caj.ca/content.php?page=ethics-guidelines accessed June 2019)

APPENDICES

Codes of practice with particular concentration on privacy and harassment

Below are details of codes of practice for print and broadcast journalists in the UK and Ireland and links to global codes. All codes are particularly concerned with accuracy, privacy and protecting vulnerable people. The press codes are generally sufficiently brief to merit reproducing in full, showing the interlinking of those issues. Broadcasting codes are much more detailed and so links to the full codes have been provided with only the privacy codes reproduced in full.

IPSO

The privacy clauses are below but the full code is available at www.ipso.co.uk where there is also additional guidance.

2. *Privacy

i) Everyone is entitled to respect for his or her private and family life, home, health and correspondence, including digital communications.
ii) Editors will be expected to justify intrusions into any individual's private life without consent. In considering an individual's reasonable expectation of privacy, account will be taken of the complainant's own public disclosures of information and the extent to which the material complained about is already in the public domain or will become so.
iii) It is unacceptable to photograph individuals, without their consent, in public or private places where there is a reasonable expectation of privacy.

3. *Harassment

i) Journalists must not engage in intimidation, harassment or persistent pursuit.
ii) They must not persist in questioning, telephoning, pursuing or photographing individuals once asked to desist; nor remain on property when asked to leave and must not follow them. If requested, they must identify themselves and whom they represent.
iii) Editors must ensure these principles are observed by those working for them and take care not to use non-compliant material from other sources.

4. Intrusion into grief or shock

In cases involving personal grief or shock, enquiries and approaches must be made with sympathy and discretion and publication handled sensitively. These provisions should not restrict the right to report legal proceedings.

8. *Hospitals

i) Journalists must identify themselves and obtain permission from a responsible executive before entering non-public areas of hospitals or similar institutions to pursue enquiries.
ii) The restrictions on intruding into privacy are particularly relevant to enquiries about individuals in hospitals or similar institutions.

10. *Clandestine devices and subterfuge

i) The press must not seek to obtain or publish material acquired by using hidden cameras or clandestine listening devices; or by intercepting private or mobile telephone calls, messages or emails; or by the unauthorised removal of documents or photographs; or by accessing digitally-held information without consent.
ii) Engaging in misrepresentation or subterfuge, including by agents or intermediaries, can generally be justified only in the public interest and then only when the material cannot be obtained by other means.

The public interest

There may be exceptions to the clauses marked * where they can be demonstrated to be in the public interest.

1. The public interest includes, but is not confined to:

   • Detecting or exposing crime, or the threat of crime, or serious impropriety.
   • Protecting public health or safety.

- Protecting the public from being misled by an action or statement of an individual or organisation.
- Disclosing a person or organisation's failure or likely failure to comply with any obligation to which they are subject.
- Disclosing a miscarriage of justice.
- Raising or contributing to a matter of public debate, including serious cases of impropriety, unethical conduct or incompetence concerning the public.
- Disclosing concealment, or likely concealment, of any of the above.

2. There is a public interest in freedom of expression itself.
3. The regulator will consider the extent to which material is already in the public domain or will become so.
4. Editors invoking the public interest will need to demonstrate that they reasonably believed publication – or journalistic activity taken with a view to publication – would both serve, and be proportionate to, the public interest and explain how they reached that decision at the time.
5. An exceptional public interest would need to be demonstrated to over-ride the normally paramount interests of children under 16.

* Reprinted with the kind permission of the Regulatory Funding Company

Impress

The code clauses regarding privacy are reproduced below but the full code and additional guidance is available at https://impress.press/downloads/file/code/impress-code-guidance.pdf accessed April 2019).

Preamble to the impress standards code

Public interest

In certain circumstances, there may be a public interest justification for a particular method of newsgathering or publication of an item of content that might otherwise breach the Code. Where a public interest exception may apply, this is identified in the relevant clause. A public interest means that the public has a legitimate stake in a story because of the contribution it makes to a matter of importance to society. Such interests include, but are not limited to, the following:

(a) The revelation or discussion of matters such as serious incompetence or unethical behaviour that affects the public;
(b) Putting the record straight where an individual or organisation has misled the public on a matter of public importance;

(c) Revealing that a person or organisation may be failing to comply with any legal obligation they have;

(d) The proper administration of government;

(e) Open, fair and effective justice;

(f) Public health and safety;

(g) National security;

(h) The prevention and detection of crime; and

(i) The discussion or analysis of artistic or cultural works.

The following provisions apply where a publisher is about to undertake an action that they think would otherwise breach the Code, but for which they believe they have a public interest justification. The action might be a particular method of newsgathering or publication of an item of content. Before undertaking the action, the publisher should, where practicable, make a contemporaneous note, which establishes why they believe that:

(a) The action is in the public interest;

(b) They could not have achieved the same result using measures that are compliant with the Code;

(c) The action is likely to achieve the desired outcome; and

(d) Any likely harm caused by the action does not outweigh the public interest in the action.

* *Reprinted with the kind permission of Impress*

5 Harassment

5.1 Publishers must ensure that journalists do not engage in intimidation.

5.2 Except where justified by the public interest, publishers must ensure that journalists:

a) Do not engage in deception;

b) Always identify themselves as journalists and provide the name of their publication when making contact; and

c) Comply immediately with any reasonable request to desist from contacting, following or photographing a person.

7. Privacy

7.1 Except where justified by the public interest, publishers must respect people's reasonable expectation of privacy. Such an expectation may be determined by factors that include, but are not limited to, the following:

a) The nature of the information concerned, such as whether it relates to intimate, family, health or medical matters or personal finances;
b) The nature of the place concerned, such as a home, school or hospital;
c) How the information concerned was held or communicated, such as in private correspondence or a personal diary;
d) The relevant attributes of the person, such as their age, occupation or public profile; and
e) Whether the person had voluntarily courted publicity on a relevant aspect of their private life.

7.2 Except where justified by the public interest, publishers must:

a) Not use covert means to gain or record information;
b) Respect privacy settings when reporting on social media content; and
c) Take all reasonable steps not to exacerbate grief or distress through intrusive newsgathering or reporting.

Ofcom

The full Ofcom Broadcasting Code is available at: www.ofcom.org.uk/tv-radio-and-on-demand/broadcast-codes/broadcast-code. Section eight, privacy, is reproduced below.

Section Eight: Privacy
The Ofcom Broadcasting Code January 2019
Principle: To ensure that broadcasters avoid any unwarranted infringement of privacy in programmes and in connection with obtaining material included in programmes.

Rule

8.1 Any infringement of privacy in programmes, or in connection with obtaining material included in programmes, must be warranted.

Meaning of "warranted": In this section "warranted" has a particular meaning. It means that where broadcasters wish to justify an infringement of privacy as warranted, they should be able to demonstrate why in the particular circumstances of the case, it is warranted. If the reason is that it is in the public interest, then the broadcaster should be able to demonstrate that the public interest outweighs the right to privacy. Examples of public interest would include revealing or detecting crime, protecting public health or safety, exposing misleading claims made by individuals or organisations or disclosing incompetence that affects the public.

Practices to be followed (8.2 to 8.22) Private lives, public places and legitimate expectation of privacy.

Meaning of "legitimate expectation of privacy": Legitimate expectations of privacy will vary according to the place and nature of the information, activity or condition in question, the extent to which it is in the public domain (if at all) and whether the individual concerned is already in the public eye. There may be circumstances where people can reasonably expect privacy even in a public place. Some activities and conditions may be of such a private nature that filming or recording, even in a public place, could involve an infringement of privacy. People under investigation or in the public eye, and their immediate family and friends, retain the right to a private life, although private behaviour can raise issues of legitimate public interest.

8.2 Information which discloses the location of a person's home or family should not be revealed without permission, unless it is warranted.

8.3 When people are caught up in events which are covered by the news they still have a right to privacy in both the making and the broadcast of a programme, unless it is warranted to infringe it. This applies both to the time when these events are taking place and to any later programmes that revisit those events.

8.4 Broadcasters should ensure that words, images or actions filmed or recorded in, or broadcast from, a public place, are not so private that prior consent is required before broadcast from the individual or organisation concerned, unless broadcasting without their consent is warranted. Consent

8.5 Any infringement of privacy in the making of a programme should be with the person's and/or organisation's consent or be otherwise warranted.

8.6 If the broadcast of a programme would infringe the privacy of a person or organisation, consent should be obtained before the relevant material is broadcast, unless the infringement of privacy is warranted. (Callers to phone-in shows are deemed to have given consent to the broadcast of their contribution.)

8.7 If an individual or organisation's privacy is being infringed, and they ask that the filming, recording or live broadcast be stopped, the broadcaster should do so, unless it is warranted to continue.

8.8 When filming or recording in institutions, organisations or other agencies, permission should be obtained from the relevant authority or management, unless it is warranted to film or record without permission. Individual consent of employees or others whose appearance is incidental or where they are essentially anonymous members of the general public will not normally be required.

• However, in potentially sensitive places such as ambulances, hospitals, schools, prisons or police stations, separate consent should normally be obtained before filming or recording and for broadcast from those in sensitive situations (unless not obtaining consent is warranted). If the individual will not be identifiable in the programme then separate consent for broadcast will not be required.

Gathering information, sound or images and the re-use of material

8.9 The means of obtaining material must be proportionate in all the circumstances and in particular to the subject matter of the programme.

8.10 Broadcasters should ensure that the re-use of material, i.e. use of material originally filmed or recorded for one purpose and then used in a programme for another purpose or used in a later or different programme, does not create an unwarranted infringement of privacy. This applies both to material obtained from others and the broadcaster's own material.

8.11 Doorstepping for factual programmes should not take place unless a request for an interview has been refused or it has not been possible to request an interview, or there is good reason to believe that an investigation will be frustrated if the subject is approached openly, and it is warranted to doorstep. However, normally broadcasters may, without prior warning interview, film or record people in the news when in public places. (See "practice to be followed" 8.15.)

Meaning of "doorstepping": Doorstepping is the filming or recording of an interview or attempted interview with someone, or announcing that a call is being filmed or recorded for broadcast purposes, without any prior warning. It does not, however, include vox-pops (sampling the views of random members of the public).

8.12 Broadcasters can record telephone calls between the broadcaster and the other party if they have, from the outset of the call, identified themselves, explained the purpose of the call and that the call is being recorded for possible broadcast (if that is the case) unless it is warranted not to do one or more of these practices. If at a later stage it becomes clear that a call that has been recorded will be broadcast (but this was not explained to the other party at the time of the call) then the broadcaster must obtain consent before broadcast from the other party, unless it is warranted not to do so. (See "practices to be followed" 7.14 and 8.13 to 8.15.)

8.13 Surreptitious filming or recording should only be used where it is warranted. Normally, it will only be warranted if:

- there is prima facie evidence of a story in the public interest; and
- there are reasonable grounds to suspect that further material evidence could be obtained; and
- it is necessary to the credibility and authenticity of the programme.

(See "practices to be followed" 7.14, 8.12, 8.14 and 8.15.)

Meaning of "surreptitious filming or recording": Surreptitious filming or recording includes the use of long lenses or recording devices, as well as leaving an unattended camera or recording device on private property without the full and informed consent of the occupiers or their agent. It may also include recording telephone conversations without the knowledge of the other party, or deliberately continuing a recording when the other party thinks that it has come to an end.

8.14 Material gained by surreptitious filming and recording should only be broadcast when it is warranted.

(See also "practices to be followed" 7.14 and 8.12 to 8.13 and 8.15.)

8.15 Surreptitious filming or recording, doorstepping or recorded "wind-up" calls to obtain material for entertainment purposes may be warranted if it is intrinsic to the entertainment and does not amount to a significant infringement of privacy such as to cause significant annoyance, distress or embarrassment. The resulting material should not be broadcast without the consent of those involved. However if the individual and/or organisation is not identifiable in the programme then consent for broadcast will not be required.

(See "practices to be followed" 7.14 and 8.11 to 8.14.) Suffering and distress

8.16 Broadcasters should not take or broadcast footage or audio of people caught up in emergencies, victims of accidents or those suffering a personal tragedy, even in a public place, where that results in an infringement of privacy, unless it is warranted or the people concerned have given consent.

8.17 People in a state of distress should not be put under pressure to take part in a programme or provide interviews, unless it is warranted.

8.18 Broadcasters should take care not to reveal the identity of a person who has died or of victims of accidents or violent crimes, unless and until it is clear that the next of kin have been informed of the event or unless it is warranted.

8.19 Broadcasters should try to reduce the potential distress to victims and/or relatives when making or broadcasting programmes intended to examine past events that involve trauma to individuals (including crime) unless it is warranted to do otherwise. This applies to dramatic reconstructions and factual dramas, as well as factual programmes.

- In particular, so far as is reasonably practicable, surviving victims and/or the immediate families of those whose experience is to feature in a programme, should be informed of the plans for the programme and its intended broadcast, even if the events or material to be broadcast have been in the public domain in the past.

People under sixteen and vulnerable people

8.20 Broadcasters should pay particular attention to the privacy of people under sixteen. They do not lose their rights to privacy because, for example, of the fame or notoriety of their parents or because of events in their schools.

8.21 Where a programme features an individual under sixteen or a vulnerable person in a way that infringes privacy, consent must be obtained from:

- a parent, guardian or other person of eighteen or over in loco parentis; and
  • wherever possible, the individual concerned;
- unless the subject matter is trivial or uncontroversial and the participation minor, or it is warranted to proceed without consent.

8.22 Persons under sixteen and vulnerable people should not be questioned about private matters without the consent of a parent, guardian or other person of eighteen or over in loco parentis (in the case of persons under sixteen), or a person with primary responsibility for their care (in the case of a vulnerable person), unless it is warranted to proceed without consent.

Meaning of "vulnerable people": This varies, but may include those with learning difficulties, those with mental health problems, the bereaved, people with brain damage or forms of dementia, people who have been traumatised or who are sick or terminally ill.

BBC

The BBC's Editorial Guidelines and guidance on those guidelines as well as other guidelines introduced from time to time are available at: www.bbc.co.uk/editorialguidelines/. Guideline seven, privacy, is reproduced below.

7.1: The BBC respects privacy and does not infringe it without good reason, wherever in the world it is operating. The Human Rights Act 1998 gives protection to the privacy of individuals, and private information about them, but balances that with a broadcaster's right to freedom of expression. In regulation, the Ofcom Broadcasting Code states *"Any infringement of privacy in programmes, or in connection with obtaining material included in programmes, must be warranted."*

Meeting these ethical, regulatory and legal obligations in our output requires consideration of the balance between privacy and our right to broadcast information in the public interest. We must be able to demonstrate why an infringement of privacy is justified.

An infringement is considered in two stages, requiring justifications for both the *gathering* and the *broadcasting* of material where there is a legitimate expectation of privacy.

Legitimate expectations of privacy

An individual's legitimate expectation of privacy is qualified by location and the nature of the information and behaviour, and the extent to which the information is already in the public domain. People in the public eye may, in some circumstances, have a lower legitimate expectation of privacy.

Location: People in public places or in semi-public places cannot expect the same degree of privacy as in their own homes or other sensitive locations. (A semi-public place is somewhere which, though private property, gives the public general access, such as an airport, station or shopping mall.)

However, location must be considered in conjunction with the activity. There may be circumstances where people can reasonably expect privacy even in a public or semi-public space, particularly when the activity or information being revealed is inherently private. For example, there may be a greater expectation of privacy when someone is in a public or semi-public place but receiving medical treatment.

There may also be occasions when someone in a location not usually open to the public is engaged in an activity where they have a low expectation of privacy, for example a sales pitch or giving public information. We do not, though, normally reveal information which discloses the precise location of a person's home or family without their consent, unless it is editorially justified.

Behaviour: There is less entitlement to privacy where an individual's behaviour is criminal or seriously anti-social.

The public interest

Private behaviour, information, correspondence and conversation should not be brought into the public domain unless there is a public interest that outweighs the expectation of privacy. There is no single definition of public interest. It includes but is not confined to:

- exposing or detecting crime
- exposing significantly anti-social behaviour
- exposing corruption or injustice
- disclosing significant incompetence or negligence
- protecting people's health and safety
- preventing people from being misled by some statement or action of an individual or organisation
- disclosing information that assists people to better comprehend or make decisions on matters of public importance.

There is also a public interest in freedom of expression itself.

When considering what is in the public interest we also need to take account of information already in the public domain or about to become available to the public.

When using the public interest to justify an intrusion, consideration should be given to proportionality; the greater the intrusion, the greater the public interest required to justify it.

Press Council of Ireland

The Press Council of Ireland's code of practice regarding privacy is below, but the full code is available at: www.presscouncil.ie

Principle 5 – privacy

5.1 Privacy is a human right, protected as a personal right in the Irish Constitution and the European Convention on Human Rights, which is incorporated into Irish law. The private and family life, home and correspondence of everyone must be respected.

5.2 Readers are entitled to have news and comment presented with respect for the privacy and sensibilities of individuals. However, the right to privacy should not prevent publication of matters of public record or in the public interest.

5.3 Sympathy and discretion must be shown at all times in seeking information in situations of personal grief or shock. In publishing such information, the feelings of grieving families should be taken into account. This should not be interpreted as restricting the right to report judicial proceedings.

5.4 In the reporting of suicide excessive detail of the means of suicide should be avoided.

5.5 Public persons are entitled to privacy. However, where a person holds public office, deals with public affairs, follows a public career, or has sought or obtained publicity for his activities, publication of relevant details of his private life and circumstances may be justifiable where the information revealed relates to the validity of the persons conduct, the credibility of his public statements, the value of his publicly expressed views or is otherwise in the public interest.

5.6 Taking photographs of individuals in private places without their consent is not acceptable, unless justified by the public interest.

Irish broadcast

The full Broadcasting Authority of Ireland code of programme standards is available at: www.bai.ie/en/codes-standards/#al-block-4 but principle seven regarding privacy is below. The code contains seven principles:

CODE OF PROGRAMME STANDARDS PRINCIPLES

The Distinction between Harm and Offence

Principle 1: Respect for Community Standards

Principle 2: Importance of Context

Principle 3: Protection from Harm

Principle 4: Protection of Children

Principle 5: Respect for Persons and Groups in Society

Principle 6: Protection of the Public Interest

Principle 7: Respect for Privacy (www.bai.ie/en//download/1285556 accessed 28–4-19)

Principle 7 respect for privacy

In fulfilment of Principle 7, broadcasters shall: – Ensure that any encroachment on the privacy of an individual in a programme or in the means of making a programme is not unwarranted, having regard to the principles of this Code, in particular, the protection of the public interest. Any such encroachment must be proportionate and limited to the degree that is required to inform the audience in the public interest.

- Have due regard to the concept of individual consent and ensure that participants in a broadcast are generally aware of the subject matter, context and the nature and format of their contribution so that their agreement to participate constitutes informed consent.
- Have due regard to the particular considerations that apply in the case of a vulnerable person or a child under 16 years of age, to ensure that the privacy of such persons is never unreasonably encroached upon. Vulnerable people are individuals whose personal circumstances or well-being require that extra care be taken.
- Obtain consent where programme material, or the means of making programme material, directly involves a vulnerable person or a child less than 16 years of age. Consent should be sought from the vulnerable person or child, if possible, and from a parent, guardian, nominated representative or person responsible for his/her primary care. It may not be necessary to obtain consent if the subject matter is trivial or the participation is minor or, based on other factors, it is warranted to proceed without consent, having regard to the principles of this Code.
- Give due consideration to requests for withdrawal of consent, having regard to the principles of the Code, in particular, the protection of the public interest and other circumstances that may arise such as contractual relationships.
- Ensure that the re-use of material, for use in different programme material or for another purpose, does not unreasonably encroach on the privacy of an individual.
- Have due regard to the impact that coverage and repeated coverage of death may have on the families and friends of the deceased.
- Have due regard for the particular considerations that apply when filming in situations of emergency or when filming victims of accidents or those suffering personal tragedy, in order to ensure that the privacy of such persons is not unreasonably encroached upon. – Ensure that surreptitious filming or recording is only used where it is warranted.

NUJ code of conduct

Members of the National Union of Journalists are expected to abide by the following professional principles:

A journalist:

1. At all times upholds and defends the principle of media freedom, the right of freedom of expression and the right of the public to be informed.
2. Strives to ensure that information disseminated is honestly conveyed, accurate and fair.
3. Does her/his utmost to correct harmful inaccuracies.

4. Differentiates between fact and opinion;
5. Obtains material by honest, straightforward and open means, with the exception of investigations that are both overwhelmingly in the public interest and which involve evidence that cannot be obtained by straightforward means.
6. Does nothing to intrude into anybody's private life, grief or distress unless justified by overriding consideration of the public interest.
7. Protects the identity of sources who supply information in confidence and material gathered in the course of her/his work.
8. Resists threats or any other inducements to influence, distort or suppress information, and takes no unfair personal advantage of information gained in the course of her/his duties before the information is public knowledge.
9. Produces no material likely to lead to hatred or discrimination on the grounds of a person's age, gender, race, colour, creed, legal status, disability, marital status, or sexual orientation.
10. Does not by way of statement, voice or appearance endorse by advertisement any commercial product or service save for the promotion of her/his own work or of the medium by which she/he is employed.
11. Shall normally seek the consent of an appropriate adult when interviewing or photographing a child for a story about her/his welfare.
12. Avoids plagiarism.

The NUJ believes a journalist has the right to refuse an assignment or be identified as the author of editorial that would break the letter or spirit of the code. The NUJ will fully support any journalist disciplined for asserting her/his right to act according to the code.

Royal charter on self regulation of the press

Agreed by parliament in 2013 and available for download at: https://assets.pub lishing.service.gov.uk/government/uploads/system/uploads/attachment_data/ file/254116/Final_Royal_Charter_25_October_2013_clean__Final_.pdf

Codes from around the world

Mediawise, a charity set up to help those affected by inaccurate, intrusive, or sensational media coverage and to deliver use-of-the-media training for the voluntary sector and devise and deliver training on ethical issues for media professionals, keeps a reasonably comprehensive and up-to-date archive of codes of conduct in English at www.mediawise.org.uk/codes-of-conduct/codes/

UK acts of parliament involving privacy

Computer Misuse Act 1990 (www.legislation.gov.uk/ukpga/1990/18/contents accessed 28–4-19)

Trespass and police powers of search: Criminal Justice and Public Order Act 1994 (www.legislation.gov.uk/ukpga/1994/33/contents accessed 28–4-19)

Protection from Harassment Act 1997 (www.legislation.gov.uk/ukpga/1997/40/contents accessed 28–4-19)

Regulation of Investigatory Powers Act 2000 (www.legislation.gov.uk/ukpga/2000/23/contents accessed 28–4-19)

Data Retention and Investigatory Powers Act 2014 (www.legislation.gov.uk/ukpga/2014/27/contents accessed 28–4-19)

Investigatory Powers Act 2016 (www.legislation.gov.uk/ukpga/2016/25/content saccessed 28–4-19)

Data Protection Act 2018 (www.legislation.gov.uk/ukpga/2018/12/contents accessed 28–4-19)

General data protection regulation

Glossary

CAA – Civil Aviation Authority

SUA – Small Unmanned Aircraft

DPA – Data Protection Act

GDPR – General Data Protection Regulations (EU regulations)

CCTV – Closed Circuit Television, now more correctly termed surveillance cameras.

APNR – Automatic Number Plate Recognition

AFR – Automatic Face Recognition

ANO – Air Navigation Order

BIBLIOGRAPHY

Archard, David (1998) 'Privacy, the Public Interest and a Prurient Public', in M. Kieran (ed.) *Media Ethics*. London: Routledge, pp. 82–96.

Aristotle (1976) *Ethics*. London: Penguin Classics.

Aristotle (1980) *The Nicomachean Ethics*. Oxford: OUP.

Beales, Ian (2012) *The Editors' Codebook*. London: PCC.

Benn, Piers (1998) *Ethics (Fundamentals of Philosophy)*. London: Routledge.

Bok, Sissela (1984) *Secrets: Concealment and Revelation*. Oxford: OUP.

Browne, Christopher (1998) *The Prying Game: The Sex, Sleaze and Scandals of Fleet Street and the Media Mafia*. London: Robson Books.

Calcutt, David (1990) *Report of the Committee on Privacy and Related Matters*. London: TSO.

Carey, Peter (2010) *Media Law*, 5th edn. London: Sweet and Maxwell.

Cohen-Almagor, Raphael (2006) *The Scope of Tolerance*. London: Routledge.

Crick, Paul and Lewis, James (2014) *Media Law and Ethics in the 21st Century: Protecting Free Expression and Curbing Abuses*. London: Red Globe Press.

Crone, Tom (2002) *Law and the Media*, 4th edn. London: Focal Press.

Culture, Media and Sport Committee (2003) *Privacy and Media Intrusion* (17 June, HC, 2002–2003, HC485-1).

Culture, Media and Sport Committee (2007) *Self-regulation of the Press* (11 July, HC, 2006–2007, HC375).

Culture, Media and Sport Committee (2010) *Press Standards, Privacy and Libel* (24 February, HC, 2009-2010, HC362-1).

Dodd, Mike and Hanna, Mark (2018) *McNae's Law for Journalists*, 24th edn. Oxford: OUP.

Dunbar, Robin (1992) Why Gossip Is Good for You, *New Scientist*, vol. 2, no. 11, pp. 2–31. London.

Duncan, Sallyanne and Newton, Jackie (2017) *Reporting Bad News: Negotiating the Boundaries between Intrusion and Fair Representation in Media Coverage of Death*. New York: Peter Lang.

Elueze, Isioma and Quan-Haase, Anabel (2018) Privacy Attitudes and Concerns in the Digital Lives of Older Adults: Westin's Privacy Attitude Typology Revisited, *American Behavioral Scientist*, vol. 62, pp. 1372–91.

Ernst, Morris L. and Schwartz, Alan U. (1969) *Privacy: The Right to Be Let Alone*. London: MacGibbon and Kee.

Evers, Huub,; Groenhart, Harmen and van Groesen, Jan (2010) *The News Ombudsman: Watchdog or Decoy?*. Diem: AMB Publishers.

Franklin, Bob (1999) *Newsak and News*. London: Routledge.

Frost, Chris (2000) *Media Ethics and Self-Regulation*. London: Longman.

Frost, Chris (2012a) 'Ethics and the Newsroom Culture', in Richard Keeble and John Mair (eds) *The Phone Hacking Scandal: Journalism on Trial*, 2nd edn. London: Arima, pp. 250–62.

Frost, Chris (2012b) Newspapers on the Naughty Step: An Analysis of the Ethical Performance of UK Publications, *Journalism Education: The Journal of the Association for Journalism Education*, vol. 1, no. 1, pp. 21–34. ISSN: 2050-3903.

Frost, Chris (2013a) 'Who Regulates the Regulator?', in John Mair (ed.) *After Leveson? The Future of British Journalism*. London: Arima, pp. 184–93. ISBN-13: 978-1845495763.

Frost, Chris (2013b) Educating for a Better Newsroom Culture in a Leveson-compliant Future, *Journalism Education: The Journal of the Association for Journalism Education*, vol. 2, no. 2, pp. 76–81. ISSN: 2050-3903.

Frost, Chris (2016) *Journalism Ethics and Regulation*, 4th edn. London: Routledge.

Galtung, Johan and Ruge, Mari (1973) 'Structuring and Selecting News', in Stanley Cohen and Jock Young (eds) *The Manufacture of News: Deviance, Social Problems and the Mass Media*. London: Constable, pp. 62–72.

Geoffrey, Robertson (1983) *People Against the Press*. London: Quartet Books.

Gluckman, Max (1963) Gossip and Scandal, *Current Anthropology*, vol. 4, no. 3, pp. 307–15.

Hartley, John (1982) *Understanding News*. London: Routledge.

Hermes, Jokes (1995) *Reading Women's Magazines*. Cambridge: Polity Press.

Hobbes, Thomas (1968) *Leviathan*. London: Penguin Classics.

Information Commissioner's Office (2006a) *What Price Privacy? The Unlawful Trade in Confidential Personal Information* (10 May, HC, HC1056).

Information Commissioner's Office (2006b) *What Price Privacy Now? The First Six Months Progress in Halting the Unlawful Trade in Confidential Personal Information* (13 December 2006, HC, HC36).

Innes, Judith (1992) *Privacy, Intimacy and Isolation*. Oxford: OUP.

Kant, Immanuel (1990) *Foundations of the Metaphysics of Morals*. tr. Lewis Beck White. London: Library of the Liberal Arts.

Kieran, Matthew; Morrison, David and Svennevig, Michael (2000) Privacy the Public and Journalism, *Journalism*, vol. 1, no. 2, pp. 145–69. London: Sage.

Leveson, LJ (2012) *An Inquiry into the Culture, Practices and Ethics of the Press* (29 November, HC, HC779).

Lewis, James and Crick, Paul (2014) *Media Law and Ethics in the 21st Century: Protecting Free Expression and Curbing Abuses*. London: Palgrave.

Lloyd, Dennis (n.d.) Some Comments on the British Television Act 1954. https://scholar ship.law.duke.edu/cgi/viewcontent.cgi?article=2745&context=lcp

Locke, John (1947) *On Politics and Education*. Toronto: D Van Norstand Co. Inc.

McGregor, Oliver (1977) *Royal Commission on the Press 1974–1977*. London: HMSO.

McStay, Andrew (2017) *Privacy and the Media*. London: Sage.

Mill John, Stuart (2008) *On Liberty and Other Essays*. Oxford: Oxford Classics.

Mills, Jon (2009) *Privacy: The Lost Right*. New York: OUP.

Monro, D. H. (ed.) (1972) *A Guide to the British Moralists*. London: Fontana.

Moore, Barrington, Jr (1984) *Privacy: Studies in Social and Cultural History*. London: M. E. Sharpe Inc.

Morrison, David, Kieran, Matthew, Svennevig, Michael and Ventress, Sarah (2007) *Media and Values: Intimate Transgressions in a Changing Moral and Cultural Landscape*. Bristol: Intellect.

Myrick, Joe Anthony (2016) www.therichest.com/rich-list/most-shocking/15-disgusting-acts-of-privacy-invasion-against-celebrities/.

Newton, Jackie and Brennodden, Lene (2015) 'Victims at the Margins? A Comparative Analysis of the Use of Primary Sources in Reporting Personal Tragedy in Norway and the UK', in Heather Savigny, Einar Thorsen, Daniel Jackson and Jenny Alexander (eds) *Media Margins and Civic Agency*. Basingstoke: Palgrave Macmillan, pp. 102–15.

Norman, Richard (1983) *The Moral Philosophers*. Oxford: OUP.

O'Malley, Tom and Soley, Clive (2000) *Media Regulation*. London: Pluto.

Packs, Patricia Meyer (2003) *Privacy: Concealing the Eighteenth-Century Self*. Chicago, IL: University of Chicago Press.

Paine, Robert (1967) What is Gossip about: An Alternative Hypothesis, *Man*, vol. 2, June, pp. 278–85.

Paine, Thomas (1993) *Common Sense and the Rights of Man*. London: Phoenix Press.

Parent, Wendy, in Chadwick, Ruth and Belsey, Andrew (eds.) (1992) *Ethical Issues in Journalism and the Media*. London: Routledge.

Petley, Julian (2013) 'Public Interest or Public Shaming?', in Julian Petley (ed.) *Media and Public Shaming*. London: I.B.Tauris, pp. 19–42.

Pratt, Walter F. (1979) *Privacy in Britain*. Cranbury, NJ: Associated University Press.

Quinn, Frances (2018) *Law for Journalists: A Guide to Media Law*, 6th edn. London: Pearson.

Rosnow, Ralph and Fine, Gary (1976) *Rumor and Gossip: The Social Psychology of Hearsay*. New York: Elsevier.

Ross, William David (1949) *Royal Commission on the Press 1947–49*. London: HMSO .

Rozenberg, Joshua (2005) *Privacy and the Press*. Oxford: OUP.

Shawcross (1962) *Royal Commission on the Press 1961–1962*. London: HMSO.

Singer, Peter (1994) *Ethics (Oxford Readers)*. Oxford: OUP.

Solove, Daniel (2009) *Understanding Privacy*. Boston, MA: Harvard University Press.

Spacks, Patricia M. (1986) *Gossip*. Chicago, IL: University of Chicago Press.

Tebbutt, Melanie (1995) *Women's Talk? A Social History of Gossip in Working Class Neighbourhoods, 1880–1960*. Aldershot: Scolar Press.

Tulloch, John (2006) *One Day in July: Experiencing 7/7*. London: Little: Brown & Co.

Tweed, Paul (2012) *The Privacy and Libel Law: The Clash with Press Freedom*. London: Bloomsbury Professional.

Venables, John (1993) *What Is News*. London: ELM Publishing.

Vincent, David (2015) *I Hope I don't Intrude: Privacy and its Dilemmas in the Nineteenth Century*. London and Oxford: OUP.

Vincent, David (2016) *Privacy: A Short History*. London: Polity Press.

Wacks, Raymond (1995) *Privacy and Press Freedom: Rights in Conflict*. London: Blackstone.

Wacks, Raymond (2015) *Privacy: A Very Short Introduction*. London: Blackstone.

Walsh-Childers, Kim, Lewis, Norman and Neely, Jeffrey (2011) Listeners, Not Leeches: What Virginia Tech Survivors Needed from Journalists, *Journal of Mass Media Ethics*, vol. 26, no. 3, pp. 191–205.

Warburton, Nigel (1998) *Philosophy: The Classics*. London: Routledge.

Webb, Diana (2007) *Privacy and Solitude: The Medieval Discovery of Personal Space*. Hambledon: Continuum.

Westin, Alan (2015) *Privacy and Freedom*. New York: Ig Publishing.

Younger, Kenneth (1972) *Report of the Committee on Privacy*. London: HMSO.

INDEX

5RB 176

accessing communications 100
After The Event insurance 138
Alfie, P. 154
Archard, David 27
archives and cuttings 122
Aristotle 11
Ash, Niema 159
Ashcroft, Lord Michael 88
Asif, Mohammed 79
Associated Newspapers: IPSO
    arbitration 89
Attorney-General v Observer Ltd 95
automated facial recognition 120
Autorité des Marchés Financier 103

BBC 148; complaints 150; Editorial
    Guidelines 14, 66, 71, 74, 150, 196;
    founder 5; Royal Charter 45, 148;
    suicide 66; tag-along raids 71; trust,
    abolition of 47
Bentham, Jeremy 15
Bessell, Peter, MP 34
Black, Lord Guy of Brentwood 44
blackmail 32
Blair, Cheri 22, 155
Blair, Tony 22
Blairs' nanny 156
Blom Cooper, Louise, QC 35
Bok, Sissella 27
Brandeis, Louis D. 26, 183
Brennodden, Lene 68

Brexit 106
Bridgend suicides 41
British Committee of the International
    Press Institute 34
broadcast media and privacy 45
Broadcasting Act 1996 46, 97, 145
Broadcasting Acts 97
Broadcasting Authority of Ireland 152;
    Code of Programme Standards 198
Broadcasting Complaints Commission
    36, 46
broadcasting of events of national
    interest 97
Broadcasting Standards Commission 46,
    143, 147
Brooke, Heather 76
Brougham, Henry 6
Browne, John, MP 35
Bulger, Jamie 61
Bunte 157
Butt, Salman 79
Buxton, Justice Richard: Loreena
    McKennitt 160
Byline 140
Byline Media Holdings Ltd: arbitration 143

Calcutt Committee 97
Calcutt, Sir David, QC 35; PCC review 37
Call Me Dave 88
Cambridge Analytica 113
camera surveillance system 119
Cameron, David, MP 43, 88
Campbell, Naomi 69

Canadian Association of Journalists: code
of conduct 186
Canadian Charter of Rights and
Freedoms 186
Canary, The 140
Cannataci, Professor Joe 24
case study: Douglas v *Hello* 159; Duchess
of Cambridge topless pics 168; Garry
Flitcroft 154; injured child photograph
171; Loreena McKennitt and her 'friend'
Niema Ash 159; Max Mosley 'Nazi'
orgy 165; Mile-high Mandy 153;
Naomi Campbell 164; Paul Weller's
children in Los Angeles 168; Prince
Harry playing strip billiards 168; Princess
Caroline von Hannover of Monaco
156; privacy invaded by false rumours
173; reporting news of a death abroad
173; royal helicopter ride 174; schoolboy
'father' 154; sex assault victim named
175; Sir Cliff Richard police raid 168;
suicide details 175; taking care in
reporting children 172; the Blairs
and their nanny 155; Theakston v
MGN Ltd 164
Cash, William MP 35
Casualty 65
Caught On Camera 120
CCTV 70, 106, 119
celebrity: definition 55; nature 49
Channel 4 97, 145
Chartered Institute of Arbitrators 143
Chester Leader 170
children, vulnerability of 98
Choudry, Ash: PCC complaint 116
Civil Aviation Authority (CAA) 120
civil rights 4
clandestine research 78
Clegg, Laura: PCC complaint 116
CMS Committee: press standards,
privacy and libel 41
codes of conduct 17
Coleridge, Justice Paul 155
Committee on Privacy and Related
Matters 35
Committee on Super-Injunctions 93
Commonwealth Games 98
Communications Act 2003 97, 143, 146
computer hacking 39
Computer Misuse Act 1990 103
Condé Nast: IPSO arbitration 89
Conditional Fee Agreements 138
consequentialists 15
Constant, Benjamin 15

contact books 58
Cooley, Judge Thomas 26
Cornick, Will 61
Coronation Street 56
Coulson, Andy 40
Court of Appeal: Kaye 35
court reporting: anonymity 69, 93
Crime and Courts Act 2013 45; S40 138
Criminal Justice Act 1988 125
Criminal Justice Act 2015 124
Crown Prosecution Service 77
Croydon Advertiser 99
Cruft, Rowan: public interest 82
Culture, Media and Sport Committee 1,
39; 2010 report 41

Dacre, Paul 1, 2, 49, 72, 163
Daily Express 1, 2, 53
Daily Herald 2
Daily Mail 1, 2, 54, 88, 174; Facebook
hoax 116; journalists 103; shaming 72
Daily Mirror 155
Daily Record 175
Daily Star 2, 53, 114, 169
Daily Telegraph 53, 76, 89
Daly, Mark: police expose 76
data collection: pseudonym 59
data protection 105
Data Protection (processing of sensitive
personal data) Order 2000 109
Data Protection Act 1984 44, 58, 59, 75,
104, 105, 106, 123
data subject, rights of 107
Davies, Gareth 99
death knock 67–8
Dee, Robert v *Daily Telegraph* 91
defamation cases in the UK 139
Denning, Lord Alfred 22, 95
deontologists 13
deontology 12
Department of Social Security 105
Derby Telegraph 171
Derbyshire County Council 171
Digital Culture, Media and Sport: Minister
of 45; Select Committee 137
digital mobile phones, introduction of 39
Director General of Telecommunications
143
door stepping 67
Douglas, Michael 159
Dowler, Milly 43
Driver and Vehicle Licensing
Agency 105
Dronecode 121

drones 78, 120
Du contrat social ou Principes du droit politique 9
Duchess of Cambridge: case study 168
Duke of York 125, 174
Dunbar, Robin: reason for gossip 51
Duncan, Sallyanne 68
Dunn, Tom Newton 101
duty of confidence 22, 96

Eady, Justice David 73, 96; Mosley case study 165; McKennitt 160
Eastenders 56
Edinburgh Evening News 114
Editors' Code of Practice Committee 129
Editors' Codebook 170
English Defence League 86
English, Kathy 124
etchings, Queen Victoria and Prince Albert 32
eudaimonia 11
European Convention of Human Rights 3, 20, 21, 85, 156
European Union 105; Data Protection Directive 110; General Data Protection Directive 110
Evans, Harold 140
Evers, Groenhart and van Groesen 177
Evolve Media Ltd, arbitration 143
ex-parte injunctions 92
extort 32
Eyles, Leonora 33

Facebook 115, 111; seeking sources 112
Fayed, Dodi 39
Federal Communications Commission 186
Ferdinand, Rio 57
FHM Magazine 124
Financial Conduct Authority 102
Financial Times 140
Fine, Gary 50
fishing expedition 79
Flickr 117
Flitcroft, Garry 83, 154
flow chart of ethical decision making 18
Foster, Geoff 103
Fowkes, Tim 159
Franklin, Ben 8
Freedom of Information Act 76
freelance journalists 106; storing data 58
Freizeit Revue 157
Fried, Charles 28

Fulford, Lord Justice Adrian 100

General Council of the Press 34
General Data Protection Regulation 106, 123; special category data 108; special purposes 109
German Federal Constitutional Court 157
glossary 201
Gluckman, Max 52
godsibb meaning 50
Goff, Lord Robert of Chieveley 95
Goodman, Clive 40–1
gossip 52–3
Grand National 98
Greater Manchester Police 76
Greene, Lord Wilfred MR 95
Guardian, The 41, 140, 156

hacking 78, 100
harassment 99
Harvard Law Review, *The Right to Privacy* 183
Hawton, Professor Keith 65
Hello! 159
Hermes, Joke 50
Herne Bay Gazette, The 114
hidden cameras 78
hidden microphones 78
High Court: privacy suits 48
Hill, Peter 1
hoax Twitter account 115
hoaxes 124
Hobbes, Thomas 5
Home Affairs Select Committee 137
Home Office, BBC 'deceit' 77
Hopkins, Katie 90, 118
House of Representatives, US 113
Huhne, Chris 101
Human Rights Act 1998 3, 4, 6, 10, 20, 38, 97
Hunt, Lord David of Wirrall 43, 44

images, public and private 56
imperatives: technical, hypothetical, categorical 12–13
IMPRESS 14, 45, 61, 128, 140–1, 190
inalienability 9
Independent, The 2, 77
Independent Broadcasting Authority 46
Independent Press Regulation Trust 141
Independent Press Standards Organisation 14, 45, 56, 80, 114, 128, 136, 159, 169; adjudications 130; arbitration scheme 88, 138; children 61; Code of Practice

83, 188; public guidance 68; public interest 80
Independent Television Commission 144
Information Commissioner's Office 5, 40, 58, 59, 103, 106–7, 110
injunctions 92–3
Innes, Judith 27
Instagram 117
Interception of Communications Code of Practice 102
intimacy 23
intrusive technology 119
Investigatory Powers Act 2016 100, 102
Investigatory Powers Commissioner's Office 100
Investigatory Powers Tribunal 101
Irish *Daily Star* 168
Irish Press Ombudsman 151
Isabel, the relict of John Luter 31

Jefferson, Thomas 8
Jimmy Savile 30, 47
journalistic material, protection of 101
journalists, personal lives 118
JUSTICE 34

Kant, Immanuel 12
Kaye, Gorden 35
Kennedy, Sir Paul 102
Kieran, Morrison and Svennevig 84
King, Justice Eleanor: schoolboy father 155
Kirby, Ruth 155
kiss and tell 70
Ku Klux Klan mask 77

Lancashire Evening Post 114
Larceny Act 1916 32
Legal Aid, Sentencing and Punishment of Offenders Act 2012 138
Leveson 2; cancelled 45
Leveson inquiry 26, 43, 45, 127; public interest 81
Leveson, Lord Justice Brian 25, 43
Libel Act 1843, S3 32
libel: chilling effect 88
Lincolnshire Echo 173
Lincolnshire police: complaint 173
Litterick, Tom, MP 35
Lloyd, Professor Dennis 46
Locke, John 6
London Assize of Nuisance 31
Lovett, Carly 173

Lyon, Alexander, MP 34

MacPheil, Alesha 61
Maguire, Audrey 61
Mail on Sunday 22, 102, 156
Mail Online 118, 168
Majeed, Mazhar 79
Major, John, MP 38
malicious access 100
Manchester Arena terror attack 114
Mancroft, Lord Stormont 34
Manson, Neil: public interest 82
Mark, Ros 22, 156
Matrimonial Causes Act 1857 32
McCann family 41
McCann, Madeleine 41
McCartney, Paul 16
McGregor, Professor Oliver 35, 37
McKennitt, Loreena 22, 87, 159
Mendus, Professor Susan: public interest 82
Middleton, Kate 40
Mile-high Mandy 153
Miliband, Ed 43
Mill, John Stuart 9, 15
Millar, Gavin, QC 57
Minnesota News Council 185
Mirror Group Newspapers 164
Mitchell, Andrew 101
Monroe, Jack v Hopkins, Katie 90
morality 4
Morrison et al. 71
Moses, Alan 80
Mosley, Max 1, 41, 96, 141, 165
Mulcaire, Glen 40
Myler, Colin 1

Nacro 124
Narcotics Anonymous 164
Nasr, Octavia 118
National Council for Civil Liberties 35
National Health Service 105
National Union of Journalists 35, 102; Code of Conduct (1936) 33; Code of Conduct 14, 65, 199; guidelines on mental health and suicide 64
'Nazi-themed' orgy 165
Neue Post 157
Newcastle: sex grooming trial 99
Newman, Brooks 79
News Chronicle 2
News International 45
News of the World 1, 40, 41, 44, 79, 96, 165

News UK 89
Newton Dunn, Tom 101
Newton, Jackie 68
Nicol, Justice Andrew 57
Nietzsche, Friedrich 16
non-straightforward methods 78
Northampton Chronicle & Echo 65, 175
Northumbria Police 99
NOS (The Netherlands Broadcasting
   Company) 178

Oakeshott, Isabel 88
Observer, The 140
Ofcom *see* Office of Communications
Office of Communications 39, 120,
   144–8; broadcasting code 14, 61,
   81, 98, 150–1, 192
Office of Communications
   Act 2002 143
OK! Magazine 159
Olympic Games 98
Operation Motorman 40, 44
Operation Sanctuary 99
Ordine Dei Giornalisti 181

Padover, Saul K. 7
Paine, Robert 53
Paine, Thomas 7
Parent, Wendy 27
Paris Court of Major Jurisdiction 180
Paul, Henri 39
payment to suppress publication 32
Pentagon Papers case 184
People, The 125; Garry Flitcroft 154
Perry, Grayson 86
personal data 104
Personal Information Protection and
   Electronic Documents Act 186
personation 78
Petley, Julian 72, 93
Phillips, Melanie 72
phone tapping 100
Piers Gaveston Society 88
Plato 11
pleasures/pain 15
Plebgate inquiry 101
Police and Criminal Evidence
   Act 1984 101
Police Information Notice 99
pranks 124
Press Complaints Commission (PCC)
   35–7, 41-43, 44, 59, 127, 169–70
Press Council of Ireland 151, 197
Press Council, the 34, 102, 139, 163

Press Recognition Panel 128; Royal
   Charter 45
Press Standards Board of Finance
   (PressBoF) 43, 44
Press, Royal Commission 1947 to 1949 33
Press, Royal Commission 1961 to 1962 34
Press, Royal Commission 1974 to 1977 35
Price, Dr Richard 9
Prichard, Harold Arthur 11, 13
Prince Albert v Strange 26, 94
Prince Harry 168
Prince William 40
Princess Diana, death of 38
prior restraint 92
privacy 1, 22, 24–6, 29, 32, 60–3, 67, 69,
   92, 98, 153, 169; Belgium 177; Canada
   186; Europe 177; false light 183; France
   179; fundamentalists 24; Germany 180;
   home and personal correspondence 25;
   Italy 181; names and addresses 69; Neth-
   erlands 177; people 61; places 62; police
   raids 70; of the post 32; pragmatists 24;
   Scandinavia 177; shame and shaming 72;
   Spain 180; statutory tort of infringement
   37; suicide 64; the dead 30; the United
   States 182; violent death 67
Privacy Act, the 186
Privacy Commissioner of Canada 186
Privacy and Related Matters,
   Committee on 35
privilege 90
Privy Council 128
Protection from Harassment Act 1997 99
Protection of Children Act 1978 125
public interest 74

Queen Victoria 26

Radio Authority 144
Reach PLC: IPSO arbitration 89
Regulation of Investigatory Powers Act
   2000 100
Regulatory Funding Company 128
rehabilitation of offenders 90
Rehabilitation of Offenders Act 1974 124
Reith, Lord John 5
Reporters Sans Frontiere 182
reputation, right to 86
revenge porn 124
revolution: America 8; France 8
Richard, Sir Cliff 98, 168
ride-along stories 70
right to be forgotten 110
Rights of Man 8

Robinson, Tommy 86
Rooney, Wayne 70
Rosnow, Ralph 50
Ross, Sir William David 13, 33
Rotterdam Dagblad 178
Rousseau, Jean-Jacques 9
Royal Charter on the Press 200; Press
  Recognition Panel 128
Russian pervert website 114, 172
Ryder Cup 98

S4C 145
Saltman Engineering v Campbell
  Engineering 94
search engines, blocking access 123
secrecy 23
Select Committee on National Heritage:
  privacy proposals 38
sexual offences, reporting 69
shame and shaming 72
Sharp, Justice Victoria 91
Shawcross, Baron Hartley 34
Simpsons, The 16
Slave Trade Act 1807 6
Slavery Abolition Act 6
Slavery, abolition of 6
Smith, Andy 102
social compact 9
social contract 9
social media 111, 113, 118; celebrity 56
Society of Editors 2
Society of Professional Journalists 184
Socrates 11
Sound Broadcasting Act 1972 46
source confidentiality 75
South Yorkshire Police 168
Spacks, Patricia: gossip 51
Sport, The 2
Sqwawkbox 140, 141
stalkers, protection from 99
Storey, Carly 57
Sun, The 54, 116, 154; Mile-high
  Mandy 153
Sunday Life 173
Sunday Mirror 57, 79
Sunday Sport 35
super-injunctions 93

Tebbutt, Melanie: gossip 50
Telegraph Media Group 89
teleology 15
Television Act 1954 46
Television Authority 46
Terry, John 57

Theakston, Jamie: *Sunday People* 164
Thompson and Venables 61
Thompson, Jenny 70
Times v Sullivan 184
Times, The 53, 89
Today 2
Toronto Star 124
Toulmin, Tim 43
*Travels with Loreena McKennitt: My Life as
  a Friend* 159
trespass 100
Trump, Donald 6, 182
Trump, Melania v *Daily Mail* 90
Tugendhat, Justice Michael 93
Tulloch, John 68
Twitter 112, 115

UK Privacy Acts 200
Ukrainian internet bride 137
UN Declaration of Human Rights 20
UN Special Rapporteur on Privacy 24
unfair treatment in programmes 98
universal laws and codes of practice 14
universal maxims 14
utilitarianism 15

Vincent, David 31
virtue ethics 11
voice mail phone tapping 39
Volkskrant 178
Von Hannover, Caroline, Princess
  of Monaco 85
Von Hannover 2 158

Wacks, Raymond 27
Waddington, David 36
Wakeham, Lord John 39
Walden, Brian, MP 35
Walsh-Childers, Kim 68
Warren, Samuel D. 26, 27, 183
Webb, Diana 31
Weller, Paul 63, 168
Welsh Authority, the 145
Westin, Alan 1, 23, 26, 113
What Price Privacy 26, 40, 103
What Price Privacy Now 26, 40
WhatsApp 111, 117
whistleblowing hotline 140
Wickham, Alex 80
Wilberforce, William 6
Wimbledon tennis finals 98
witness contributors 116
Wittams, Sophie, Tory PR girl 79
Wolfe, David, QC 128

Woman's Own 33
women's magazines 50
Woolf, Lord Justice Harry
    83, 154
World Cup 98
World Wide Web 98, 105

Yaxley-Lennon, Stephen 86
Younger Committee 97
Younger, Kenneth 35

Zeta-Jones, Catherine 159
Zuckerberg, Mark 113

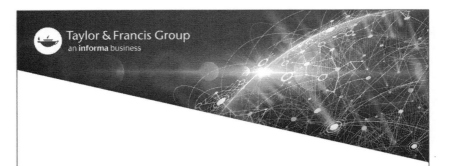